RUBBER CHEMICALS AND PROCESSSING INDUSTRIES

A complete encyclopaedia on Rubber Chemicals & Processing Industries which deals with new technologies, processing, formulations, project profiles and directory section. The book is covering with the 32 detailed chapters including directory section & details of machineries & equipments for rubber processing industries. Apart from the processing industries, the book also provides plenty of informations about the manufacturing of Rubber Chemicals.

Written By :

EIRI CONSULTANTS & ENGINEERS

and

Compiled By

SUDHIR GUPTA

A WORLD RENOWED CONSULTANTS WORKING OVER 21 YEARS

ENGINEERS INDIA RESEARCH INSTITUTE

4449, Nai Sarak, Main Road, New Delhi - 110 006

Phones : 291 8117, 291 6431, 292 0361 Fax : 91-11 - 291 6431

PRINTED & PUBLISHED BY

ENGINEERS INDIA RESEARCH INSTITUTE

Regd. Office : 4449, Nai Sarak, New Delhi - 110 006 (INDIA)
Tel : 291 8117, 291 6431, 292 0361 • *Fax* : 91-11-291 6431

DISTRIBUTED BY

SMALL INDUSTRY RESEARCH INSTITUTE
New Delhi (INDIA)

ISBN : 81- 86732 - 15 - 2
Printed in New Delhi (INDIA)

Rs. 400

Printed & Published by Sudhir Gupta for "Engineers India Research Institute" and Laser Type Set by **Puneet Malhotra** at Engineers India Research Institute, and printed at 'Sanjeev Offset Printer', Krishan Nagar, New Delhi - 110 051

Preface

The book **RUBBER CHEMICALS AND PROCESSING INDUSTRIES** contains most valuable informations & technologies including various formulations to manufacture the rubber chemicals & processed goods industries. Few names are Natural Rubber, Acrylic Rubber, Butyl Rubber, Rubber Powder, Colours & Pigments, Rubber Blowing Agents, Latex Dipped Goods, Foam Products, Adhesives & Solutions, Rubber Moulded Articles, Rubber Rollers, Rubber Beltings, Rubber Footwear, Tyre & Tubes, Rubber Gaskets, Auto Parts, Various Other Important Formulations including Compounding, Polymers & Processing Methods. Apart from these the book also deals with the Testing & Trade Names & Chemical Compositions.

The book is covered with 33 detailed & exhaustive chapters. At the end of the book, it also provides various Project Profiles for the dynamic entrepreneur, who are venturing for the lucrative project related to Rubber Chemicals & Processing Industries.

Rubber Goods Manufacturing Industries have recorded a steady growth in the past 50 years. Today India is the 4th biggest producer of Natural Rubber (NR) after Thailand, Indonesia & Malaysia. It ranks first among major producers in terms of productivity. The rapid growth in production was sustained because of a quick growing Industrial sector, which was ready to consume all the domestically produced rubber, whereas the major producers are exporting the bulk of their output, India's share with China, the unique position of consuming the entire domestic output of NR.

However, while demand has increased, production has not kept pace with it. The growth of rubber goods manufacturing industry has been no less impressive. Consumption of NR has shot up from less than 20,000 tonnes in 1950-51 to 5.61 lakh tons in 1996-97. During this year, this is estimated to increase to 6.10 lakh tons recording a growth rate of 8.6%.

It is hoped that this book will serve as a ready referencer to all those who are engaged in the field of Rubber Chemicals & Rubber Products Industry, be it is a technologist, a corporate planner or a businessman planning to setup a new projects.

Director
ENGINEERS INDIA RESEARCH INSTITUTE
Nai Sarak, New Delhi.
Fax : 91-11-291 6431

CONTENTS AND SUBJECT INDEX

Chapters	Page No.

Details of Rubber Processing Equipments and Machineries 290-310

PRINTING, PACKAGING AND METALLURGICAL

37. Hand Book of Printing Processes Technologies & Industries
38. Hand Book of Screen Printing
39. Hand Book of Metallurgical & Engineering Industries
40. Hand Book of Packaging Industries
41. Plastic Processing and Packaging Industries
42. Stationery Paper Converting & Packaging Industries

PAINT, VARNISHES AND LACQUERS

43. Hand Book on Varnishes, Paints and Lacquers
44. Paint Varnish and Lacquer Technology

PLASTIC AND RUBBER INDUSTRIES

45. Plastic Processing & Packaging Industries
46. Hand Book of Plastic Projects
47. Hand Book of Plastic Industries
48. Selected Profitable Plastic Industries
49. Small Scale Paint, Plastic & Rubber Goods Industries
50. Hand Book of Rubber & Rubber Goods Industries
51. Rubber Chemicals and Processing Industries

FOOD, BAKERY, CONFECTIONERY AND AGRO FOOD

52. Food Processing & Agro Based Industries
53. Agro Based Industries Hand Book (Plantation & Farming)
54. Agro Based & Food Processing
55. World Importers Directory of Agro Based & Food Industries
56. Hand Book of Food Industries
57. Hand Book on Confectionery Industries
58. Hand Book on Bakery Products
59. Canning & Preservation of Fruits & Vegetables
60. Food Processing Industries
61. HI-Tech Food & Food Products Industries
62. Agro Based & Processed Food Technology Hand Book

ELECTRICAL, ELECTRONIC AND COMPUTER

63. Electrical and Electronic Goods Industries
64. Electrical, Electronic and Computer Based Industries
65. Hand Book on Electronic Industries

SOAPS, DETERGENT, COSMETICS, CANDLES AND PERFUMES

66. Soap Detergent & Perfume Industry
67. Hand Book of Soap Detergent & Glycerine
68. Acid Slurry and Detergent Powder Industry
69. Hand Book on Cosmetic Industries (Herbal & Synthetic)
70. Perfume Flavour & Essential Oil Industries
71. Small Scale Manufacture of Soap & Detergents
72. Manufacture of Perfumes Cosmetics and Detergents
73. Handbook of Candle Industries

PULP, PAPER AND STATIONERY

74. Stationery, Paper Converting and Packaging Industries
75. Hand Book on Pulp and Paper Industries

INDUSTRIAL DIRECTORIES (TRADE DIRECTORIES)

76. World Importer Directory of Agrobased & Food Processing
77. World Importers Yellow Pages (All Trade Buyer's Directory)
78. '*SIRI*' Directory of Industries in India
79. ***All India Industrial Yellow Pages Directory***
80. Delhi and Around Industrial Directory
81. All India Directory of Machinery Manufacturers
82. Directory of Food Products/Industries
83. Directory of Plastic & Polymer
84. Directory of Automobiles and Auto-Components

TERMS & CONDITIONS

- Ask the Price for each Book either through Phone or by Post.
- Send **Rs. 300/-** as an advance in favour of **'ENGINEERS INDIA RESEARCH INSTITUTE'** Delhi for all above mentioned Books and postage **Rs. 35/-** extra for each **Book** should be added up and balance amount shall be charged by **V.P.P.**

10 % DISCOUNT ON BUYING THE BOOKS WORTH RS. 5000/- OR MORE AT A TIME

ENGINEERS INDIA RESEARCH INSTITUTE

4449, Nai Sarak, Main Road, New Delhi - 110 006

Phones : 291 8117, 291 6431, 292 0361 Fax : 91-11 - 291 6431

1

Natural Rubber

Introduction

Natural rubbers *i.e.* substances which are able to stretch to several times their original length and snap black to roughly the original length on removal of force, are obtainable from large number of trees, shrubs, etc. of tropics. Because of its shape, type of bark and adoptability to plantation together with high yield and outstanding excellent rubbery properties of the product obtained from the Hevea Tree, the latter has emerged as the main source of natural rubber. Now-a-days natural rubber means Hevea Rubber. It is cis-poly isoprene having the following structure :

$$\left(CH_2 - \overset{\displaystyle CH_3 \atop |}{C} = CH - CH_2 - \right)_n$$

Latex is a emulsion of rubber obtained from the rubber tree. It is tapped from the bark by making a special type of cut through the bark. It gets collected into a metallic, plastic or earthenware cup attached containing a small amount of preservative to prevent coagulation. Latex is collected in a routine way and is carried in buckets to the collection centre where it is sieved to remove particles of dust and bark. Latex is to be properly preserved; otherwise the action of bacteria makes it acidic resulting in coagulation. Usually 0.5 to 1% ammonia is added for this purpose for killing the bacteria and making it alkaline.

Latex is coagulated with acids, acidic salts and alcohol etc. Acetic acid is widely used for this purpose.Formic acid is used in smaller quantities and gives rubber of improved colour. Sodium bisulphite, calcium chloride, stronsium chloride and magnesium chloride are some of the salt coagulants . Usually a mixture of various coagulants is used. A good coagulant is 20 parts spirit and 30 parts acetic acid.

The coagulated latex is passed through roller, passed, washed sheeted, dried and baled in sizes of 250 lbs. These are dusted with talc or chalk to prevent self adhesion during transportation and storage. Drying is a slow operation, whether done in smoke houses or modern drying tunnels and takes about 4 to 5 days and longer at ambient temperature. The drying temperature is generally not raised above normal temperature of 40° to 50° C so that darkening of light-coloured rubber by heat does not take place.

Properties of Natural Rubber (NR)

Pure rubber is odourless, elastic and transparent; but it is not easy to get pure rubber. For this purpose crude rubber has to be freed from proteins, resins and other impurities. Usually crude rubber of a specific odour and colour is used. It softens at about 120° C and dissolves in naphtha, toluene, benzene, carbon disulphide and petrol etc. Its specific gravity varies from 0.915 to 0.930. The better grades of natural rubber contain at last 90% of the main hydrocarbon *i.e.* cis-1, 4-polyisoprene together with impurities described above. The composition varies and the high yielding types give higher acetone extract and protein content. Typical analysis reveal acetone solubles 2.5-4.5%, nitrogen 0.4-0.6% and ash 0.2%. The molecular weight of the polymer varies between 5,00,000 to 10,00,000.

In the presence of solvents rubber first swells giving a gel (requiring about 10 to 40 times its weight of solvent) and then this gel dissolves in the solvent. If the rubber solution is kept for long, protein and some other impurities separate out and settle to the bottom carrying with them some rubber. Rubber solution is highly viscous and its viscosity is affected by mastication, light, heat and mechanical action.

Grades of Natural Rubber

Internationally recognised market grades of natural rubber are given below :

Type	*Grade*
Ribbed smoked sheets	IX RSS, RSS No. 1-5
Thick pale crepes	IX, 1,2,3
Thin pale crepes	IX, 1.2.3
Estate brown thick crepes	IX, 2X, 3X
Estate brown thin crepes	IX, 2X, 3X
Compo crepes	1,2,3
Thin brown crepes (Remills)	1,2,3,4
Thick blanket crepes (Ambers)	2,3,4
Flat bark crepes	Standard, hard
Pure smoked blanket crepe	Standard

Processing Methods

Rubber is mixed with compouding ingredients and then it is followed by extrusion, calendering, moulding, vulcanisation and finishing etc.

Mastication & Mixing

Roll and banbury mixtures are used for mastication and compounding of rubber. Mastication eases the processing operations, as viscosity is lowered. Mixing of compounding ingredients is a must. Temperature of mill is about 50°C. Formulated material is known as the compound.

Compounding Ingredients

Compouding ingredients can be mainly divided into anti-oxidants, fillers, extender oils and vulcanising agents etc. Generally the mixing order is as follows, antioxidants, oils and then vulcanising agents; other ingredients can be added in any order preferred. Fillers are generally added for cost reduction and sometimes for reinforcing. Softening agents or plasticizers are used to impart plasticity. These are paraffin oils, naphthenic oils, aromatic oils, asphalts, vegetable oils and synthetic ethers e.g. DOP, DBP, DOA, DBS and TCP Zinc oxide is used as lcanizing aid. Sulphur is used at the rate of max. 3phr. except for nite, as vulcanisation agent. Vulcanisation accelerators e.g. MBT, T ETC. are used. Various types of carbon blacks are used for forcement. Other compounding ingredients such as tackifiers, peptisers, cessing aids, colourants and blowing agents etc. are used as asion demands.

rther Processing

For extrusion the compound is warmed and then fed to the extruders. us desired shapes are moulded from moulds of extruders. L/D of ubber extruders is smaller than that of plastic extruders and are from 5 to 12. Calendering is used for rolling, profiling, embossing, forcing, doubling, frictioning and topping and so on. Moulding gives most of the products such as tyres and footwears etc. Vulcanisation is carried out usually at about 150°C; this removes the plasticity and the compound retains its rubber elasticity. Injection machines are also are also sometimes used instead of vulcanising presses when necessary. In this case, care should be taken for burned marks on the surface of product.

Uses

Natural rubber by itself or its blend with synthetic rubbers are used for making all types of rubber products. Some of the more important applications include automobile, aeroplane, cycle, carts tyres and inner tubes; soild tyres; conveyer belts; transmission belts; hoses, tubes for gases chemical and other fluids; soles, heels and footwear; balls toys and other items of games and sports; prophylactics, condoms; gloves; nipples and teats; handles and other teats; handles and other heat and electrically insulating components for appliances; moulded industrial parts; vessels, pumps and other lined equipments; rubberised fabrics for rainproof clothing and tents etc. mattings; gaskets, washers, bellows, rollers, diaphragms; insulation and sheathing cover for all types of wires and cables; flooring tiles; medical instruments; corks and stoppers; hot water bottles; foams and sponges for cushions etc. Apart from these there are thousands of other rubber gods made by issuing natural rubber.

Typical Vulcanisate Properties of ISNR Grades

Tread Recipe

Compound formation	*Parts by weight*
ISNR	100
Zinc oxide	5.00
Stearic acid	2.00
HAF black	45.00
Santoflex IP (antioxidant)	1.50
Aromatic oil	5.00
Santocure CBS (cyclohexyl benzthiazole sulphenamide)	0.50
Sulphur	2.50

ISNR - Processing Parameters

Properties	*ISNR 3CV*	*ISNR 3L*	*ISNR 5*	*ISNR 10*	*ISNR 20*	*IS. 50*
Compound Mooney Viscosity ML (1+4) at 100°C	57	75	66	65	65	56
Mooney scorch time (minutes to 5 units rise above minimum at 120°C)	25	19	22	16	18	17
Monsanto Rheometer at 140°C						
Optimum cure t90 (minutes)	25	21	24	21	20.5	22
Cure rate t90 - 12 (minutes)	6	5.5	5.8	4.5	5.3	4.8

ISNR - Physical Vulcanisate Properties

Properties	*ISNR 3CV*	*ISNR 3L*	*ISNR 5*	*ISNR 10*	*ISNR 20*	*ISNR 50*
Cure conditions at 140 (min.)	25	21	24	21	20.5	22
Modulus at 300% (kg/cm)	165	170	175	168	173	156
Tensile strength (km/cm)	270	273	268	258	249	216
Elongation at break (%)						

After ageing at 70°C for 14 days						
a) Tensile strength (kg/cm)	235	237	235	219	200	175
b) Elongation at break (%)	420	420	420	403	339	340
Hardness (shore A)	59	58	60	61	60	61
DIN abrasion Loss (mm)						
Load 10 N	64	63	64	68	79	79
Dunlop resilience (%)	55	56	55	55	55	53
Tear Strength (km/cm)	130	120	108	105	100	95
Compression set (%)						
(22hrs. at 70°C)	38	36	36	36	32	32
Demattia Flexing						
Crack Initation (K Cycles)	58	39	41	28	30	29
Crack failure (K cycles)	350	355	350	332	332	332
Goodrich heat build up						
dynamic compression set (%)	6.0	8.5	8.6	8.5	9.9	9.9
Temperature rise after 25 mnt.	28	28	27	26	28	27

Substitutability of ISNR at a glance

Sl.No.	Product	Conventional grades generally used	Equivalent ISNR which could replace conventional grades
I.	Tyres & Tubes		
	1. Automobile tyres & tubes :		
	a) Tread & carcass	RSS III, IV, V including superior grades of EBC	ISNR 20
	b) Tubes (NR)	RSS I	ISNR 5
	2. Aero tyres	RSS IX	ISNR 3 CV
	3. Off the road tyres & ADV tyres	RSS III, IV, V	ISNR 20
	4. Cycles tyres & tubes :		
	a) Tyres	RSS III, IV, V & lower grades of EBC	ISNR 20
	b) Tubes	RSS I	ISNR 5

II.	Footwear :		
	1. Quality items	RSS II, III, IV	ISNR 10 &20
	2. Cheap items	RSS V & lower grades of EBC	ISNR 50
III.	Conveyor Belting :		
	1. Food	RSS I	ISNR 5
	2. Other	RSS III, IV, V	ISNR 20
IV.	Hoses :		
	1. Extruded hoses	RSS II, III, IV	ISNR 10 & 20
	2. Handmade hoses	RSS V & Lower grades of EBC	ISNR 50
V.	Moulded Goods :		
	Injection bottle caps & such other items	RSS IX, PLC	ISNR 3L
VI.	Bushes	RSS V & lower grades of EBC	ISNR 50

SYNTHETIC RUBBER

Introduction

Synthetic rubbers are produced in two stages, first monomer or monomers is produced which is then polymerised. A single substances may be polymerised into synthetic rubber, or two or more basic substances may be copolymerised to form a synthetic rubber having superior properties to those obtain able from one substance alone.

Synthetic rubbers are broadly classified as general purpose synthetic rubbers and special purpose synthetic rubbers compounds styrene butadiene, polybutadiene, polyisoprene, butyl, poly-chloroprene, nitrile, EDPM etc. Use of these rubbers is mostly made by blending with natural rubber and/or reclaim rubber. Many rubber goods could be made wholly from synthetic rubber.

Various important synthetic rubbers, their properties, uses and general compounding and processing aspects are given below :

1. Acrylic Rubber
2. Acrylonitrile Butadiene Rubber (NBR)
3. Butyl Rubber (IIR)
4. Silicone Rubbers
5. Urethane Rubbers

2

Acrylic Rubber

Introduction

Acrylic rubbers are usually copolymers of ethyl acrylate and a small proportion of a second monomer containing chlorine e.g. 2-chloro ethyl vinyl ether. Sometimes even chlorine containing monomer is not incoroporated. They have excellent heat, weather and oil resistance.

Manufacturing Process

Rubber is prepared by emulsion, bulk and suspension polymerisation and also by solution polymerisation. Organic peroxides, ammonium persulphate and potassium persulphate are used as polymerisation initiators and dodecyl mercaptans are used as polymerisation modifier, the polymerisation temperature being in range of 70-80°C.

Properties

Acrylic rubber has execellent heat and ozone resistance due to saturated carbon bond. Fuel oil and fatty hydrocarbon reistance is good due to polarity of the carbonyl group. The outstanding feature is their ability to perform in sulphur modified oils at even above 180°C.

Vulcanisates are superior in resistance to hot hydrocarbon oils, extreme pressure lubricants, transmission and hydraulic fluids, ozone sunlight and weathering. It can be used intermittently upto 180 to 200°C. It has excellent flex life and can be used upto 20°C.

Processing

General rubber processing machines are available but the processibility is very poor. Hence stearic acid is first applied to the surfaces of roll mills when milling. The same fillers may be used as that for general rubbers. Reinforcing agents such as carbon black and certain white inorganic pigments are necessary to bring out optimum physical properties. Zinc oxide, clays and camel black are generally avoided. FEF black is generally used and synthetic graphite may be incoroporated in compounds for rotating shaft seals and reinforcing silicates are used in non-black mixes. During extrusion barrel temperature is maintained at 40 to 55°C and die temperature at 75°C. Good smooth extrusion requires more loading and lubrication than that for moulded goods. Addition of 20 parts of styrene-acrylonitrile resin gives excellent extruding compounds. For calendering also a temperature of 40°C to 55°C is the best. In mill mixing, high temperature of 40 to 55° C is the best. In mill mixing, high temperatures will cause sticking and splitting. Mill warm-up is necessary and 15-mill films are possible.

Unlike other rubbers, generally, the combination is of polyamines e.g. hexamethylene-diamene carbonate, triethyl trimethylene triamine and triethylene tetramine, and lead oxide as vulcanising agents. The vulcanisation being slow, a secondary vulcanisation should be carried out

Uses

Acrylic rubbers can be used in appplications requiring high heat and oil resistance. They are, thus, used in oil hoses, auto-gaskets, search -light gaskets, O-rings, especially in contact with sulphur containing and high pressure lubricants, beltings and tank-linings etc. These rubbers, now-a-days, find general use in automotive applications such as transmission seals. As they are soluble in alcohols, ketones, toluene, MEK perchloroethylene, benzene, ethyl-butyl acetate etc., their solutions have interesting possibilities for use in paint and adhesive industries.

3

Acrylonitrile Butadiene Rubber (NBR)

Introduction

Nitrile rubber (NBR or Buna-N) is first introduced by Germany in 1934. Various trade names of nitric rubber are as follows : Perbunan , Baypren, Chemaprene, Chemigum N etc. Its structure is given below :

$$(-CH_2-CH=CH-CH_2-)_X-(-CH_2-\overset{\overset{\displaystyle CN}{|}}{CH}-)_Y$$

Manufacturing Process

Butadine and acrylonitrile are polymerised using emulsion technique. In the case of hot polymerisation (emulsion polymerisation 40°C) inorganic peroxides are used as initiators while in the case of cold polymerisation (at 10°C) redox initiators are used. Alkylmercaptans are used as modifiers while anionic surfactants, rosin acid soaps and fatty soaps are used as emulsifiers . Hydroquinones and dimethyl dithiocarbamates are used as polymerisation short stops.

Properties

The greatest characteristics of NBR are excellent oil resistance and solvent resistance and fuel oil resistance. Resistance to oils , fuels, greases and solvents increases with the increase in the nitrile content; but low temperature flexibility, resilience and elasticity decrese. Thus, a compromise between oil resistance and low temperature properties is necessary. A grade of nitrile rubber, blended with PVC is also available which has better weather and ozone resistance, bright flame resistance gloss, colours etc. Low nitrile NBR are cheaper and also have low resistance to ozone.

Processing

NBR is not broken down by mastication in the same way as natural rubber. Thus money viscosity of rubber has imporatnt effect on its processing properties, in addition to polymerisation temperature. "Hot" NBR is more difficult to process than "Cold" polymerised NBR. Low money NBR absorb fillers and plasticisers more easily than high mooney grades; and also there is less heat build-up during mixing and faster extrusion rates can be achieved. Soft compositions utilise small amounts of fillers and large amounts of plasticizer, hence high mooney NBR is preffered as strength retention will be better.

Nitrile rubber is compounded in similar manner as that for NR and SBR. Ester series plasticisers should be used due to compatibility reasons. Dispersion of sulphur is more difficult and thus magnesium carbonate coated sulphur should be used. Ester and polymeric plasticisers give better processing, hardness, low temperature flexibility and oil resistance. All types of carbon blocks and other fillers may be used, but semi-reinforcing types are preffered as they give suitable physical strength coupled with low cost. Phenolic resins may also be used as reinforcing fillers. Channel and reinforcing furnace blacks are generally used to gave optimum tensile strength, abrasion and tear resistance Thermal and semi-reinforcing furnace blacks permit higher loadings for equivalent hardness stocks, thus resulting in cheaper compounds. TMTMS with sulphur is an excellent general purpose vulcanisation system for nitrile rubber.

Nitrile rubber has poor compatibility with natural rubber but with SBR, it can be blended successfully in all proportions. It reduces overall oil resistance but imparts resistance shrinkage. During extrusion care should be taken to prevent scorching as high heat is generated during extrusion. calendering is similar to that of SBR.

Uses

NBR is used in oil resistant boxes, petroleum industrial parts and boots, rubber rolls for printing, sealing materials, gaskets for transformers, packings. O- rings, rubberised fabrics, rolls for paper manufacture, rubber sheets, oil resistant soles, linings of fuel tanks, auto-parts (packings, seals and fuel hose) , oil resistant belts, oil resistant hose with low temperature resistance, oil transport pipes, hydraulic brake cups, adhesives and modifier for plastics.

4

Butyl Rubber (IIR)

Introduction

Butyl rubber (IIR) is a copolymer of isobutylene and isoprene, the presence of latter making the polymer vulcanisable. Butyl rubber has the following structure :

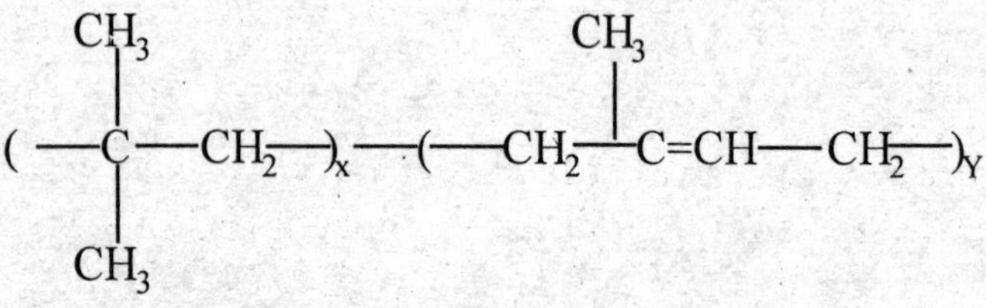

Manufacturing Process

Isobutylene and isoprene (few percent) are polymerised in liquid phase at low temperature (about 100°C) using anhydrous aluminium chloride as catalyst.

Grades

IIR is produced in several grades ranging in isoprene content from 0.5 to 3%. Butyl rubbers are characterised by molecular weight, degree of unsaturation and whether the A.O. is staining or non-staining.

A system of numbering has been devised to indocate these features, but unlike SBR system, it is not yet common to all manufacturers. Now-a-days various modified grades of butyl rubbers particularly the halogenated ones are also coming more and more in to light. Halobutyl rubbers i.e. cholorobutyl or bromobutyl rubbers are better able to be blended with general purpose rubbers and convulcanisation is greatly improved.

Properties

IIR vulcanisates have higher tensile strength than those of BR but lower than those of NR, SBR, CR and EDPM. Tear strength also follows the same trend. Compression set is similar to that of EDPM but is lower than that of NR, SBR, and CR. IIR has basically excellent heat, weather and ozone resistance due to low degree of unsaturation. It shows softening type degradation in high temperature if sulphur vulcanisation method is used while vulcanisation by quinoids improves this phenomenon. IIR rubbers show very excellent resistance to acids, alkalis, bleaching agents and detergents. Its oil resistance is similar to that of SBR.

IIR rubbers have most excellent electrical properties among all rubbers. Their gas permeability is very low. Their rate of vulcanisation is slow due to small degree of unsaturation. The adhesive property with other polymers or metal is inferior because of nonpolarity.

Processing

Butyl rubbers can be processed on general rubber processing machines. Compounding ingredients are almost similar to those of NR and SBR. The temperature of roll mills should be 75°C, the nips should be narrowed and the nerve should be lowered because of poor wrapping onto the roll mills. Butyl rubber is not compatible with other highly unsaturated rubbers and such plasticisers and fatty acids, hence low unsaturated oils and waxes should be used as softeners and process-aids with butyl rubber compounds. Hydrocarbon plasticisers increase resilience and ozone resistance is invariably impaired. Paraffin is ineffective upto 20 phr.

Reinforcing agents may not be necessary in order to strengthen the tensile strength because IIR is a crystalline rubber, but will become necessary for tear strength, abrasion resistance and good processibility. Fillers most commonly used are carbon black and mineral types. Lower unsaturation grades are used for applications requiring high resistance to ozone and weather while the higher unsaturation grades are used for applications requiring high aging and heat resistance. For steam hoses and belts good heat resistance is required and fillers used are furnance or thermal type carbon blocks. For good chemical resistance low filler loadings and fine particle size inert fillers should be used. For use in tyres, abrsion resistance is required, and MPC black and plasticiser oils to increase softnesss are employed. For low gas permeability e.g. for inner tubes, low plasticiser level, furnace blacks, and high filler loadings are required.

Nickel dibutyl dithiocarbonate is an effective antioxidant for butyl compound. Strong vulcanisation condition is necessary because of low degree of unsaturation. Vulcanisation may be carried out by sulphur, quinone oximes or resins. Sulphur gives better physical properties, and same accelerators as those of natural rubber are used. Quinone oximes give rapid cures but scorching becomes a problem. Curing with resins (*e.g.* P-F resins) gives vulcanisates with excellent ageing and heat resistance properties. Chlorinated compounds are used as polymerisation accelerators.

Smooth extrusions can be obtained by loading the compound with at least 20 volumes of carbon black or 30% of mineral fillers. For extrusion, barrel and die temperature should preferably be about 120°C. The extruder feed stocks should be stored before extrusion, preferably for at least 24 hours otherwise control of dimensions and surface finish of the extrudate will be difficult. The warm up and feed mills should operate at about 70°C and optimum extrusion temperature varies betwen 105 to 130°C. For calendering sheeted stock is fed at about 85°C and the roll tempeartures may be, top roll 98 to 110°C, middle roll 70 to 82° C and bottom roll 82 to 105°C. This will give sheeting of excellent quality at the output rate of about 20 M/min.

Uses

Low air impermeability makes it suitable for inner tubes, football bladders and air tight components of some equipment etc. Due to high heat resistence it is used in tyre curing bags, bladders and other goods. Resistance to ozone, weathering etc. are utilised in roofing and reservoir membranes, electrical insulation and auto-components. The very low resilience makes it suitable for vibration damping e.g. body mount system for cars and trucks. It is also used in axle bumpers, radiators hoses, accelerator bellows, and window seals etc. Butyl tyres have greater resistence to tread groove and side wall cracking. Actually transport items take up about 80-85% of butyl rubber production.

Its comparitively low cost and some outstanding qualities are making it more and more important. Some other important applications of butyl rubber are : road cushions, tie pads, chemical hose, beater hose, diaphragms, rubber balls, rubber boats and other important use in auto tyres & tubes.

5

Nitrile Rubbers

Manufacture

This rubber is obtained by copolymerisation of butadiene and acrylonitrile by emulsion polymerisation using free radical catalyst.

$$\underset{\substack{\text{Butadiene}\\(60\text{-}85\%)}}{CH_2 = CH\text{-}CH = CH_2} + \underset{\substack{\text{Acrylonitrile}\\(40\text{-}15\%)}}{CH_2 = CHCN} \longrightarrow$$

$$(\text{-}CH_2\text{-}CH = CH - CH_2 - CH_2\,\underset{\substack{|\\CN}}{CH}\ \text{-})_n$$

Acrylonitrile can be prepared by passing acetylene and hydrogen cyanide over heated carbon. Table lists Producers of Nitrile rubber in the world with their **Trade Names**.

Procedure of Nitrile Rubber with Trade Names

Producer	Trade Name
Copolymer Rubber and Chemical Corp.	Nysen
BFGoodrich Chemical Company	Hycar
Goodyear Tyre and Rubber Company	Chemigum
Uniroyal Chemical Division of Uniroyal, Inc.	Paracril
B.P.Chemicals Ltd. (UK)	Breon
Huels Mexicanos, S.A. (Mexico)	Humex
Japan Synthetic Rubber Co. (Japan)	JSR
Mcbay (Germany)	Perbunan
Nippon Zeon Company (Japan)	NIPOL
Polysar Ltd. (Canada)	Krynac

Compounding

Basically nitrile rubbers are compounded in much the same way as N.R. or SBR. Reinforcing fillers are necessary to obtain optimum properties. Vulcanisation can be achieved with sulphur and accelerator or peroxides when transparent compounds are obtained.

Properties

Oil resistance is the most important property of nitrile rubber. It is available in several grades of oil resistance based on the acrylonitrile content of the polymer. As the acrylonitrile content increases oil resistance, tensile strength, hardness, abrasion resistance, heat resistance and gas impermeability increase while low temp. flexibility, resilience and compression set decrease. it resists both aliphatic and aromatic hydrocarbons and is second only to sulphide rubbers in this respect.

Applications

Based of oil and chracteristics, nitrile rubber finds uses in applications where these properties are required such as gasoline hoses for automotive, marine, aircraft, industrial air hose, carburetter parts, oil-drilling industry, adhesives, cements and brake linings.

A typical composition of Fuel-Hose Compound based on nitrile rubber is given in the table

Automotive Fuel-Hose Compound

	Parts
Hycar 1092-80	100.0
Zinc oxide	5.0
Stearic acid	1.0
Antioxidant	1.5
Hard clay	30.0
N774 Black	90.0
Plasticiser	15.0
Sulphur	1.5
Accelerator	1.5
Mooney viscosity 80,	
Acrylo nitrile 33%	
Expected Properties :	
Tensile strength (psi)	2000
Elongation (%)	300
Hardness	70

6

Silicone Rubbers

Introduction

It is a class of polymers containing long chain polymers of methyl or methyl phenyl-polysiloxane. Sometimes vinyl groups are also included to make it easily vulcanisable.

Manufacturing Process

Silicone rubber is made by reacting metallic silicone and alkyl chloride at about 300°C. Dialkyl chlorosilane thus obtained is hydrolysed to get cylic dimethyl siloxane. It is heated with acid or alkali to get polymerised product.

Properties

The most important and outstanding property of silicone rubbers is the exceptional thermal stability, little change in chemical and the electrical properties between 80°C and 250°C. compression set is equal or superior to that of any of the natural and synthetic rubbers. These rubbers are chemically inert, tasteless and odourless. They are not effected by light, moisture and ozone. Their electrical properties are excellent.

The tensile and tear strength are much lower than those of other rubbers. They also have low pure gum strength and low adhesion to metal.

Processing

Due to low pure gum strength reinforcement with silica is a must; carban black is not used due to various reasons. Fine powder, foggy or hydrated silica are used for this purpose. Silicas pretreated with cholorosilanes and washed with hydrochloric acid improve water resistance and electrical properties. Poly-tetrafluoroethylene (PTFE) is a valuable additive at low loadings to improve tear resistence.

In silicone rubber compounds accelerators, softners, anti-ozonates and plasticisers etc. are not required. their low viscosity, stickiness and non-black colour necessitate careful handling and precautions against contamination; even traces of impurities may cause vulcanisation failures. Benzoyl peroxide is the standard vulcanising agent for silicone rubber, other peroxides, *e.g.* dicumyl peroxide and teritary butyl peroxides etc. may also be used.

During mixing filler is added to the gum, followed by the vulcanising agent; to prevent scorching the water cooled rolls should not be hotter than 45°C. General rubber procesing machinery is usuable, but larger the L/D of extruder, the better the processibility. Curing of extruded or calendered products is done at 110-160°C followed by a post cure at 200-250°C in a well ventilated oven to remove products of the reaction and impart the full properties particularly heat resistance, although somegrades are now available which do not require any post cure.

Uses

Due to its outstanding properties silicone rubber finds the following applications. In automobiles it is used for gaskets such as spark plugs, ignition cord, boots, torque convertors, O-rings and engine blocks oil seals for transmissions and bearings. It is also used in industrial, paper and printing industry rolls due to non-sticking and good release properties. It is used in ships, guns, aircrafts for gaskets, vibration dampers, O-rings and seals etc.

Silicone rubber finds applications in edge seal of heaters, seal of steam irons, high temperature controlled electric wire, cord of heaters, electric wire for spare plugs, electric wire for aircrafts and ships, electric heater wire for refrigerator defrosters and packings. Silicone rubber is also used in pressure coker gaskets. It is used in health services for rubber plugs, blood transfusion tubing, injection materials for breasts, cheeks and nipples for infants. Belts of tape recorders are also made of silicone rubber.

Silicone rubber does not have all the outstanding properties of all the rubbers and also it is costly. But its properties remain almost constant at temperature extremes, hence it is finding speciality applications and its uses are increasing fast.

7

Synthetic Polyisoprene Rubber

Introduction

Home and Coworkers polymerised isoprene to mostly cis-1, 4-polyisoprene using Al-Ti catalyst in 1963. This was made possible by the discoveringof Ziegler and co-workers of stereoregular catalysis earlier.

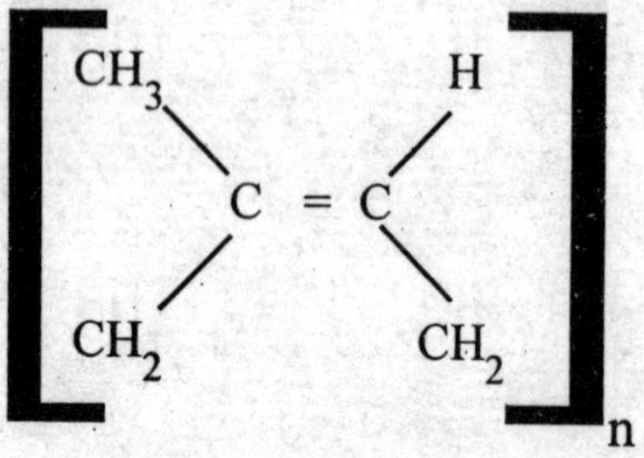

cis-1, 4-polyisoprene

Manufacture

Isoprene is derived from petroleum. It is mixed with a hydrocarbon solvent such as n-pentane. Two types of catalysts can be used. One is based on a coordination catalyst of titanium tetrachloride and an aluminimum alkyl such as triisobutyl aluminimum. (Al-Ti) while the other anionic catalyst is butyl lithium.

Reaction takes place at 50°C and moderate pressure. The process makes use of solution polymerisation.

Structure

The polymer made by coordination catalyst has a molecular weight distributionn similar to that of natural rubber whereas one made using butyl lithium is higher in molecular weight and requires longer mastication than natural rubber.

The synthetic cis.-1, 4-polyisoprene with Ziegler type Al-Ti catalyst is almost similar rubber in its crystallisation behaviour and has identical crystal structure.

Properties and Application

The properties of cis.-1, 4-polyisoprene are nearly identical with those of natural rubber and this polymer is preffered because of greater clealiness and uniformity. It is virtually colourless due to high purity and freedom from contamination and is used for medical purposes. it has high elongation break which leads to its use in rubber threads for golf balls. Tensile strength and tear resistance are somewhat low as compared to natural rubber, other properites viz. ageing, hysterisis are similar to natural rubber.

Polybutadiene Rubber

Formerly butadiene was made from alcohol. However, now it is derived exclusively from petroleum.

Structure

The presence of two double bonds in butadiene can be give risse to a number of configuration of the resulting polymer. However it is cis.-1, 4-polybutadiene which is the most important as a rubber.

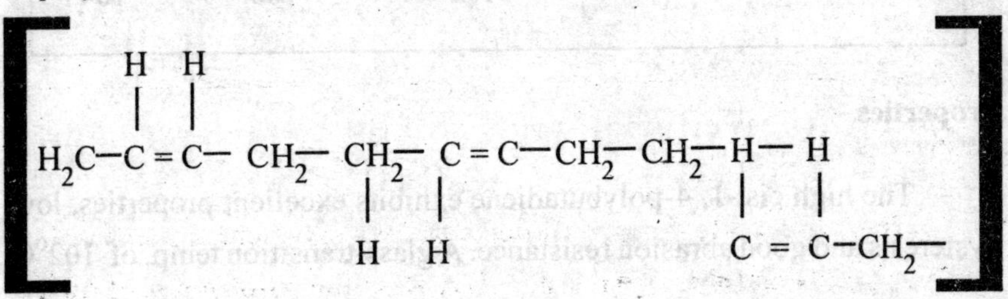

Manufacture

It is manufactured similar to polyisoprene employing solution polymerisation using pure monomer and hydrocarbon solvents. Organic lithium compounds or coordination catalysts containing metals in reduced valence states are employed. Care has to be taken to eliminate completely air, moisture and impurities which can have detrimental effect on the properties of the resultant polymer.

Compound	A	B	C
45-percent vinyl PBD	68	—	—
cis-4 1203	—	—	35
SBR 1712	32	100	6.5
Styrene, %	7.5	23.5	15.3
Vulcanizate Properties			
300% modulus, kg/cm²	91	91	98
Tensile strength, kg/cm²	202	207	197
Elongation, %	560	550	510
Shore A hardness	59	58	59
T, °C at 15 min	42	42	39
Yerzley resilience	58	55	59
Blow-out time, min.	60	17	15
Crescent tear 100°C, kg/cm²	37	37	44
Abrasion Index			
12875 km	106	100	137
Wet-Skid Index			
40 km/hr	102	108	104

Properties

The high cis.-1, 4-polybutadiene exhibits excellent properties, low hysteresis and good abrasion resistance. A glass-transition temp. of 102°C is reported for this polymer which accounts for its excellent low temperature, performance, high resilience and abrasion resistance. It also processes well in blends with other polymers e.g. natural rubber and SBR. It should not however be used more than 40-50%, above which it imparts poor skid resistance.

Table shows properties of blends resulting by the incorporation of polybutadiene into SBR, when significant improvements in abrasion resistance and tear strength are noticed.

8

Urethane Rubbers

Introduction

Urethane rubbers are the rubbers prepared from polyesters or polyethers and isocyanates. They are known by various trade names *e.g.* Adiprene, Urepan, Genthane etc. Commercial urethane rubber is divided into 3 classes namely, casting type and thermoplastic type.

Manufacturing Process

Polyurethanes are prepared by addition polymerisation from discoyanate and polyester, polyester amide or polyether. Propolymers from liquid to soild are prepared by kinds of raw materials related to moleculer weights.

Properties

Urethane rubbers have outstanding abrasion resistance and load carrying capacity, which is more than any other rubber. Load carrying capacity of urethane rubbers is almost 4 times that of NR and abrasion resistance is about 10 times. They show good resistance towards many oils, solvents, ozone and weather, and maintain flexibility at low temperatures. They have high tensile strength, hardness and elasticity. The polyester series urethane rubber show better oil and heat resistance and adhesive properties with metals, than polyether series; but the latter has better water and low temperature resistance.

Processing

The casting type polyurethanes have isocyanate group at the terminal and are cured by adding main chain extenders sfter casting. In the case of millable type, when terminal group is isocyanate group, water and glyocol etc. or when it is hydroxyl group, polyisocyanate may be added and mixed by rubber rolls and then is cured at high temperature. General rubber processing methods are employed. In the case of thermoplastic type, the machines used for thermoplastics are used.

Uses

Due to their high cost and their processing and curing difficulties coupled with difficulty of blending with other rubbers, they are not used in tyres, except for making caster and lift truck wheels where their high abrasion resistance is worth their high cost. Due to the same reasons , they are used for pads for metal forming and impellers for abrasive slurry pumps etc. They have damping characteristics also. They are being used in footwear industry.

Urethane rubbers find use in auto-parts such as packings, O-rings, stearing packings, silent blocks and plate springs etc., grips for rock drills, guide rolls of conveyer belts, head plates of steel hammers, vibration insulation and sound proof gears of mixers, soles, heels, sponges for vibration insulator, whetstones and rolls for rice hullers.

The common use of polyurethane rubbers is in the manufacture of foams, known as U-foams.

9

Rubber Powder

Introduction

Rubber powder has got tremendous demand now-a-days. The trend now a days is towards automation in production of rubber goods during handling, mixing and processsing. The liquid and powder forms of rubber are very easy to be handled. Liquid form of rubber is perhaps the most revolutionary but liquid rubber compounds tend to be very viscous and because of this are difficult to manipulate by the methods normally used to transfer, store and meter viscous liquids; such as heating as the liquid compounds will be containing active ingredients.

The advantages of powder processing have been recognised and include (a) rapid and inexpensive mixing ; (b) flexibility in compounding. Powder handling equipments are used in plastics industry also ; hence those equipments can be utilised for compounding of powdered rubber before actual processing.

Manufacturing Technology of Rubber Powder

Powdered rubber can be made from bale rubber or from latex. From bale rubber it can be made by grinding into small particles using 10 to 30% of a partioning agent. But this method has a number of disadvantages.It requires a high percentage of a partioning agent or lubricant to assist grinding. Secondly, being elastomeric in nature, it requires a high power consumption. Also it gives coarse particles, uneven and relatively large in size. But one advantage is there, that of purity. Bale produced powders contain less non-rubber impurities than those produced from latex, as rubber is subjected to considerable washing after coagulation where as the latex particle contains all the impurities present in polymerisation recipe (in case of synthetic latices) and natural latex. Therefore, these also are present in any rubber powder made from latex.

Spray Drying of Latex

This consists of introducing the latex into a chamber by means of a high speed rotating disc. This converts the latex into small droplets which meet a stream of hot gas, usually air, in the chamber. The water is immediatly removed and the dried rubber which is now in the form of a fine powder is left suspended in the gas stream and is seperated by the passage through cyclone seperator.

Flash Drying

It is similar to spray drying but the speed of drying is much more. It takes about 4 seconds compared to 20 seconds in the spray drying. Much higher temperature are used. Here also the product is left in the gas stream.

Freeze Drying

Certain rubbers can be obtained in powder form by freeze-drying technique. Polyuretherene powders are particularly prepared by this process. The process consists of spraying the latex into a cold chamber (below–30°C) under vacuum. The water sublimes off and a very fine powder results, even as small as 0.1 micron.

All these three processes namely, spray drying , flash drying and freeze drying require expensive equipments.

Co-precipitation Method

Prepraption of powdered SBR and NBR has been reported, where partioning agents such as starch xanthate have been successfully added to the synthetic latex to prevent particle reagglomeration during coagulation starch-xanthate systems based on tapioca starch can be incorporated into ammonia stabilised field natural rubber latex to get powdered NR. The method essentially consists of dispersing the rubber latex in a starch xanthate solution at a pH of 12. This dispersion is then acidified under oxidising conditions and the rubber is coprecipitated with the starch in the form of a powder of uniform particle size.

Preparation of Starch Xanthate

162 g Tapioca is dispersed in water at about a 10% level and converted into a homogeneous gelatenous mass by adding 1 mole or 40 gm of NaOH per mole of anyhydrous glucose unit. When this dough of starch is ready carbon disulphide is added to it. The amount of carbon disulphide added depends upon the final degree of xanthation desired. Addition of 0.75 moles (57gms) of carbon disulphide yields a product with a degree of substitution (DS) of 0.35. The mixture is stirred vigorously for about 3 hours and stored at $5^{o}C$ for a minimum period 24 hrs. before use.

Preparation of Rubber Powder

The natural rubber latex stabilised with 1% ammonia is used for this purpose. The level of NH_3 is first brought down to 0.2%. The latex is then diluted to 10% solids content. To this latex is added the above starch xanthate solution. Sodium nitrite is then added to this mixture at the rate of 1 mole of sodium nitrite per mole of xanthate. Coprecipitation is then brought about by the addition of 1 mol. of H_2SO_4 which destabilises the latex and forms nitrous acid which in turn oxidatively cross links the starch xanthate to starch xanthide. The mixture should be stirred vigorously during this period to facilitate the formulation of small crumbs. The mixture is filtered through cheese cloth, and the crumbs are washed and dried.

The crumbs after separation from the liquid are washed and dried in such a way that agglomeration during drying does not take place. For this purpose the wet crumbs are washed with atleast 2% zinc stearate on rubber content of the masterbatch. If Zinc stearate is not used reagglomeration during drying takes place and if inspead of it alcohol is used for washing then reagglomeration is reduced to only some extent. The washed material is air dried with hot air.

The starch loadings are kept between 20 to 40 phr. Degree of substitution should be aimed at 0.75 (DS). Sodium nitrite should be added to give a molar equivalent of 1/10th the actual DS. 2% talc on the DRC is added to the particles in suspension to prevent them forming clusters during drying.

A typical powder blended nitrile rubber compound will give the basic idea of compounding :

NBR, powdered	100 parts
SRF black	50
Zinc oxide	5
Stearic acid	0.5
DBP	5
Sulphur	2
MBTS	1.75

The possible areas of application for starch powdered rubber are : general purpose moulding compounds, general extruded goods and oil resistant soleing compounds etc. The areas where powdered rubber compounds will make first impact are mechanical goods such as injection moulded gaskets, seals, shock absorbers etc. and also the extruded products such as window seals, door seals, cables and hoses etc.

10

Rubber Reclamation

Introduction

Reclaimed rubber is used as an extender in rubber compounds. It is cheaper than natural and is mostly used in making auto and cycle tyres. There are bright prospects for the tyre industry. Hence the reclaim also has a good scope.

During reclamation combined sulphur is not removed and some of the good properties of reclaimed rubber are attributed to this fact. Free sulphur, of course, gets removed during reclaimation. The following points are noteworthy regarding the chemistry of reclamation. The chemical unsaturation of the rubber hydrocarbon of the reclaim is similar to that of the original vulcanised scrap. Reclaiming agents in the proportion from 0.5 to 20% of the weight of scrap are used to speed the devulcanisation and to impart desirable processing properties to the finished product. Well-known reclaiming agents are dipentene, naphtha, unsaturated resin oils obtained during petroleum refining, and various chemicals such as alkylated phenol sulphides, aliphatic and aromatic mercaptans, alkyl and aryl amines. The defibouring agents whether acids, alkalies or metallic chlorides, influence the reactions during reclamation. The natural rubber is more responsive to reclaimation than SBR types and its plasticity increases continuously. Synthetic rubbers on the other hand first increase in plasticity but then begins to reharden.

Properties and Applications

Reclaimed rubber is used in various recipes as a partial replacement of fresh rubber due to its following advantages :

1. Reclaimed rubber is cheaper, stable in price and contributes to consistency in qualties of the products.
2. Reclaim rubber speeds up mixing operation, breaks down quickly, wets the pigments and blends the mixture together with ease. Due to pigments in already dispersed state, power consumption is less.
3. Reclaimed rubber imparts firmness to compounds making the processing easier. It permits faster and safer extrusion and calendering. It reduces sagging and loss of shape.
4. Reclaim decreases shrinkage of uncured compound before and during curing. Curing is made faster thus reducing mould or press time.
5. Introduction of reclaimed rubber imparts excellent ageing properties.
6. Reclaimed rubber is plastic and may be worked with solvent, usually in the presence of resins to form useful, high solid cements.
7. Reclaimed rubber is helpful in modifying the recipes to suit individual customer requirements, with respect to physical and chemical properties, colour, cost, size of package etc.
8. Less heat is developed mixing and subsequent processing compared with compounds based on new rubber. This is an important property especially in compounds containing high carbon black loadings, which are sometimes scorchy if too high a temperature is allowed to develop.
9. Extruder die swell and calender shrinkage are minimised by the proper use of reclaimed rubber.

Reclaimed rubber has excellent ageing properties, when used in either the cured or uncured condition. The severe treatment to which it has already been subjected includes oxidation, heating digestion, washing and mastication in air and these appear to stablise the hydrocarbon against further changes. But, the tensile strength modules, resilence, tear resistence and abrasion are all reduced as the proportion of whole tyre reclaim is increased. Reclaim is extensively used in friction tape, where retention of tackiness is important. Due to maximum processing efficiency it is used in the manufacture of tyres, auto floor mats and auto hard rubber battery containers. It is also used in articles such as tubings, hoses and weather proof items. Reclaimed rubber is satisfactory used in many articles such footwear, which have to withstand constant tear.

In some cases 'where the aim is to have items of which the longest wearing life reclaimed rubber cannot be used. From the cost angle it gives the most miles per rupee, in case of tyes, Light coloured rubber scraps are now scarce and more expensive comparitively. Thus to a great extent, economics limits the use of light coloured reclaims to applications where their processing advantages and advantages in the finished products are especially important.

Red tube reclaim finds use in cement dispersions and adhesive compositions. Black tube reclaimed rubber is used in moulded goods, hose and tubing, flaps, footwear, cheap tyres for cycles and rickshaws. In a number of automotive goods such as bumpers, mountings, couplings, hoses, fender flaps, glass run rubber, primary and ignition wires, reclaim ventilator strips, auto channels, tubing and stearing wheels, reclaimed rubber is an important ingredient, and large amount of reclaim is consumed for these items.

Manufacturing Methods

The following are the 4 principal processes in use today, but the first namely, the digester and reclaimator procesess are the most important and will be described in detail :

1. Digester Process
2. Reclamator Process
3. Heater or Pan Process
4. Engelke Process

The raw material for reclaimed rubber is scrap rubber in a wide variety of forms, but tyres form the major quantity. The first stages, in all processes are the cracking and grinding of the scrap rubber to reduce it to a crumb passing through a 20-30 mesh screen. Scrap tyres are fed to a cracker, which consists of two heavy corrugated steel rolls revolving at unequal speeds, exerting a powerful tearing and grinding action on the ground material is sifed through fast vibrating screens. Larger pieces are sent back to the cracker whereas the finer material is sent to storage bins. Big truck tyres cannot be handled directly by a cracker and are therefore first cut down to size on a splitter which cuts the tyre in half longitudinaly. The ground scrap is passed under a magnetic separator for removal of ferrous metal which might have been picked up and may damage the further processing equipments

Digester Process

Digester process is a wet process in which the fibre is chemically decomposed and washed away. It is the most imporatnt reclaiming process. The ground waste is loaded into a digester along with water, reclaiming oils, and other additives, such as activated black (for minimum staining grades). The digester is a cylindrical jacketed pressure vessel fitted with a horizontal agitator, and steam can be supplied to both interior and jacket, thus enabling a uniform temperature throughout the mass. Reclaiming agents are naval stores, petroleum and coal tar based oils and resins; varoius chemical softners; defibouring agents are chiefly caustic soda and zinc and calcium chlorides. The temperature range for digester is 190 to 210°C and the digestion time is 5-12 hours. During this time rubber becomes devulcanised and fibre gets hydrolysed.

The digester is then 'blown down' to continuous screens on which water is sprayed to wash the rubber free from digester liquor and decomposed fibre. The washed rubber is sent to dewatering press to squeeze out the excess water. The rubber is then dried to control mioisture in a 3-stage hot air drier. At the same time diluted wash liquor is settled to recover some of the low rubber content which is used as a filler in cheaper reclaims. The dried rubber is blended with small proportions of reinforcing and processing agents etc. in a Banbury Mixer or Ribbon Blender. These ingredients are chiefly clay, carbon black and softeners which aid in smoothing the dried stock and in obtaining uniformity with a high productivity rate. These ingredients also help in controlling the sp. gravity of the finished reclaim. The rubber is then sent for preliminary refining. This refiner is similar to a mixing mill but the rolls are kept together under great pressure. This smooth out the particles of rubber and give throughly dispersed product. The 0.01 sheet obtained from it is cut off from the fast take off roll by a scraper knife.

Material is then passed through a strainer or extruder equipped with a screen. It removes foreign matter and non-magnetic metal, and the material comes out of it in the form of rods which are cut off by rotating knives. This is sent to a 'finishing refiner' which is similar to 'preliminary refiner' but here the rolls are set to a much smaller opening viz. 0.003 to 0.005. This removes hard, improperly devulcanised particles which are useful form of rubber for low price moulded compounds, but are objectionable for smooth products. The reclaimed rubber, obtained thus, is in the form of a paperthin endless sheet, which is wound up on a drum and cut off as a slab about 1" thick. The slabs are dusted and then stored.

Reclamator Process

In the reclamator process the fabric of the rubber is removed by mechanical means, whereas in the digester process it is destroyed by chemical means in a water medium. In the reclamator process water is not used ; thus all washing and drying steps are eliminated. Ground vulcanised rubber heated in a temperature range of 120-200°C undergoes a rapid initial increase in plasticity and on continued heating passes through an inversion point and until after prolonged heating, a further but slower increase in plasticity is attained. This is a general characterstic behaviour depending somewhat on the type of rubber ; reclaiming agents and physical conditions used.

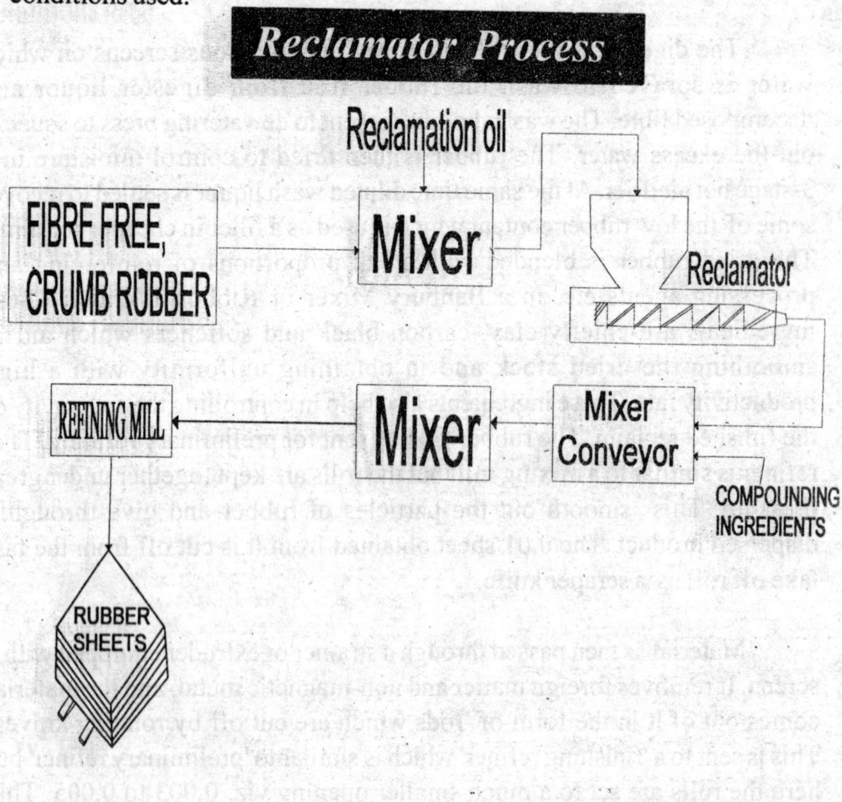

In other processes the whole cycle is enacted in the process but in reclamator process, the reaction is carried out essentially at the initial lowest point, in the presence of plasticisers, oxygen and catalysts. The rapid heating of the rubber while it is being worked mechanically gives the desired plasticity in a matter of 3-6 min. The total cycle time is only 30 min., hence it is called short cycle process, and the process is entirely dry.

In this process crack-sifted-metal-free scrap as earlier is sent to a disintegrator where a series of hammers beat the material and loosen much of the fibre. The scrap is then blown to a centrifugal separator where most of the loosened fibres are whirled to the top, while the heavier material containing both rubber and fibre spins down to another machine known as a beater ; here again further separation takes place. Vibrating tray further effects separation. The final feed fibre drops into the hopper of a Garnetting Machine which untwists most of the cords, combs out almost all of the remaining rubber, and delivers the product to a Baler, or first to beaters which removes still more rubber. Meanwhile the feed rubber is ground uniformly fine and mixed continuously with chemical reclaiming agents and conveyed to the Reclamator.

Plasticity vs. Time Curve for Rubber

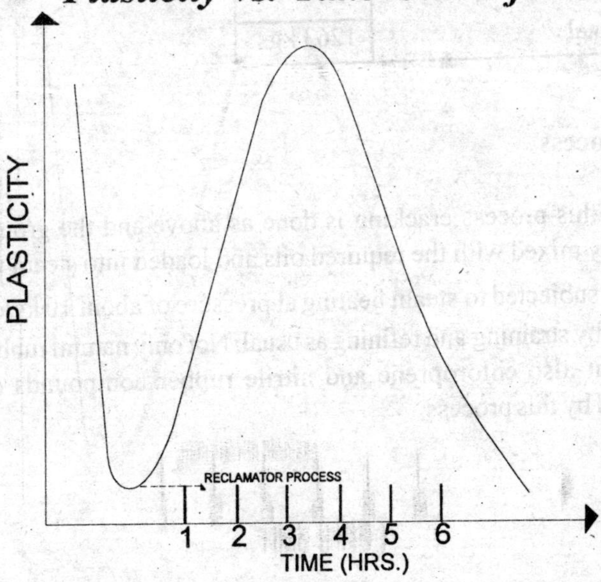

The reclamator machine, from which the process gets its name, is of the screw extrusion type with a hopper at one end into which the crumb mixed with other ingredients is automatically fed at a predetermined rate. It generates its own heat for depolymerisation by mechanically working the finely divided rubber crumb under pressure, and then discharges it as reclaimed rubber. Clearnaces near the discharges end are adjustable in order to control the process reaction. The temperature range is 175 to 205°C and is controlled by alternating oil and water jackets. The transit time is 1 to 4 minutes.

Stock temperature is reduced at the discharge end. Devulcanised material compound, mixed, refiner-sheeted, extruded in slab form as usual or powdered handling machines.

Following raw materials are required for 1 tonne of reclaim rubber.

Scrap tyres etc.	1,100 kgs.
Sweller	21 kgs.
Permanent plasticiser	44 kgs.
Pine Tar	44 kgs.
Asphaltic	42 kgs.
Perptisers	3 kgs.
Mineral fillers	9 kgs.
Total	1263 kgs.

Pan Process

In this process cracking is done as above and the ground waste is intimately mixed with the required oils and loaded into steam vulcanisers. Here it is subjected to steam heating at pressure of about 10 kg/cm^2. This is followed by straining and refining as usual. Not only natural rubber and SBR scraps but also chloroprene and nitrile rubber compounds etc. can be reclaimed by this process.

Engelke Process

This process is quite simple as it requires no wetting of the stock or elimination of the fibre. Scrap rubber containing fibres is subjected to very high temperature for short periods of time such as 10-20 min. in small autoclaves. This carbonises the fibre. The cracked stock, when necessary can be premixed with plasticising oils and peptisers. The reclaim is strained and refined as usual.

11

Pigments and Colours

Introduction

A number of inorganic pigments are available for colouring rubber compounds. They are usually chosen for their stability to curing conditions and their complete freedom from staining and bleeding. They have good covering power and are resistant to dry heat and cheap.

Inorganic Pigments

White Pigments

Lithopone, zinc oxide and titanium dioxide are the compounds which give white colour. Titanium dioxide is the best for this purpose as it impart 5 times the whiteness given by other white pigments. Being of fine particle size it has greater covering power. This comes in two grades the Anatase and Rutile, the difference being in the crystalline structure. The Rutile grades have more covering and whitening power than the Antase grade. About 1 to 5 % is used for brightening of coloured goods and 10 to 25% for white goods. This pigment is useful for natural and synthetic rubbers. Titanium dioxide and barium sulphide mixture known as 'Titanium White' gives a very good white colour. But barytes, barium sulphate, magnesium carbonate and calcium carbonate though are white in colour, do not have any whitening properties. Lithopone is also a white pigment and is obtained by the action of zinc sulphate over barium sulphide. It is actually a mixture of barium sulphate and zinc sulphide and is used in cheaper compounds.

Red Pigments

Iron oxide is the main inorganic red pigment. It comes in various shades ranging from yellow to brick red and dark red. Naturally occuring iron oxides have undesirable impurities such as manganese, hence they are synthetically produced by calcining ferrous sulphate. The iron oxide produced thus is ground and thoroughly bleached and washed before the final drying and grinding, as a trace of acid results in bad ageing properties.

Other inorganic red pigments are antimony sulphide and cadmium selenide but they have little use since good, non-fading, non-bleeding organic red pigments became available. They give much brighter reds than iron oxide but cannot compare with the organic reds from either colour or cost stand point. Antimony sulphide has two grades. Crimson antimony is antimony trisulphide which may contain some free sulphur and sometimes antimony tetra-sulphide. It gives strong colours with a crimson base, and imparts good resistance to ageing. Golden antimony is antimony trisulphide which may contain free sulphur and sometimes calcium sulphate. It gives colours of a red orange type. Antimony sulphide is non-poisonous and thus can be used for gaskets used in bottles for lemonade and soda etc. and other food containers and also some druggists sundries and tubings. It gives bright shades to rubber goods; coloured ebonite could be made using antimony sulphide alongwith pigment to cover the ebony colour of ebonite. Among the inorganic pigments mercury sulphide or vermilion gives the brightest shades of colours ranging from orange to deep red. It is a costly pigment and is used in brightly coloured ebonite.

Yellow Pigments

The best of inorganic yellows is cadmium lithopone which gives a bright clear colour. It is made similarly to white lithopone except that cadmium sulphide is precipitated on the barium sulphate base. Cadmium sulphides are available in shades ranging from yellow to orange and give brilliant shades. These are non-bleeding and heat resistant and could be used for coloured ebonite. Nickel titanate gives yellow colours of extremely high stability to heat, light and chemicals. Yellow iron oxide gives a dull, dirty colour, but it is cheap and is used sometimes for shading tans. Zinc yellow or zinc chromate has a very low covering power and is no longer used to any extent.

Green Pigments

Chromium oxide is the principal green inorganic pigment used in rubber compounds. It is made by fusing sodium dichromate with boric acid. It is quite cheap, inert and stable particularly at high temperatures. It gives a rather dull green.

Blue Pigments

Ultramarine blue is the principal blue pigment, it is obtained by calcining and extracting mixture of clay, charcoal, soda ash and sulphur. The colour obtained vary from a deep blue to greenish shades. The colour of rubber compounds is subject to appreciable change during cure. It fades badly during steam cures and bleaches out completely when rubber comes in contact with acids.

Organic Pigments

Inorganic pigments usually give rather dull colours in rubber compounds, hence for brightly coloured compounds synthetic organic pigments are used. They are available in very large range of colours and shades. Organic pigments are quite expensive and are compared on a cost covering power basis. Oragnic pigments used in rubber goods should be light-fast. Pastel shades are generally obtained by combining such materials with light coloured inorganic fillers, notably titanium dioxide. Organic colours are of various types e.g. lakes, toners, insoluble pigments colours and indigo derivatives etc. They are available in the form of dry powders, oily pastes or as masterbatches in rubber. Dry powders are not convenient for mixing because of their tendency to fly and contaminate other batches. Paste colours mix readily but present awkward handling problems. Masterbatches greatly assist in dispersion and lead to appreciable economics in the amount needed to produce the colour required in the final compound. certain dyestuffs soluble in rubber are also used to produce delicate shades in translucent materials.

Colours of organic types are often the most expensive ingredient in a compound. But very small quantities are needed i.e. 0.5 to 1% to give bright shades. Colours are sensitive to cure conditions and other materials present in the compound. In NR compounds it is preferable to use pale crepe in place of smoked sheet rubber. If a synthetic rubber compounds is to be made, only non-staining type synthetic rubbers should be used. Accelerators should be carefully chosen, as some of them can not be used with certain shades while others change the shade during cure. Curing should be done at somewhat lower temperatures to avoid the risk of dulling of the shade.

As mentioned earlier incorporation of some light coloured inorganic fillers e.g. titanium dioxide (1 to 3%) brightens the shades, particularly for pastel shades. Care should be exercised to avoid the incorporation of more than the sufficient quantity of white pigment as otherwise much large quantities of colour will be required to get a given shade, thus resulting in higher cost of the compound. Organic colours are not useful for the production of ebonite, as they fade during the long curing periods used for ebonite manufacture. Specially produced colours are available for use in the rubber industry.

Colour matching in rubber compounds is somewhat of an art, and, in case of difficulty, valuable advice can be obtained by consisting the manufacture of the colours.

12

Rubber Blowing Agents

Introduction

Rubber Blowing Agents are the chemicals, inorganic or organic, which under well defined conditions liberate gases giving expended closed cell or open cell structure rubber product. The most commonly used inorganic blowing agent is sodium bicarbonate, though ammonium carbonate and bicarbonate are still in use. These liberate CO_2 and yield an open pore structure. Ammonium carbonate is one of the earliest blowing agents used for production of sponge rubber and is still used for toilet sponge. Sodium bi-carbonate is still quite popular bacause of its low cost compared to organic blowing agents. It is used in quantities upto 10%. A high dose of stearic acid is normally used to facilitate decomposition of the bi-carbonate, before the curing starts, in the production of open cell sponge rubber.

Few important organic blowing agents are as follows :

1. Benzene Sulphonyl Hydrazide

It is the simplest aromatic blowing agent under the class of sulphonyl hydrazides. It is available under the trade name of Celogen BSH (Bayer). It is a white crystalline solid melting and beginning to decompose at near 105°C. It releases nitrogen producing both open-cell and closed-cell sponge rubber. The decomposition temperature is lowered by the presence of basic materials like urea and ethylene glycol. It liberates about 100 c.c. of gas per gm. and is widely used for the production of soft microcellular slippers and sandals.

2. p Toluene Sulphonyl Hydrazide

TSH is similar to BSH except that the melting point and decomposition temperature are higher (120°C and higher).

3. p P'Oxybis (Benzene Sulphonyl Hydrazide)

This rubber blowing agent is free from odour problem. It is a while crystalline solid melting and decomposing at about 164°C. It is widely used in rubber and plastics in the extrusion of cellular polythene for wire insulation, in expanded rubbers and in rubber resin blends. It is free from odour, toxicity or discolouration problems. It decomposes to produce gas in an alkaline latex system at steam temperature, giving acidic products which coagulate or gel the latex in the foamed state. This provides a unique method of producing an expanded rubber product. Impregnation of paper or non-woven fabric with latex so treated can produce an interesting fibre reinforced rubber article.

4. Diazoamino Benzene

It is one of the earliest organic blowing agents used for rubber. It is soluble and capable of producing an extremely fine unicellular structure in rubber but the decomposition products produce a dark colour in the expanded product and also may stain other other materials with which it may come in contact. Diazoamino benzene melts with decomposition near 100°C. It is claimed to be carcinogenic and is no longer used as a rubber blowing agent.

5. Azoisobutyronitrile

Azoisobutyronitrile or AZDN was first introduced for the production of sponge rubber latices but was later used for expanding PVC. It is completely non-discolouring and non-staining giving white PVC foam of fine uniform cell structure. Decomposition occurs rapidly at temperatures above

100°C. The decomposition residue is a toxic substance and good ventilation is necessary to eliminate the hazard.

6. Dinitroso Pentamethylene Tetramine

Dinitroso pentamethylene tetramine also known as DPT or DNPT. This is the most important and popular nitrogen blowing agent used for the production of soft, medium and hard tyres of microcellular soling. When heated alone or in the presence of inert diluents, this chemical decomposes near 195°C, but when used in rubber or plastics in the presence of certain activators produce gas within a temperature range of 130 to 190°C. The decomposition is accelerated and temperature lowered to even 120°C by acidic substances such as stearic acid, salicylic acid, benzoic acid and phthalic anhydride, these are commonly used as activators. DPT produces a large volume of gas, about 200 c.c. per gram and is very economical to use, in this respect. Goods produced with DPT have a fishy odour when fresh, which disappears on storage. The odour is reduced to a considerable extent by the presence of ethylene glycol, benzoic acid and urea in the compound.

7. N, N'-Dinitroso-N, N'-Dimethyl Terephthalamide

This material is a weak explosive and is used in desensitised form with mineral oil, but still care should be taken to protect it from sparks and open flames. It melts with decomposition at 105°C. Prolonged heating at 80 to 90°C, leads to sustain and rapid formation of nitrogen gas. This blowing agent is unique in the fact that the low decomposition temperature permits the expansion of a vinyl plastisol prior to gelation at 95°C. Subsequent curing of the fragile foam at 175°C produces open cell vinyl foam. The products are free of colour.

Azo Dicarbon Amide

Azo dicarbon amide or AC is a yellow solid decomposing at 195°C to give a high yield of gas (220 to 240 c.c./gm at STP). This temperature can be lowered using a variety of activators e.g. lead, cadmium, zinc and barium salts etc. Unlike most other blowing agents, azodicarbon amide does not support combustion and is self-extinguishing. The white decomposition residue is odourless, non-toxic, non-discolouring and non-staining.

9. Sulphonyl Semicarbazides

These are one of the newest blowing agents now being used in U.S.A. p-toluene sulphonyl semicarbazide and p-p'-oxybis (benzene sulphonyl semicarbazide) come under this category. The latter one has a decomposition temperature of 215°C. They can be used for rubber expansion since activators lower their decomposition and comparitively high gas yields (about 145 c.c./gm at STP) are obtained.

10. Others

Related to azodicarbonamide are the alkyl esters of Azocarboxylic acid. They are soluble in the usual plasticisers. They give little gas on heating even upto 240°C but under the presence of activators. They decompose to give a mixture of gases even at as low as 100°C . Among the salts of azodicarboxylic acid the barium salt is available as blowing agent. It is a yellow crystalline solid decomposing at 240 to 250°C with the evolution of nitrogen and carbon monoxide gases and barium carbonate.

13

Latex Dipped Goods

Introduction

Articles manufactured by immersing, a former into a suitably compounded latex, and withdrawing it in such a way as to leave a uniform deposit on it, is known as 'Dipping'. This is an old process and the seamless rubber articles thus obtained are known as '***Dipped Goods***'. Previously, dipped goods used to be manufactured by dipping into a solution of milled rubber, but after the advent of concentrated latex (60% and above), solution technology has been replaced by the latex technology. Use of latex has various advantages over solutions viz. high solids non-inflamability, lower capital expenditure, no solvent loss, non-toxicity, and hazard free operation etc. Apart from this latex dipping gives thicker deposits per dip as compared to those obtained from solutions. Solvent solutions have very high viscosity at even low rubber content, which is not the case with latex compounds. The manufacture of teats, surgical investigatory fingers, bags, balloons, surgical gloves, household and industrial gloves, shoes, bathing caps, contraceptives/condoms etc. are some of the rubber articles produced by the dipping process using latex compounds.

Dipping System

The simplest dipping machine consists of a carrier member arranged to slide up and down the vertical; guides. This movement is manual through a system of wire cables, pulleys, or chains and sprockets. The formers, fixed in boards are placed in the carrier member which lowers them into the dipping tank; the speed of dipping and withdrawal is manually controlled. This kind of machine is quite simple and satisfactory for small scale operation. In the improved version of the machine, the carrier member may have two sets of formers with arrangement for inverting them. In this case the first set can be dipped and then inverted while the set on the opposite side is being dipped. With the help of a motor drive, a uniform speed of immersion and withdrawal can be arranged, ensuring evenness of deposit and uniformity in the weights of individual batches. The drive can also be designed to make it possible to the operator to select different speeds for immersion and withdrawals. When articles of complicated shape are being dipped, it may be possible to vary the speed of withdrawal, so as to obtain a uniform surface speed over the straight and curved parts of the formers.

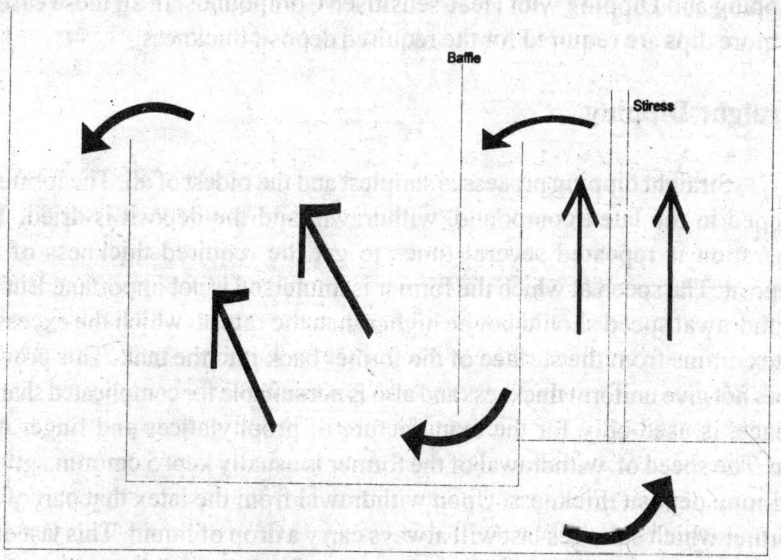

Circulating Dipping Tank

The size and number of formers that can conveniently be dipped at one time, determine the size of the dipping tank. If a fairly viscous compound is used with a straight dipping process, a skimming board is also required. This board is passed lightly over the surface, every so often, to remove the skim coagulum over the liquid surface. A continuous stirrer is also provided at one corner of the tank to keep the contents of the tank in gentle circulation; this prevents sludging and skimming. The tank is usually made of metal. It should be resistant to ammonia and other alkalies present in the latex compound. Stainless steel is the most suitable material for this purpose but is rather costly. Mild steel can also be used, provided the inner surface is protected with an alkali-proof and rust-proof paint, bitumen coating or lining of PVC. Wood impregnated with paraffin wax is quite cheap and satisfactory. The temperature of the dipping tank should be maintained between 15° to 20°C so as to prevent the changes in viscosity, loss of ammonia and to slow down pre-vulcanisation.

Dipping Methods

Various methods for getting a deposit on the former by dipping a former in the latex compound are available, *viz.* Straight Dipping, Coagulant Dipping and Dipping with Heat-sensitised Compounds. In all these cases 2 or more dips are required for the required deposit thickness.

Straight Dipping

Straight dipping process is simplest and the oldest of all. The former is dipped in the latex compound, withdrawn, and the deposit is dried. The operation is repeated several times to get the required thickness of the deposit. The speed at which the former is immersed is not important. But the withdrawal speed should not be higher than the rate at which the excess of latex drains from the surface of the former back into the tank. This process does not give uniform thickness and also is not suitable for complicated shapes, hence, is used only for the manufacture of prophylatices and finger cots etc. The speed of withdrawal of the former is usually kept 5 cm/min., giving a 1 mm. deposit thickness. Upon withdrawal from the latex that part of the former which emerges last will always carry a drop of liquid. This last drop represents a comparatively large quantity of latex which has to be evenly distributed so as not to prodduce an objectionable local thickening at the tip. It is sufficient merely to invert the formers and allow the drop to flatten out and spread.

Coagulant Dipping

In this method the depositing of latex is facilitated witrh the aid of a coagulant such as acids mainly acetic and formic and some metallic salts *e.g.* calcium nitrate or chloride. The former is first dipped in a solution of a coagulant; calcium nitrate in alcohol solution is the preffered coagulant. This former carrying a film of coagulant is next dipped into the latex compound. The action of coagulant causes a relatively thick solid deposit to congeal on the surface of the former. Usually, the time of immersion does not exceed 30 seconds. To ensure complete wetting of the former by the coagulant solution a wetting agent e.g. methyl alcohol or acetone is included in the formula. Sometimes finely divided talc or diatomaceous earth is added in the coagulant solution to serve as a stripping aid. When heavy walled articles 0.7 mm and thicker are desired, it will accelerate the process, if the form is removed after a dwell of 1 to 2 minutes and is reimmersed in the coagulant. This speeds up the gelation of the first dip and adds a new supply of coagulant ready for the next latex dipping. No stripping aid is used in the coagulant when it is applied between the layers of rubber. In a slight modification of this process the former is first dipped into the latex, followed by the coagulant dip. The initial rubber deposit acts as carrier for the coagulant. The initial film adheres to the form and helps to prevent sagging when heavy films are coagulated upon it. This modified process is used for dipped coatings where the rubber remains permanently on the former as part of the final product. An example of such a product is a metal tool having a rubber coating on the handle for insulation purposes. Caogulant dipping process gives uniform deposits on elastomers of complicated shape such as gloves.

The following coagulant solution has been found to be quite satisfactory :

Methyl alcohol	50 parts
Water	27
Calcium nitrate	20
Acetic acid, glacial	3

The latex compound in this process is similar to that used for straight dipping when metal salt solution is used as coagulant, but if acid solution coagulant is used then the latex compound should have low ammonia (0.15%) content.

Dipping with Heat Densitised Latex

In this process latex compounds that show reasonably good stability at normal room temperatures, but which coagulate spontaneously when the temperature is raised to about 70° to 80°C, are used. The heat sensitising, agents such as ammonium sulphate, ammonium persulphate, DPG and Zinc ammonium complex are used for making the latex compound sensitive to heat. In such a compound a heated former can be inserted and a coagulum will form around it just as if the former had a coagulant on it. As the continuous dipping of hot formers will bring about an increase in the temperature of the dipping tank, a cooling jacket is necessary, so as to maintain the temperature at 14°C - 18°C, particularly for getting uniform results. Even so, irregularly shaped objects will dissipate heat at differing rates with a resulting variation in coagulum thickness. Dipping process based on heat sensitised latex compound is as simple as straight dipping and gives quicker, heavier and even deposits. A heat sensitising agent usually zinc ammonia complex, for example, is produced as per the following formulation :

Zinc oxide	2 parts
Ammonium benzoate	5
28 Be' ammonia	14

This mixture is mixed with 180 parts of latex.

Compounding

Natural latex is normally used; neoprene latex is chosen where heat, oil or ozone resistance is required. SBR latices are not usually employed because their unsupported films are not too strong when dry and their wet gels are very weak. Neoprene gives a strong wet gel almost like that with natural latex. As usual accelerator, antioxidant , pigments, waxes etc. are incorporated. Stabilisers are kept to the minimum so that coagulant could be most effective. Little or no mineral loading is employed in dipping stocks because of poor wet gel strength and tendency to sludge.

Now some of the specific dipped rubber goods are given below :

Toy Balloons

Straight dipping process is used for cheaper balloons while good quality balloons are made using coagulant dipping process. 10 to 15% calcium nitrate solution in alcohol containing a stripping aid is used as coagulant, followed by dipping for 10 to 20 secs. in the latex compound, to get a dried deposit thickness of 0.15 to 0.25 mm. After leaching with water and drying at 70-80% for 30-45 min. bead is made. Soap solution or talc is applied as a stripping aid and the balloon is stripped off. Balloons, in partially infllated condition, can be stamped using a solvent solution of rubber colour master batch. Multicoloured or 'jazz' patterned balloons are made by dipping white or light-coloured balloons, while still on the dipping form, in a water bath on the surface of which small quantities of bright-coloured rubber solutions have been floated, some of these adhere to the balloon as it is withdrawn forming very striking and swirling patterns.

The latex compound for balloons should be such as to give maximum elongation, easy inflation and adequate permanent set. Zinc-bearing accelerators are preffered and zinc oxide is kept at the minimum. Antioxidant, stabliser and sometimes wax, are present. A small quantity of lithopone may be incoroporated if an opaque balloon is required.

General Balloons Formulations

	1	2	3
Rubber	100	100	100
Sulphur	1	1	1
Zinc oxide	1.5	1.5	1
Accelerator 552	0.5	—	0.38
ZDC	0.5	—	—
MBT	—	—	0.3
Antoxidant	1	1	1
TiO^2	5	—	—
Organic Pigment Colour	2	2	—

All these ingredients are in the form of dispersions and latices.

Another formula is given below :

60% Natural Latex	167 parts
10% KOH solution	5
20% Pot. caprilate solution	2.5
50% Zinc oxide dispersion	1.25-1.5
50% ZDC dispersion	1-1.2
50% Antioxidant dispersion	1.5
50% Sulphur dispersion	1.25-1.5
50% Vegetable oil emulsion	5-10
50% Colour dispersion	As required

Various dispersions are prepared as usual.

Prophylatics

These articles are very thin and thus can be made by the dipping process only, with only one or two dips. The formula A below gives low toughness and high extensibility while formula B gives tightly cured products:

	A	B
Rubber (60% latex)	100	100
Sulphur	1	2.5
Activator	0.5	1
Antioxidant	1	1
Accelerator	0.75	1

More formulations for contraceptives :

	1	2	3
Rubber	100	100	100
Sulphur	2.5	2	0.6
Mineral oil	5	—	—
Zinc oxide	—	0.5	1
Stearic acid	—	0.5	—
ZDC	0.5	0.5	0.75

Due to very low wall thickness and high quality, extreme cleanliness during manufacture has to be observed.

Footwear

One piece rubber footwear, both ladies' toe and conventional types may be made from latex. The latter may be dipped on an engraved form and reserved so that the pattern will appear on the outside; the upper thus formed is cemented to a milled rubber calendered sole. More complex boots are made by cementing the inner dipped rock into the other portions. All these footwear dipping compounds should be high in rubber content to give maximum resiliency, durability and stretch. A tight cure is desired. A suitable compound on dry basis is given below :

Rubber (in latex)	100 Parts
Sulphur	1.75
Zinc oxide	5
Thickener	0.5
Kaolin	7
MBT	1.2
Colour	2

Gloves

Gloves are of various types, according to their use *e.g.* surgeons', electricians', industrial workers' and housekeepers' etc. Surgeons' gloves must be thin, strong and should stand repeated sterilisations. As water soluble materials should not be present the latex used should be of high purity. Accelerator etc. should be properly chosen and also the antioxidant. A fairly weak coagulant may be used. Plasticiser is incorporated to lower the toughness so as to reduce the strain on hands.

Surgeon's Gloves

The finish of the outer surface is either rough or smooth The gloves are transparent or transculent. No colouring ingredient is mixed. They donot contain any ingredient, harmful either to the wearer or the person they come in contact with. The gloves are provided with a bead not more than 3mm and have a rolled wrist. The thickness of rubber is 0.24 ± 0.6mm. The tensile strength and elongation at break are 180 kgs/cm2 and 7 times respectively. These gloves are produced in sizes 6,6-1/2, 7,7-1/2 and 8. The pair weight varies from 20 to 33 gms. depending on the size.

General Formulation

Rubber (in 60% latex)	100 parts
Sulphur	1.5-2
Activator	0.5-0.75
Accelerator	0.5-1
Dispersing (mineral or castor oil)	1-5
Antioxidant	1
Stabiliser	1

Postmortem gloves also have almost similar formulations and just like surgeon's gloves, these are also made using coagulant solution. The gloves have the wrist edges rolled up or straight cut, reinforced with rubber straps. Their tensile strength and elongation at break is 140 kg/cm^2 and 6 times respectively, before heat treatment.

Disposable Free Size Surgical Gloves :

Disposable as well as sterilizable surgeon's rubber gloves can now be prepared easily by automatic dipping machine making use of concentrated latex solution (60% and above). The product gives very fine finish and smooth surface, desired thickness and weight, high flexibility, are non-toxic and non-inflammable. No solvent is required for the production. The use of automatic dipping machine gives the advantages of higher production capacity, low cost of production, lesser man-power, less space utilization and easy & safe operation.

Disposable surgical gloves are free of size, ambidextrous and non-sterile, available in uniform size for both hands. They are about half in weight compared to surgeon's gloves (weighing about 16 to 20 gms per pair). These gloves are completely hygienic because of their one time use and offer 100% immunity against virus transfer.

Household Gloves

In this case also the thickness is very much as compared to that surgical gloves. Their thickness is about 1 to 12 mm and the weight is about 100 gms. They are generally made in 3 sizes viz. small, medium and large. These gloves are generally pigmented and sometimes contain blooming wax. To further improve the surface chlorine vapour or sodium hupochlorite treatment may be given. This gives a slight case hardening to the surface and imparts a smooth feel with reduced rubbery drag. Bromine solution may also be used for the same effect. Two general formulations are given below :

	A	B
Rubber (in latex 60% latex)	100	100
Sulphur	2	1
Activator	1	1
Antioxidant	1	1
ZDC	0.75	0.5
China clay	10-20	—
Stabiliser	—	0.2
Pot. hydroxide	—	0.5
Lithopone	—	10
Colour/pigment		As required

If heated formers are to be used, then the latex compound is made heat sensitive by incorporating ammonium sulphate, DPG etc. Mineral content may be reduced by using 1 part TiO_2 in place of 10 parts of lithopone. Compound cost may be reduced by using 1 part TiO_2 and 10 parts clay in place of lithopone. Neoprene latex may be used for oil, grease and solvent resistance.

Industrial Gloves

Various types of industrial gloves are available. Light-duty gloves are similar to household gloves, about 1-25 mm thick, while heavy duty industrilal gloves may be even 2 mm thick; in this case beading is not required. The weight of a pair of those gloves is about 200 gms. In the case of industrial gloves, formulations of household gloves may be used; in place of colour some lamp-black may be used. For good moisture-resistance water-solubles should be minimum and even some paraffin wax may be incorporated. Very - heavy - duty industrial gloves are made of fabric dip-coated with latex which is, usually of neoprene type. The compound used in this case is of high viscosity to reduce fabric penetration. The fabric glove is fitted on to the former and then dipped into the latex compound. Coagulant dipping method may be used. Antifoam may be incorporated to reduce webbing. A general formula for such gloves is given .

These types of gloves are used for gardening and other rough domestic work also.

Rubber (in latex 60%)	100
Thickening agent	0.25-0.75
Sulphur	2
Activator	1
Antioxidant	1
Accelerator	0.5-1
China clay	15-25
Lamp black	Small amount

Gloves by Lamination Dipping

As mentioned earlier for oil, grease and solvent resistance special latices such as polychloroprene or nitrile latices are used, but this increases cost; to offset this lamination dipping process may be used. In this process bulk of the glove is made using natural latex followed by dipping in neoprene or nitrile rubber latex. The natural latex compound does not contain free sulphur so that this coat may withstand the high temperature curing required with neoprene.In one method a smooth former is used, having a solvent-roughened surface to fingers, thumbs and palms, and is heated to 65°C. It is dipped in the following coagulant solution :

Calcium chloride	10 Parts
Calcium nitrate	10
Industrial methylated spirit	60
Acetone	20

After drying the former is dipped for 1 minutes in the natural latex compound. The latex coating is allowed to go 'dull' and it is then dipped in the neoprene latex compound for 45 seconds. The time between natural and neoprene dipings should not be more than required, otherwise the two coatings will have a weak bond and delamination shall take place during service. Immediately after the neoprene dip, it is dipped for 30 seconds in a solvent rippling or roughening solution containing 5% glacial acetic acid in toluene. It is then dried for 1 hour at 70°C followed by 1 hr. at 120°C to full-vulcanise the two deposits. In the second method an engraved former is used and this requires the glove to be dipped inside out; i.e. first neoprene dip is given followed by the natural latex dip. The former is first coated coagulant as therefore. It is then dipped into neoprene latex and withdrawn immediately. The firm is partially dried for 15 min. at 70°C, followed by dipping for 1 minute in the natural latex compound. The composit deposit is dried for 1 hr. at 70°C followed by 1 hr. at 120°C.

To ensure good coagulant pick-up the pH of the neoprene later should preferably be about 10.7; if pH is high glycine (solution 18%) is added; and if pH is lower, it is adjusted by using KOH solution.

These two processes of lamination dipping give a film thickness of 0.4 mm for natural latex and 0.15 mm for neoprene latex. By varying the dipping time and coagulant solution composition, the film thickness may be controlled. In both the processes water-leaching is carried out before drying and curing.

	Natural latex compound	Neoprene latex compound
Narural latex (60%)	167 parts	
Neoprene latex (60%)	—	167
Sod. oleyl, p-anisidine sulphonate (10%)	2	2
Casein solution (10%)	—	3.25
Pot. hydroxide (10%)	0.25	—
Zinc oxide dispersion (50%)	6	10
TMTD (33%)	9	3
Thiourea (10%)	10	—
Sodium dibutyl dithiocarbamate (50%)	—	2
ZDC (50%)	2	—
Antioxidant (styrenated phenol) (50%)	2	4
Lithopone dispersion (50%)	10	—
Filler dispersion (50%)	—	60
Colour/pigment		As required

The filler dispersion for neoprene compound is as follows :

Lithopone	25 parts
Clay	50
Whiting	75
Sodium alkyl naphthalene Sulphonate (10%)	150

Surgical Investigatory Fingers

The surgical investigatory fingers or finger coats are used by surgeons. These are made in a set of five. A set weighs about 25 gms or 5 gms each. Straight dipping process is used in this case. The former is dipped in the latex compound for 30 seconds twice. The entire process is as usual. Following formula may be used :

Rubber (latex 60%)	100 parts
Sulphur	1
Activator	0.5
Antioxidant	1
Accelerator	0.75
Plasticiser	3

Teats and nipples are also made by dipping process but rubber is used in place of latex.

The various chemicals used in the formulations are as follows : Activator - zinc oxide or zinc carbonate; stabiliser - Vulcastab L.S. (ICI); dispersing agents - Dispersol LN (ICI), and antioxidant - Nonox D, PBN etc. and their equivalent unless specified.

14

Latex Foam Products

Introduction

Latex rubber foam products have got good demand now-a-days. Cushions of this foam rubber are used in chairs, pillows, beddings automobiles furnitures etc. for luxurious living.

The first cellular rubber to be made from latex was made by coagulating the latex in the presence of a chemical blowing agent and subsequently causing the tough coagulum to 'rise' like bread before fixing this structure by vulcanization. Thus the technique was 'first coagulate then blow'. The principle now is 'first blow then coagulate'

Thc two modern routes to latex foam products concern the way in which the foam is made. They are : (i) Chemical foaming, which has proposed to use every possible reaction for generating gas in the latex to cause it to foam. (ii) Mechanical foaming, in which the latex is whisked like white of egg and thus whipped into a foam. This is the chief method used in modern production.

The mechanical frothing processes used today on such a large scale for the production of latex foam goods use, for the most part, a concentrated natural rubber latex prepared by one of the processes involving partial removal of the non-rubber substances as well as concentration of the rubber (*e.g.* processes such as centrifugation or creaming). Successful operation of latex foam processes normally demands a concentrated latex one containing a minimum of 58% rubber is convenient. It is usual to reduce the ammonia content of the latex, during compounding, to a value between 0.1% and 0.25%. This facilitates gelation and the control of the process and is usually done by stirring and blowing a current of air over the surface of the compounded latex as part of the 'maturing process'.

The following formulaes are used for compounding :

(a) Castor oil soaps solution, obtained by slow boiling of the compounds in quantities until the solutions clears. Enough water should be added to make up to original volume.

	Parts by wt.
Water	829
Castor oil	371
Potassium Hydroxide	75

(b) Stabilizer solution, consisting of :

Water	250
A dispersing agent like Darvan, Dispersol etc.	5
Vulcastab T.M.	25
Notax L.M.	20

(c) Accelerator-antioxidant dispersion prepared by ball-milling together :

Water	30
10% Casein solution	30
10% Darvin solution	10
An antioxidant, PPD (Piperidine-pentamethylene dithiocarbamate)	20
Sulphur	40
Zinc salt of mercapto-benzothiazole (ZMBT)	35

(d) Zinc oxide dispersion, obtained by ball-milling :

Water	22
10% Casein solution	30
10% Dispersing agent solution	10
10% Sodium Silicate Solution	5
Zinc oxide	100

(e) Sodium silico-fluoride dispersion, made by

	Parts by Weight
Continuous ball-milling :	
Water	304
Bentonite	16
Sodium Silico-fluoride	80

With all the above mentioned solutions ready. The procedure follows these steps : one part of solution (a), 3 parts of solution (b), 8.75 parts of dispersion and (c) 166 parts of 60% latex are mixed in a tank with a slowly stirring mixer. Mixing is carried out for about 18 hrs, now give a foam. The speed of the stirrer is reduced when the mixture becomes sufficiently foamed. 8.35 parts of dispersion and (d) 2.5 parts of 10% casein solution are then added, mixing is repeated and finally 7.5 parts of dispersion (e) are added.

The size of the mixer or foamer will depend on the scale of production. Small amounts (0.25 parts) of ammonium oleate may be added to increase foaming rate and to insure good setting. The foam thus prepared is then moulded in moulds of various designs, which are made generally of cast aluminium fitted with cored tops. After the foam is poured into moulds, the lids are immediately sunk into the proper position, and the setting taking approximately 5 minutes. The foamed latex is then vulcanised in steam under no pressure by passing the moulds through a heated chamber. A curing time of 30 minutes is sufficient to prevent subsequent deformation. Some further curing may be accomplished in the drier. The foam is then washed in water and then squeezed through ringer rolls several times. Drying is done in hot tunnels, the temperature of which increases from 60° at the begining to 80°C at the end of the tunnel.

15

Latex-Based Adhesive and Rubber Solution

Introduction

Rubber in solution form is used as an adhesive or cement. When two materials are to be joined with a flexible joint rubber solutions is employed. Rubber solutions are used in joining two or more rubber layers, various shoe parts and soles etc. Rubber solution is used by automobile tyres and tube repairers.

Natural and reclaimed rubber solutions and adhesives are widely used for bonding paper labels to tins and bottles, rubber, plaster, board, floor tiles, wood, leather and metals. They form the basis for many pressure sensitive tapes; blended with asphalt, rubber adhesive are used for joining non-metalllic parts. In building trade they are used for weather proofing, damp prevention and sealing. They are used for tiling and sealing of wood defects. Ceramic tiles, plastic sheetings, and resin-bonded decorative veneers may be attached to plaster, brick, wood, steel; and linoleum and vinyl floor-tiles may be attached to wood or floor.

Formulations of Rubber Solutions & Latex Based Adhesives

A simple rubber solution is given below :

Smoked sheet	10 parts
Solvent Benzene	15 "

An improved solution is given below, dichloro-ethylene reduces the flammability and viscosity

Smoked sheet	10 parts
Di-chloro-ethylene	30 "
Solvent benzene	70 "

Tubes Joining Solution

Natural rubber	100
Calcium silicate	20
Coumarone resin	5
Zinc oxide	20
Stearic acid	1
PBN	0.5
HFN	0.5

The compound is dissloved in naphtha. A thin coat is applied at the end of the tube to be joined. After careful drying, one end is dipped, in sulphur chloride diluted with toluene, For a moment, and both the ends are pressed together immediately. The final joint is allowed to rest for 8 to 10 hours to ensure a good bond. Sulphur chloride solution in toluene should not be too strong; otherwise the bond will fail due to overcure.

Lamination Adhesive

It is based on SBR and contains well sealed tack producing resins :

SBR	100 parts
Zinc oxide	5 "
Titanium dioxide	10 "
P-F resin	12 "
Ester Gum	40 "

Paraffin oil	25 "
Coumarone resin	40 "
Yellow pigment	0.3"
Heptane	300 "
Alcohol	10 "

Metal to Metal or Rubber Adhesive

Based on SBR	100
SBR	Variable
Carbon black	3
Zinc oxide	8
Sulphur	3.2
MBT	3
PBN or IPPD	3
Plasticiser	1000
Xylene	

Nitrile Rubber Base Adhesives

Nitrile rubber adhesive have good self-stability, high temperature properties and oil resistance. Blended with phenolics they are used to, laminate aluminium and stainless steel, bond brake linings to brake shoes, laminate leather and attach soles in shoe manufacturing. They are used to bond cork, card board, fibre board, nylon and other polymeric films to themselves and to each other. Some of the adhesives based on nitrile rubber are given below :

General Purpose Black Curing Cement

Nitrile rubber	100 parts
Zinc oxide	5
Sulphur	3
Carbon black	50
Phenolic acid	5
Coumarone resin	25
Refined coal tar	25

Leather Adhesives

Nitrile rubber	100 parts
Vinyl chloride/acetate copolymer	100
Zinc oxide	5
Stearic acid	1.5
Calcium silicate	2

Adhesive for Boiling Vinyl to Fabrics

Nitrile Rubber	100 parts
Calcium silicate	40
Titanium dioxide	10
Refined coal tar	25
Coumarone resin	25
Chlorinated rubber	100

Adhesive are made by dissolving in suitable solvents.

Neoprene Based Cements

Numerous Adhesives are being made from polychloroprene or neoprene, they are being widely used in shoe manufacture industrial rubber goods, bonding of rubber to metal goods and bonding of decorative laminates to the table tops. Zinc oxide is used with vulcanising ingredients in a solvent of benzene and trichloroethylene to form the adhesive. Bentonite Clay and diatomaceous earth are employed as fillers. Isopropyl acetate is the usual thinner employed for neoprene adhesives. As is the case with other simple and modified adhesives, the solid content of this type of cement is also maintained at about 20 to 25% by volume.

Pressure Sensitive Adhesives

The required chief chracterics of these adhesives is permanent tacky surface. Adhesive tapes of scotch type, medical type, packaging type and marking type come into this category. Some of these formulations are given below :

Formulation 1

Butyl rubber	100 parts
Carbon black	90
Whiting	20
Phenolic resin	10
Cuprous oxide	2
Paraffin process oil	5

It is a black composition to be calendered on to the vinyl film for use as industrial pressure sensitive tape to be used for wrapping underground pipes.

Formulation 2

Beta-naphthol modified rubber	100 Parts
Pale crepe rubber	100
Rosin	180
Chlorinated paraffin wax	50
Toluene	1000

Formulation 3

Pale crepe rubber	100 parts
Zinc oxide	50
Ester gum	150
Rosin	50
Antioxidant	1
Solvent	500

Latex Based Adhesives

Latex based adhesives are of special importance for cementing porous surfaces due to their ability to wet such surfaces. On the other angle the porosity allows the latex adhesive to dry out thus producing a strong coherent film. Sodium silicate, Glue, albumen, gums and starch etc. are compatible with natural latex and exert a stabilising action. The latex rubber in the adhesive film imparts flexibility and strength and protects and bond against dynamic fatigue.

Advantages of Latex Adhesive over Rubber Solutions

1. Reduced coagulation of suspended matter.
2. Non-flamibility and absence of toxic solvents.
3. Wide range of solids content and viscosities possible.
4. Wets and penetrates the porous surfaces.
5. Deposit higher molecular weight material of super ageing resistance.

Disadvantages of Latex Adhesives

1. Low rate of drying and its irreversibility. The dried film cannot be removed by washing with water or with dilute alkali.
2. Inferior water resistance and electrical properties of the dried films.
3. Possibility of contamination with metallic impurities.
4. Susceptibility to freezing and tendency of latices to shrink textiles and to wrinkle paper.

The latex-based adhesives are used mainly in the leather shoe industry. Latex adhesives are used in making paper products such as bags, milk cartons, envelopes, drinking straws and gummed tapes etc. In both these types of applications the latex adhesives can be used even when the surfaces are moist; this is an advantage over solution adhesives. Latex adhesives may also be used to bond hard surfaces such as metals, glass etc. but in this field they are not the important. Latex adhesives find important use in bonding rubber to textiles.

Latex based adhesives contain a rubber latex, adhesion modifiers, plasticisers, curatives, fillers such as whiting and kaolin, thickener e.g. cellulose derivatives and other additives e.g. antioxidants, surfactants, antifoams (octyl alcohol, silicones), antifreeze, stabilisers, corrosion inhibitor, colourants, deodourants and redeoudrants etc. All these ingredients are not present at a time, but only some of them are used according to requirements. A simple leather foam latex adhesive is given below :

NR latex, 60%	100 parts (actual)
NaEDTA (20%)	2.5
Antioxidant, (50% dispersion) *e.g.* polymerised trimethyl Hydroquinone	2.5

This formulation is a clean, unfilled, low viscosity latex formulation containing EDTA as a chelating agent to protect it against metal catalysed oxidation. It can be thickened with some thickener e.g. a 10% solution of ammonium caseinate or gums, like karaya, arabic or tragacanth. If a purely synthetic material is desirable then polyvinyl alcohol, ammonium polyaizylate etc. may be used. When manufacturing convenience requires the latex to dry fairly thoroughly before combining, particularly with thickener present, a tackifier is desirable.

High Viscosity Leather Foam Adhesive

NR latex (60%)	100	Actual weight
Sod. EDTA	25	
Antioxidant	1	
Methyl cellulose (5% solution)	2	
Tackifying resin Dispersion	10-20	

Paper and Leather Latex Adhesives

	1	2
NR latex (60%, ammonia preserved)	167	167
Ammonium caseinate (15%)	-	100
Zinc oxide (50% dispersion)	4	4
Sulphur (50% dispersion)	4	4
ZDC (50% dispersion)	2	2
Nonox CI (25% dispersion)	4	4
Starch (15% dispersion)	667	-
Koalin (50% dispersion)	-	100

The quantities given are actual parts by weight. The solid content of the first formulation is given about 24% and that of the second is 45%.

The following latex adhesive compositions are based on SBR latices either alone or with natural rubber latex. These adhesives are extensively used in footwear, paper, leather, textile and tyre industries, and also as general purpose adhesives.

General Purpose Cement

Natural rubber latex	83 parts (actual)	50 parts (dry)
SBR-2000 latex	120	50
Carbon tetrachloride	4	4

Waterproof Cement

SBR-2000 latex	100 parts
Glue	100
Water	100
Formaldehyde	30
Alpha -Naphthol	7

Adhesive for Paper and Leather

	1	**2**
SBR-2000 latex	100	100
Sodium alkyl sulphate	0.5	1
Sodium polyacrylate	1	0.5
Zinc oxide	3	3
Sulphur	0.75	0.75
ZDC	1	1
PBN	1	1
Kaolinite clay	-	100

Adhesive for Bonding Soles and Foxing to Canvas

Natural latex (60%)	70 parts (dry basis)
SBR-2000 latex	30
Zinc oxide	3
ZDC	0.5
ZMBT	0.5
A.0.2246 (Bayer)	1
Sulphur	1.2

SBR latex is added to NR latex by slowly stirring. Compounding ingredients are added as 50% dispersions in water made in ball mills using sodium naphthalene formaldehyde sulphonate as dispersing agent.

General Purpose Choloroprene Latex Adhesives

	1	2
	Parts by wt. (wet basis)	
Polychloroprene latex (50% high gel polymer)	200	200
Zinc oxide (50%)	30	40
Thiuram E (50%)	3	–
Tepidone (25%)	6	–
Vulcafor TC (50)	–	3
Santowhite crystals (50%)	4	6
Kaolinite clay (67%)	–	15
Pptd. CaCO3 (67%)	–	15
Sod. metalisilicate (10%)	2.5	2.5
Aquarex WAQ (33%)	2.5	3
Total solids content	**49%**	**51%**

The first formula takes about 60 minutes and the second about 80 min. for curing at about 100°C.

16

Rubber Moulded Articles (Goods)

Introduction

Rubber moulded goods (articles) are used in day to day life in household, electrical, surgical and automotive and other applications. Several thousands of types of moulded goods are being produced. A few of these are : bottle stoppers, pump valves, mallet heads, grease and oils seals, O-rings, grommets, dust masks, handle grips, pedal pads, vibration absorbing units, bulbs, balls, electrical equipment parts, sockets and other parts having metal inserts, erasers, gaskets, tyres, hot water bottles, footwears, shoe heels, bumper pads, cycle paddles, ice bags etc. etc.

There are various moulding proceses but all of them are basically similar. The ways of introducing the materials into the mould distinguish one moulding process from another. The three moulding processes are namely; compression moulding, transfer moulding and injection moulding. The material is placed into a mould and there it is compressed, excess material flows out and the rubber object is formed which is cured by heating. Injection and transfer moulds do not require any provision for excess material flowing out of the mould, simply an escape route for the volume of air in the cavities, which the parting faces provide. These two methods give parts which carry little or no flash adhering to them at the parting lines of the mould.

Moulds

The most important item of equipment required for moulding is a good mould. Moulds are generally made of steel, and usually consists of two or more flat metal plates of varying thickness, which are so shaped that when kept together, they form one or more closed mould cavities; the shape and volume of cavity depend upon the end product dimensions. Single moulds having more than even one thousand cavities are in use. Apart from steel, the moulds are made of aluminium alloy and white metal also. In some cases, For example, in the manufacture of rubber ink pads, moulds of plaster of paris are also used. White metal consists of 80% lead, 10% tin and 5% antimony. White metal moulds are easier to make and are cheaper. They are employed for moulding shoe soles and heels, bottles, cycle handles, etc. Main advantage is that white metal moulds can be used for about 250 mouldings and after that they can be melted and reused for making fresh moulds. Moulds made of mild steel can be hardêned by chilling. Multiple moulds are sometimes necessary to increase the production rate. The moulds are carefully designed and finished to get products of correct dimensions and surface finish.

In compression moulding, to ensure dimensional consistency it is necessary to allow the excess material to move away from the edge of the cavity so that the 'lands' can contact with minimum thickness of rubber between them, thus flash can be kept to the minimum. Spew grooves and channels are provided of sufficient dimensions to accomodate this excess, and also to allow the escape of air from the mould cavity. In the case of complex shapes, it is necessary to provide extra venting to allow air to escape from a 'blind' area, where it is likely to be trapped. In transfer and injection moulds no escape route for the excess material is provided. Only an escape route for the air in the cavities is there.

The shrinkage of rubber compound and that of mould steel should be kept in mind if the moulded goods of correct dimensions are to be produced; and the mould has to be carefully designed keeping this in view. Shrinkage is the term used to describe the difference in the dimensions of the mould and the article produced from it; this shrinkage takes place because the coefficient of thermal expansion (volume) for steel is 0.3×10^{-4} per ^{o}C while that for rubber compounds vary between 4 to 7×0^{-4} per ^{o}C. Linear shrinkage of rubber compounds vary between 1.5 to 3% and thus moulds are made larger, by this factor, than the size of the moulding to be produced.

The question of mould lubrication is an important one to ensure easy extraction of the moulded component from the mould cavity. Detergents, soaps, wetting agents, silicone emulsions, aqueous dispersions of mica, talc and fatty acids etc. are used for this purpose and are known as mould lubricants or mould release agents. These materials are applied by means of spray or brush. 'Dry' lubricants are also available, based on teflon, polythene and are applied as aerosols. These lubricants should be applied in minimum quantities depending upon the mould complexity, type of lubricant and polymer in the mix. Release agents result in build-up of a solid deposit on the mould surface, this will cause pitting if not removed frequently. If mould lubricants are not used carefully, the rubber to metal bonds in the moulding will not be good.

To ensure the manufacture of the good moulding having good surface finish, frequent cleaning of moulds is necessary. Steel, wood, abrasives and wire brushing, is suitably for cleaning of simple moulds, while the complicated mould may be cleaning by girt blasting, vapour blasting and electrolytic oxidation in salt baths. In girt balsting ground nut shells of 10-30 mesh are used. Vapour blasting consists of high pressure application of detergent solution. Salt baths are used in big plants, they are efficient but hazardous. Ultrasonic cleaning yields flashless moulds; moulds are immersed in hot water detergent solution at about 80°C and is subjected to ultrasonic cleaning action, generated by a generator at a frequency of 25 kcycles/sec. Moulds are then washed with water at 90°Cand dried.

Various Formulations

Erasers

Rubber erasers can be made by extrusion or moulding process. They can be individually moulded or moulding can be carried out in desired thickness of sheets which can be then cut to size and finished. Pencil erasers do not damage the surface of the paper and remove the graphite-mark due to its adhesion to the rubber; the other constituents of the pencil erasers are the first diluents and cheaping agents. But in the case of typewriter or ink eraser rubber plays the part of the binding material for the other ingredients e.g. glass powder, sand, pumice etc., which remove the paper with the ink mark by tearing the paper surface. The compound is sheeted by a calender and vulcanised in at low temprature but more often in frame moulds in the hydraulic press. These sheets are cut into eraser pieces which are shaken in rotating drum to round off their sharp edges and corners. They are then stamped and packed. For embossing, the vulcanised sheet is cured in moulds, the metallic bottoms of which are engraved with the desired design. In selection of compounding ingredients for the erasers, the cost factor should be kept in mind as the cheaper erasers seem to be the most in demand. White or drab erasers are generally more popular than the coloured ones. Barytes, emery powder, lithopone, pumica powder, whiting and zinc white are the popular white pigments used.

Pencil Eraser : Good quality

Smoked sheet	100 parts
Factice	78
Mineral oil	5
Antioxidant	2
Zinc oxide	3
Heavy calcined magnesia	3
Titanium dioxide	5
Red oxide	10
Barytes	120
Whiting	60
kaolin	120
Sulphur	3

Pencil Eraser : Good quality

Smoked sheet	100 Parts
Zinc oxide	10
Lithopone	20
Pumice powder	50
Whiting	100
Magnesium carbonate	5
Magnesium oxide	25
White factice	200
Light mineral oil	30
Sulphur	10
MBTS	2
DOTG	1

It is press cured for about 20 minutes at 150°C.

Ink Erasers

	I	II	III
Smoked sheet	100	100	100
Rubber substitute	—	100	50
Reclaimed rubber	—	50	100
Zinc oxide	5	50	50
Lithopone	20	—	—
Pumice powder	50	—	40
Glass powder	50	200	50
Whiting	150	20	50
Magnesium carbonate	30	—	—
French chalk	—	20	—
Light mineral oil	30	—	—
Sulphur	2.5	10	10
MBTS	1.5	1.5	1.5

Curing takes 20 minutes at 150°C.

Bottle Rubber Stoppers

Three Formulaes are given below:

	I	II	III
Pale crepe rubber	100	—	50
SBR-1502	—	100	50
Barytes	100	—	100
Clay	50	70	50
Calcium silicate	—	30	—
Paraffin oil	5	—	10
Zinc oxide	5	4	5
Stearic acid	1.5	1	1.5
Naphthenic oil	—	10	—
Paraffin wax	1	—	1
A.O.PBN	1	—	—
A.O.SP	—	1.5	—
ZDC	1.2	—	0.75
MBTS	—	1.6	—

	I	II	III
DPG	—	0.4	—
DEG	—	2	—
Sulphur	2.5	1.75	2.2

These compounds take about 8-10 minutes for press curing at 150°C. Their specific gravities vary between 1.35 to 1.55 and colour may be introduced if desired.

Rubber Parts & Sheets

Resistant to electric current upto 15 KV and above.

SBR-1502	50 Parts
Smoked sheet	50
Hard clay	40
Activated $CaCO_3$	60
Zinc oxide	15
C.I.R	7
Talc	40
Flexon 641	5
A.O.PBN	1
A.O.DNP	0.5
Paraffin Wax	4
Stearic acid	0.5
TMT	2.5
Sulphur	0.7

Curing at 140°C takes about 7 minutes.

Nitrile Rubber Compound for Oil Resisting Rubber Parts

NBF	100 Parts
GPF	60
DOP	15
Nonox D	1
Zinc oxide	5
Stearic acid	1.2
MBTS	1.5
Sulphur	1.8

Curing takes about 10 minutes at 150°C.

Butyl Rubber Compounds

Polysar Butyl 301	100 Parts
Zinc oxide	5
Petroleum jelly	2
EPC black	50
Clay	60
MBTS	1.5
p-Quinone dioxide	2

Curing takes about 5-8 min. at 150°C

The following two moulding compounds based on butyl rubber are suitable for making rubber spatulas and valves etc.

	A	B
Polysar butyl-301	100	100
Zinc oxide	3	3
Stearic acid	1.5	1.5
Paraffin wax	3	3
Petroleum jelly	3	3
FEF black	60	30
SRF black	—	30
TMT	1.5	—
MBTS	1	—
Accelerators thiuram/thiazole blend	—	1.5
ZDC	—	1
Sulphur	1.75	1.75

Formula A takes about 20 minutes and the *formula B* takes about 15 minutes for cure at 160°C.

17

Rubber Beltings

Introduction

Rubber beltings are mainly used for two purposes namely conveying and transmission. Conveyor belts are used for conveying various items such as coal, ash, ore, grain, sand, packed goods and other industrial inputs and outputs. They are used in elevators also, employed for lifting of passengers at railway stations and air-ports etc. Conveyor beltings are produced in long lengths, are wide and run at slow speeds over large rollers. Transmission beltings are used for transmitting power from prime overs to machines. Transmission belts may be flat or V-type. They run faster than conveyor beltings over smaller pulleys. V-belts are used for short centre drives and are run in V-groove pulleys.

Conveyor Belts

Conveyor belts consist of a body, made up of a number of plies of rubberised fabric; this is known as carcass. Fabric as mentioned above above is cotton or synthetic. The selection of fabric depends on the end use of belting. The carcass has a covering of the same or similar rubber to protect the failure against the damage, both mechanical and chemical. For satisfactory performance quality conveyor belts should meet *IS Specifications 1891* : Grade R and S and B.S.S. 490 : grade M and N.

Conveyor belts are now-a-days designed for specific applications and purposes. Heat resistant beltings are used for carrying hot sinter and coke: oil resistant types etc. for carrying oily products and non-toxic for use with food products. Belts are also made with a moulded rough or chevron surface for incline conveying. Fire-resistant, heavy duty, antistatic belting is used for underground use in the coal mines etc.

Various designs of conveyor belts are in use today. At the edges of the belt the fabric may be folded back upon itself, producing a belt with rounded edge, which is usually identified as 'folded edge' or it may form a square foldless edge, a sealer being applied to protect the exposed duck edges. The latter construction is most commonly called '*raw edge*' . In the cord type of construction, the stress-bearing member is usually composed of textile cords running lengthwise, each surrounded by rubber; and if more than a single layer is used, each is separated from the next by rubber. This construction is weftless, there being no cross threads. Top and bottom plies of the textile reinforcement are of woven duck. While it is customary to cut the edge square, for special applications the duck is folded back. When the folded structure is used, there is one longitudinal seam for each two plies in belts upto 26" wide, two seams in wider belts. Edges of the fabric are enclosed in a strip of breaker fabric and tie gum that unites the ply edges, skim coat rubber (between plies), and the rubber cover. In a typical belt of this type, the central plies are composed of textile cords running lengthwise. On the bottom side of this central core are usually two fabric plies, and on the top, a ply consisting of transverse cords. The plies are bonded by rubber into unit and the outer covering is applied as in the all fabric belts. Steel cord conveyor belt consists of steel cable instead of multiple layers of textile cord.

Cross Section of a Cord-type Belt

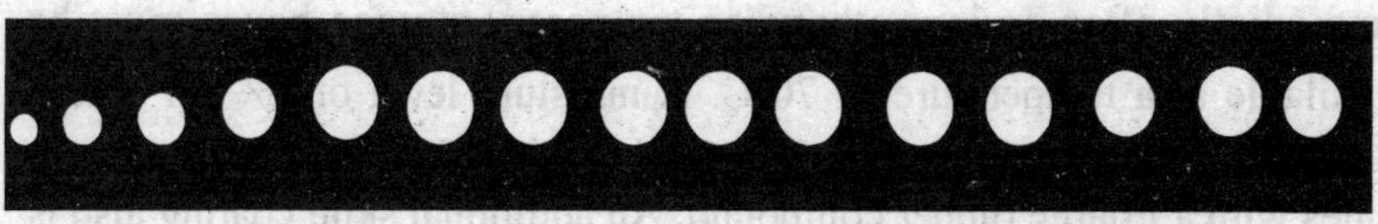

Standard and Folded Jacket Conveyor

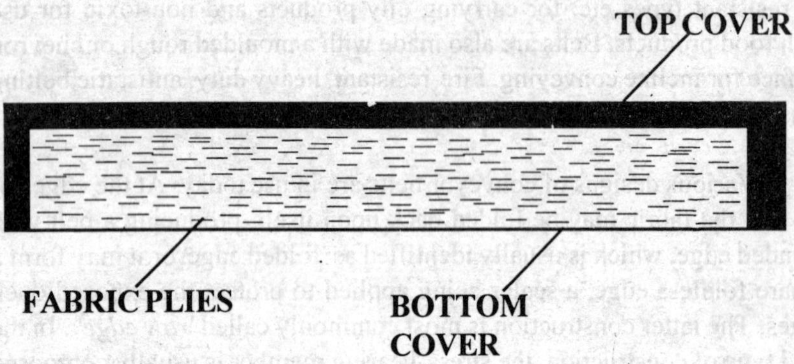

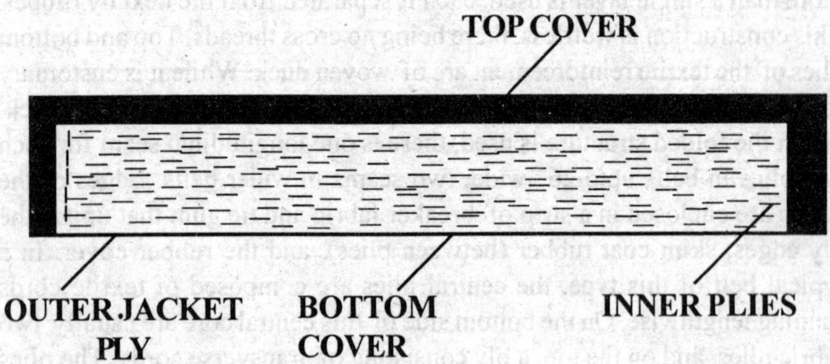

Process of Manufacture

Drying of the fabric is necessary to avoid blowing of the laminate occuring during the vulcanising operation. The fabric is dried with the help of hot rollers or in steam heated dryers. The dryer compartment temperatures are kept at 110°-120°C. Coating of rubber is carried out immediatly after drying; otherwise temporary storage boxes must be available at a temperature of 70°C. A moisture level of 1% for cotton containing fabrics is required. The fabric is then friction coated on both sides with a Pliable rubber compound. An additional skim coating also is applied in the case of heavier fabrics to make the beltings more flexible.

To obtain good adhesion, synthetic fibre fabrics are either pre-spread with isocyanate based solutions or RFL dipped prior to calendering (friction coating). A topped skim coating of rubber only is then required. 4-bowl calender can do this operation at both sides in one operation. Rubber coating is carried out on hot fabric. In a 3-roll calender the bottom rolls revolves at a slower speed than the other rolls. The intermediate roll rotates at double the speed of the bottom roll. The top and middle rolls are maintained at 80-90°C and the bottom one is maintained at about 60°C. Rubber is fed between the two upper rolls and the duck is fed between the bottom rolls and the rubber sticks to it. The rubberised fabric is stored in cotton liners to prevent sticking. Recent development in carcass building techniques, no pretreatment (isocyanate) of the fabric is required, the bonding being achieved by special bonding agents added to friction or topping compounds.

The frictioned and topped fabric layers are plied up together on a building table. Doubling rollers are used for consolidation of the plies. When the required number of plies are built up, the top cover and the bottom cover are also applied, using doubling rollers. The top and the bottom cover rubber is separately sheeted out in a calender. The machines used for pressing the plies together are of the same nature as those used for making rainproof clothes. The joints should be as far from each other as possible. No more than two transverse joints are allowed within 500 ft. and there should not be any joint with in 50 ft. The rubber squeezing out of the sides is pressed there itself. The completely built belt is then pressed through pricking rollers to remove any trapped air. The covers may also be calendered directly on to the belt carcass using 3 or 5 bowl calender. The finished raw belt is stored in a cotton or polyethylene lining, or chalked to prevent sticking prior to the vulcanisation operation.

Preheating

The latest development is the introduction of preheating step, by means of microwaves, before vulcanisation by Press Curing or Continuous Drum Curing. Preheating results in upto 50% saving in vulcanisation time and also reduction in strain during vulcanisation conditions lead to a better quality product. Rubber has high dielectric characteristics and thus absorbs energy of very high frequency, generating uniform heat within the material. Frequency used is at the level of 2000 MHz. The preheater is worked in conjuction with the press by automatic electronic controls.

Vulcanisation

The finished raw belts are cured in a long belt vulcanising press. The presses may have single or double daylights and one or two belts could be pressed at the sáme time. The presses usually water-cooled ends to prevent over-cure of the portion of the belt which receives two cures, which happens when the portion of the belt at the back end of the press is moved forward for curing the next stage. The belts are also stretched, at each stage, before closing the press for curing, by suitable devices attached to the ends of the press, to prevent stretching of the belt in service. Belt is pressed from the sides by metal irons during cure. Belts are so pressed from the sides that a 10% reduction in thickness (of raw belt) results during cure. A pressure of about 21 kg/cm^2 is used. The cure time for each pressing is 15 to 25 minutes at 145 to 150°C, depending on the thickness of the belt.

In continuous belt vulcanisation, the belt is passed between a rotating steel drum and an endless high tensile steel band, heat is applied to both sides of the product, from the internally heated drum and through the steel hand by contact with steam heated shoes. The curing speeds range from 5 to 50 M/hr. giving curing times of from 3.5 to 50 minutes. The belt is fed through the vulcaniser with initial tension and stretch properly and accurately maintained.

Compounding and Formulations

Conveor belts are used for carrying sand, ore, coal etc. and hence have to be highly abrasion resistant and also flexing and ageing resistant. The compounds used are very similar to high grade tyre tread compounds. Compounds for frictioning and skim coat are highly flexible and contain very small quantities of non-reinforcing fillers. Friction compounds contain a good amount of plasticisers and should have good adhesive properties. Flat curing accelerators are used to prevent overcure of the portions which receive double cure. For abrasive materials a natural rubber tread type compound is used (BS 490 Grade N), for high resistance to cutting, as in the case of belting conveying ores, a highly resilient and abrasion resistant rubber cover is used (BS 490 Grade M). Heat resistant covers for carrying hot foundry sand etc. are made from SBR, IIR blends with natural rubber. For oil resistance compounds neoprene and nitrile or PVC-NBR blends are used which are fire resistant.

1. Conveyor Belt Formulations from NR & SBR

	Friction & Skim			Cover		
	1	2	3	1	2	3
Smoked sheet	10	—	80	100	—	50
SBR-1500	—	100	20	—	100	50
Stearic acid	3.5	1.5	2.0	1.5	2	2
Pine tar	—	7	3	5	7	3
Antioxidant	1	1.5	1	2	1.5	1.5
Coumarone resin	—	10	3	—	10	3
Zinc oxide	5	10	4	10	10	4
Wood rosin	—	7	—	—	—	—
SRF black	10	—	10	20	30	30
FEF black	—	40	—	—	20	—
Whiting	15	—	60	—	—	—
TMT	—	3	—	—	3	—
CBS	—	—	0.6	—	—	0.8
MBTS	0.5	—	—	1	—	—
ZDC	0.1	—	—	0.2	—	—
Sulphur	2.75	0.25	0.25	2.25	0.5	2.1
Microcrystallline wax	—	—	—	1	1	1

Curing time (min.) at about 152°C.

2. Formulations for Conveyor Belts (BS 490 Grade N & M)

	Cover		Heat resistant Cover	Friction
	A	B		
Smoked sheet	100	100	50	100
SBR-1500	—	—	50	—
Zinc oxide	10	10	5	5
Stearic acid	2.5	2.5	2	1
HAF-LS	40	50	45	—
Calcium carbonate	—	—	—	25
Pine tar	2.5	3	2.5	3

Process oil	2.5	3	2.5	—
Coumarone resin	—	—	3	—
HBS	0.6	0.6	—	0.6
BSM	—	—	1.4	—
TMT	—	—	0.6	—
Sulphur	2.5	2.5	0.33	2.5
Antioxidant				
HSL/Nonox BL	1	1	1	1.5
Nonox DPL	0.5	0.5	0.5	—

Curing is done at 4 kg/cm² for 15 to 20 minutes

3. Formulations for Conveyor Belts (BS 490 Grades N & M)

	Carcass	Cover	
		Grade N	Grade M
Natural rubber	100	—	80
SBR-1500	—	100	20
HAF black	—	50	—
ISAF black	—	—	45
Whiting	20	—	—
Zinc oxide	5	5	5
Stearic acid	1	1.5	1.5
Process oil	3	3.5	5
Pine tar	3	3.5	—
Coumarone resin	—	5	—
MBT	0.4	—	—
MBTS	0.4	—	—
HBS	—	0.75	0.5
Sulphur	3	2	3
Retrader	0.5	—	—
Antioxidant	1.5	1.5	1.5
Antiozonant	—	1.5	1.5

Curing for 17 minutes at 145°C.

4. Conveyor Belting Compound Based on Butyl Rubber

	Friction	Skim	Cover
Polysar butyl (101)	100	100	100
Aluminium silicate	30	30	50
Pine tar	—	6	6
Zinc oxide	10	10	10
Stearic acid	1	1	1
TMT	2	2	2
MBT	1	1	1
Sulphur	1.5	1.5	1.5

For friction and skim compounds bromobutyl rubber is preferred to butyl rubber.

5. Nitrile Rubber Based Conveyor Belt Cover

When only oil resistance is required then normal vulcanisation system with high scorch resistance is recommended. When oil resistance at high temperatures is required then EV system is preferred. But this will impair flexing resistance, hence Semi-EV system is preferred.

	Oil-Resistant Cover	Oil and Heat Resistant Cover
Nitrile rubber-3309X	100	100
FEF black	50	50
Hard Clay	20	20
DOP	20	20
Coumarone indene resin	7	7
Zinc oxide	4	4
Stearic acid	1	1
A.O.PBNA	2	2
ETDO Type A.O.	0.5	0.5
CBS	1.2	1
TMTD	—	1
Sulphur	0.5	0.5

Curing time is 20 and 10 minutes respectively at about 155°C

Rubber V-Belts

As the name itself indicates these power transmission belts have the V-type cross-section. They have various advantages over flat belts *e.g.* compactness, quite operation, non slipping grip between belt and sleeve, absorption of shock, smooth starting, cleanliness, long service life, low cost and light bearing load. The internal structure of standard V-Belts varies considerably. Cords are the 'backbone' of V-belts. They are located in the upper wider portion. These cords in the best belts are impregnated and embedded in a rubber compound which reduces friction between individual strands or fibres and retard heat build up. This is known as cushion rubber. This is embedded in a mass of solid rubber ; it is known as core. Core of the belt improves flexibility and increases shock absorption. In starting, momentry stresses greater than those encountered in running must be withstood, and this core rubber acts as an absorber for the sudden pull thus protecting the cords and cover. When the belt travels around a sleeve, the narrower portion is compressed, and the solid rubber must withstand such distortion without accumulating excessing heat. Special cool running compounds have been developed. The whole thing is enclosed in a rubber fabric jacket or cover which acts as an envelope to resist wear and protects the inner structure.

V-belts are specially useful for silent drives between short centre distances and are used for fractional horsepower drives for domestic appliance and for automotive fan belts. They come in five standard sizes A,B,C,D,E. The top width of A is 12.7 mm (1/2 inch) and that of E is 38 mm (1-1/2") and the thickness varies between 8 and 24 mm (29/32") between the different sizes. When power transmitted is heavy multiple belts are used in pullies having a number of grooves as required. More, recently, premium industrial belts known as 3V, 5V and 8V belts or wedge type belts have been introduced. In these the ratio of depth to the top width is greater than in the standard sections, giving a more compact drive. These constructions are made possible by the use of high tanacity materials such as polyester cord.

V-BELT CONSTRUCTION

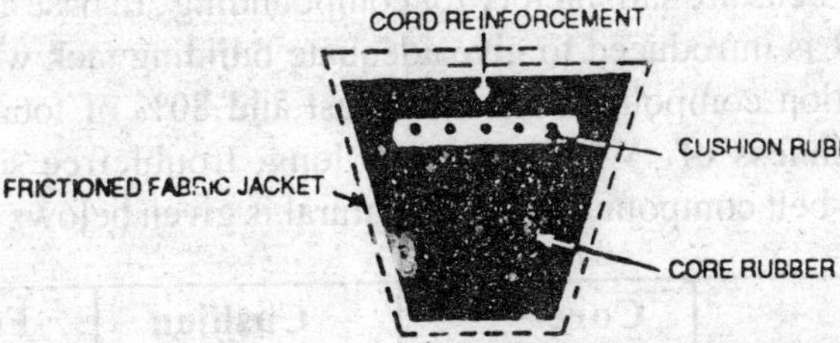

Cross-sectional Dimensions of Standard Multiple V-belts

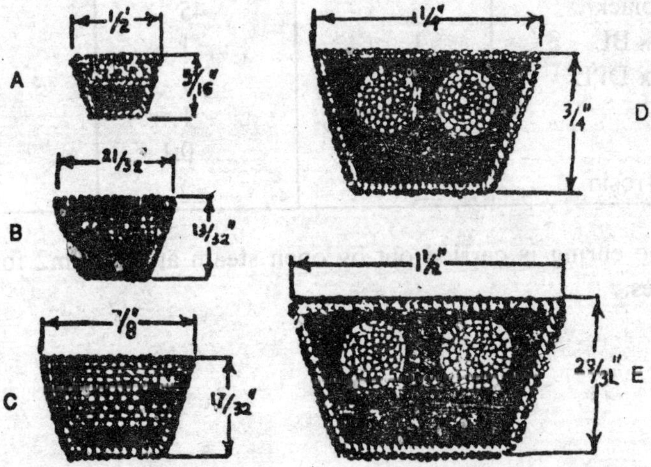

Manufacture

Compounds for 'V' belts should withstand high speed, flexing and heat, as well as age resistance. Natural and SBR blends for diferent sections of 'V' belts are satisfactory for compounding . In base and cushion compound NR is introduced to give adequate building tack where as for skim and friction compounds NR is a must and 80% of total rubber is NR. The toughness of V-belts ensures long, troublefree service. An example of V-belt compound based on natural is given below :

	Core	Cushion	Friction
Natural rubber	100	100	100
Zinc oxide	30	10	10
Stearic acid	1.5	1	1
Paraffin wax	0.5	—	—
Process oil	3	—	—
Pine tar	—	5	3
SRF black	70	—	—
GPF black	—	45	35
Nonox BL	1	1	1
Nonox DPL	1	1	1
BSM	1	1	1
TMT	0.1	0.1	0.1
Wood rosin	—	—	1

The curing is carried out by open steam at 4 kg/cm2 for 20 to 30 minutes.

The following formulation utilises a blend of SBR and natural rubber:

	Base	Cushion	Skim	Friction
Synaprene-1500	85	70	60	20
Natural rubber	15	30	40	80
SRF Black	100	60	40	10
Pptd, CaCo3	—	—	—	50
Naphthenic oil	10	5	7	2
Coumarone resin	5	5	5	3
Zinc oxide	4	4	4	4
Stearic acid	2.5	2.5	2	2
Antioxidant PBN and DPPD	1	1	1	1
Antioxidant ketone amine	1	1	1	1
CBS	1.4	1	0.8	0.8
TMTD	0.2	—	0.1	—
Sulphur	2	2	2	2.5

Cure time for base, cushion and skim compounds is 15 minutes and for friction compound it is 10 minutes at 152°C.

18

Rubber Rollers

Introduction

Rubber rollers are extensively used in pulp and paper, card board, strawboard, textiles, fabrics, plastics and film industry. Many other industrial products like laminates, coverings and tapes use rubber rollers for some purpose or the other. In textile industry, they are used in printing finishing, bleaching, mercerising, dyeing sizing, waxing, waterproofing etc. They are also used to apply inks, lacquers, paints and varnishes etc. to paper, cardboard, plastics and textiles etc. Other uses include agricultural equipments, leather machinery, polishing rolls, printing rolls, plating rolls, wringers, waxing rolls, sheet metal rolling and various other specialised applications.

Process of Manufacture

Building

The compounding ingredients according to the recipe are mixed and masticised in a roll mill or Banbury internal mixer. The compound is extruded in the form of a thick sheet which is then calendered to a uniform thickness. The calendered sheet is then applied to the prepared metallic roller generally in a direction opposite to the grain in roll building, although some rolls of smaller sizes may be plied up directly from the calender.

A clean fresh surface free from dirt is essential in successful rubber metal bonding. In case the rubber compound cannot be freshly sheeted or extruded before assembely, the surface of rubber sheet in contact with the prepared metal core should be brushed lightly with an aromatic solvent or xylene. The rubber is then applied over the cores previously coated with adhesive and cement.

Curing

Curing of rubber rollers is done in open steam. The rolls are spirally wrapped with wet cotton tape or strips of cotton cloth in long lenghts. A few wrappings are done to ensure consolidation of rubber due to pressure. Ends of the rolls should be held with disc to prevent the overflowing of the rubber edges during wrapping and curing. Wrapping cloth may be wetted with soap solution to prevent its sticking to the rubber. Nylon tape is preferred to that of cotton. Wet tape on drying contracts and exerts pressure. The rolls are put on trolly and cured by steam in chamber at the required pressure. Smaller rolls with chemical bonding require less curing time than the larger rolls with ebonite bonding. Thus in the latter case the roller compound should be so formulated that curing takes place slowly and no overcure takes place. After curing the temperature is reduced and wrapping is removed. In wrapped steam curing the roller is first heated up very gradually during 3 to 6 hours according to the size of the roller or the thickness of rubber, being afterwards slowly vulcanised at 135°C. for 8 to 12 hrs. The temperature should not be alllowed to drop before vulcanisation sets in, or the outer coatings may become porous or spongy, places of unequal hardness being formed. After vulcanisation the roller should be allowed 12 hours to cool down, or more according to its size, after which it can be unwrapped and sent for finishing. In the case of small rolls, which are cured between moulds in between the platens of a press, finishing is not required as their size and surface are as required.

Finishing

As mentioned earlier rollers are built up to a size slightly bigger than the final required dimensions. The surface is ground by means of a cylindrical grinding machine large enough to accomodate the roll shaft or in a precision lathe. Very rough stones are used for grinding soft rubber. Grinding is finished in 2 or 3 passes but for abrasion resistant rollers, several passes are required. After grinding to the finished dimensions the rollers are finished to a smooth surface by a fine emery paper with periodic application of talc, in between the polishing operation.

Compounding

The roller compound should be formulated from raw materials of good fitness and purity, and they should be free from grit and foreign matter. This is a must as all the applications require a roller surface free from blemishes. Powders such as sulphur which have a cake forming tendency are used in the surafce coated form, to ensure uniform mixing. The compound is passed several times between the tight nip of mixing mill or through strainers. The compound should preferably be sheeted out in a calender and wound with inter-layer of liners and stored for subsequent use.

Printing Rollers

Glue composition rolls were being used earlier for printing. But now-a-days rubber rolls are used because of their good performance on high speed machines. Printing rolls are usually very soft ranging in hardness of about 15 to 45. They are made from chloroprene or nitrile rubber to ensure good resistance to oils and solvents to oils and solvents which are present in the inks. In anline printing and duplicator rolls, natural rubber is used. The following formulas are of various hardness; A being soft whereas C is the hardest. Nitrile rubber of the type Butakon A 3003 is used as it has low mooney viscosity which ensures easy processibility. To help processing and to control the properties of the compound, more plasticisers are incorporated. Polymeric plasticisers e.g. PPA are preferred as they are not easy to be extracted by solvents as the ester type monomeric plasticisers e.g. DOP. For easy processing usually a blend of monomeric and polymeric plasticisers is employed.

	A	B	C
Butakon A 3003	100	100	100
Zinc oxide	5	5	5
Stearic acid	1	1	1.5
Aluminium silicate	25	—	50
GPF black	—	25	—
PPA	50	50	15
DOP	25	15	—
Brown factice	50	40	5

	A	B	C
China clay	—	20	30
Coumarone resin	3	3	5
Diethylene glycol	1	—	2
Titanium dioxide	5	—	5
HBS	2	2	2
Nonox B	1	1	1
Sulphur	2	2	2

Two or more formulas for printing rollers are given below using SBR rubber.

	Premium Quality	Medium Quality
Synaprene 1513/1514	50	—
Synaprene 1712	—	100
NBR (high nitrile)	50	—
FEF black	20	30
Precipitated $CaCo_3$	20	—
Brown factice	35	20
Petroleum jelly	10	5
Aromatic oil	—	20
Napthenic oil	20	30
DBP	20	—
Coumarone resin	4	7
Zinc oxide	5	4
Stearic acid	2	1.5
PBN	1	1
MBTS	1.5	0.8
MBT	—	0.5
Sulphur	2	1.7

Curing time is 90 minutes for each at 40 psi in open steam for 1" thickness.

Chloroprene based printing roll formulations are given below :

	Black	White	Tie-stock
Baypren 210	100	100	100
Light magnesium oxide	4	4	4
Factice	40	40	—
Aromatic oil	10	—	5
Naphthenic oil	—	10	—
Stearic acid	1	1	1
A.O.PAN	1	—	1
A.O.KSM	—	1	—
A.O.DNP	0.25	0.25	—
DOP	40	40	5
SRF black	10	—	60
Diatomaceous earth	—	10	—
Coumarone resin	5	5	5
Vulcacit NPV	1	1	0.8
Zinc oxide	5	5	5
Hardness (shore)	25	25	75

These are wrapped and cured in open steam at 4 kg/cm^2 for about 1 to 1-1/2 hours depending on thickness.

Printing roll formulations based on natural rubber are given below:

	A	B	C
Smoked sheet	100	100	100
Zinc oxide	5	5	5
Stearic acid	1	1	1
Light mineral oil	15	10	5
SRF black	35	50	—
Precipitated silica	—	—	75
Rosin	1.5	1.5	1.5
Nonox B	1	1	—
Nonox SP	—	—	1
Nonox CI	0.25	0.25	0.25

	A	B	C
Sulphur	0.25	0.25	0.25
TMT	2.5	2.5	2.5
MBTS	0.5	0.5	0.5
Hardness (shore)	**40**	**50**	**60**

It is wrapped and cured in direct steam at 4.5 kg/cm^2 for about 1 to 1-1/2 hours depending on thickness.

Typewriters Rollers

These rollers are characterised by high hardness and moderate to low resilience. Natural or unnatural and SBR rubber blends may be used as the polymer with high filler loadings.

	Black	**White**
Smoked Sheet	25	100
Synaprene 1500	60	—
Synaprene 1958	15	—
Zinc oxide	5	10
Stearic acid	2.5	1
Magnesium carbonate	—	30
Forcal S	—	70
China clay	100	75
Talc	100	—
GPF black	25	—
Aluminium silicate	—	60
Diethylene glycol	—	1
Coumarone resin	10	—
Paraffin wax	1	0.5
Nonox SP	—	1
Nonox D	1	—
Vulcafor F (Thiazole/Guanidine blend)	—	1.2
TNT	—	0.1
HBS	1.5	—
Sulphur	3	3

These are wrapped and cured at 4 kg/cm^2 steam for a time depending on the thickness. White compound takes lesser time for curing. Antioxidant of the non-staining or non-discolouring nature e.g. styrenated phenol type (nonox SP) is used in white compound, where as phenyl beta- naphthylamine (nonox D) type is satisfactory for the black formulation.

Whereas the typewriter rolls are made by loading SBR or NR-SBR blends, the wringer rolls are prepared directly by moulding or vulcanising an extruded tube on a mandrel. Two formulations are given below :

	Typewriter roll	Wringer roll
Synaprene-1502	80	80
Smoked sheet	20	20
Hard clay	4	150
Precipitated chalk	60	60
Aluminium silicate	—	25
Light magnesia	10	—
Coumarone resin	8	10
Petroleum jelly	—	5
Zinc oxide	10	6
Stearic acid	1.5	1.5
Titanium dioxide	—	15
Antioxidant SP	1.5	1.5
MBTS	0.8	1.2
MBT	0.5	—
TMT	—	0.3
Sulphur	2.5	2.5

The wringer roll takes about 15 minutes and the typewriter roller abou 45 minutes to cure at about 152°C.

Rice Mill Rollers

Heat and abrasion resistance are the most essential requirements o the rice mill rollers as the rolls run hot during dehusking and polishing and th surface is spoiled by abrasion. The surface is acted upon by rice bran o also, hence natural rubber alone does not function satisfactorily. NR an SBR based compounds can be used to achieve the desired degree c abrasion resistance but incoroporation of nitrile rubber imparts oil resistance and neoprene is also sometimes included to improve heat resistance. In the following formula combination of Nonox D and Nonox B are used as antioxidants to give optimum heat resistance to the compound. Diorthotolyl-thiourea (DOTT) has been added to cure neoprene.

Neoprene WX	50 Parts
Synaprene-1500	40
Synaprene-1958	10
Zinc oxide	10
Stearic acid	1
HAF black	50
BOC oil 50	10
Light calcined magnesia	2
Nonox D	1
Nonox B	1
HBS	0.6
TMT	0.5
DOTT	0.5
Sulphur	1.5

Synaprene can be partly replaced by smoked sheet rubber. The slab cured at 152°C. for 30 minutes shows excellent abrasion resistance and superior heat ageing. The hardness IRHD is about 75, sp gravity 1.32 and resilience at 50° C is 51.14.

Paper & Textile Mill Rollers

These rollers are required to have high mechanical strength and resistance to acids and alkalies. They are usually made from natural rubber in the hardness range of 50 to 90. In some applications ebonite is used and when the rolls come in contact with fat liquors and dyestuffs nitrile rubber is used in place of natural rubber as the latter is attacked with these materials. A few formulations of different hardness are given below:

Heavy Duty Paper Mill Roller

RMAI	70
EBC-2X	30
Zinc oxide	5
Stearic acid	1
Nonox SP	0.5
A.O.Ketone amine type	1
CBS	0.8
Sulphur	2.5
Titanium dioxide	5

It is cured for 20 minutes at 140°C. The hardness of the roller is about 75 IRHD. Natural rubber is chosen as it offers outstanding fatigue resistance under constant heavy load.

Paper Mill Rollers (Black)

	1	2	3
Natural rubber	100	100	100
EPB-OE	—	—	40
Stearic acid	1	1	1
Zinc oxide	40	40	40
SRF black	100	60	90
Precipitated silica	—	30	—
Mineral oil	5	5	5
Rosin	3	3	3
Sulphur	6.5	6.5	6.5
DOTG	0.5	0.5	0.5
MBTS	0.1	0.1	0.1
Antioxidant	1	1	1
Hardness	90	90	85

It is cured for 4 hours in steam at a pressure upto 3 kg/cm^2 in stages.

High Speed Paper Mill Rollers

	A	B
Natural rubber	100	100
Diatomaceous earth	100	75
Precipitated silica	25	—
Titanium dioxide	5	5
Coumarone resin	5	5
Naphthenoc oil	10	10
Zinc oxide	5	5
Stearic acid	1	1
Antioxidant	1	1
TMT	2.5	2.5
MBS	1	1
Sulphur	0.2	0.2

Formula A gives shore hardness of 75 and B gives shore hardness of 50 when cured in steam at a pressure upto 3 kg/cm^2 reached in stages.

Textile Mill Rollers

	A	B	C
Smoked sheet	100	100	—
SBR	—	—	100
China clay	55	70	75
Precipitated silica	25	32	40
Titanium dioxide	5	5	7
Coumarone resin	5	5	5
Naphthenic oil	5	5	7
Zinc oxide	5	5	5
Stearic acid	1	1	1
Antioxidant	1	1	1
MBTS	1	0.2	0.5
TMT	2,5	—	—
DPG	—	0.7	1.5

The hardness of A is 60, B is 65 and that of C is 75. For thick rollers step up cure is given as usual. As expected the compound C containing SBR gives better resistance to heat and oxidation.

19

Rubber Footwear

Introduction

The rubber footwear industry is only next to tyres, in importance. Various types of rubber-containing shoes are being made now a days. Heavy industrial gumboots, fashion boots, rain boots, sport shoes and carnals with canvas uppers, slippers and rubber soled leather footwear with solid or microcellullar soles and heels are getting popular as compared to, purely leather footwear on account of their low cost and water resistance, coupled with good look. Traditionally rubber footwear was manufactured by hand assembling preshaped parts on lasts and vulcanising the assembly in an autoclave, the finished article will appear as if it has been moulded. This method is still used and is quite popular as the machines are quite costly. Now-a-days direct Moulding or direct vulcanising process (DV process) and the injection moulding machines are getting popular, giving the complete shoe in one operation.

General Compounding Considerations

The quality of footwear varies widely due to economic and competitive considerations; hence specific formulation considerations can not be given. Only a general guidance can be given. Various types of polymers and its blends are used in footwear industry to achieve the specific combinations of properties *e.g.* lightness, wear-comfort, stiffness and durability also kept in mind. In compounds meant for hand assembling natural rubber is used due to good building tack and reduced shrinkage. Adhesives for hand built shoes are also based on natural rubber. For good quality thin upper compounds, where flexing is a critical factor, best quality natural rubber is used; while for soles and heels lower grade rubber may be used. In moulded products synthetic rubbers *e.g.* non-staining low Mooney SBR, oil extended SBR and butyl rubber etc. are extensively used. Nitrile rubber is used for oil and heat resistant compounds. Various blends are also used. Nitrile and polychloroprene blends are used, mainly in compounds for hand assembly, due to their high tack. Bromobutyl rubber and NR blends give better abrasion and flexing resistance than NR alone, but the tensile strength is lowered, though ageing properties are superior. Bromobutyl containing compound requires less curing system.

Whole tyre reclaim (WTR) is used extensively in black soling and moulded black uppers. Finely ground vulcanised rubber crumb reduces cost and porosity. In black compounds carbon black is used as a reinforcing filler, but for good quality non-black compounds reinforcing silicas are used. whereas for cheap non-black compounds aluminium silicate or calcium silicate may be used. Clays and activated calcium carbonate may be used as reinforcing fillers for natural rubber but in the case of SBR rubbers silica fillers are a must. Whiting and cheap clays are used as diluents and titanium dioxide is used for whiteness. Thiazole type accelerators are normally used together with guanidine, thiuram or dithicarbamate types secondary accelerators. As usual nonstaining antioxidant should be used in white or light coloured compounds.

Injection Moulding of Soles and Heels

Injection moulding of heels and soles is a modern mass production process. Injection moulding is an important process in the plastics industry and has been adopted in the rubber industry. An injection moulding machine basically consists of a reciprocating screw working within a pre-plasticising cylinder. The number of the moulding stations vary depending upon the machine design 4-, 6-, 10-station injection moulding machines are usually employed. At the begining of the cycle, the screw rotates and moves to the back end of the cylinder, and the compound in the form of strip or pellet is fed into the unit. The rotation of the screw plasticises the compound and the screw then acting as ram forces the compound through the nozzle into the closed mould. Pressure is maintained for a few seconds to fill the mould. The injection unit then retracts, and the rotary table brings the next station in front of the unit and the cycle is repeated during which the previous station opens and moulded material is removed from the cavities. Each station carriers individual temperature controls so that cure temperatures for mouldings of different sole and heel thickness can be achieved. Screw and cylinder are also fitted with independent temperature regulators.

Formulations of Rubber Footwears

Heat Built Boot Upper

Good quality Smoked sheet	80 Parts
Polyisoprene rubber	20
Zinc oxide	8
GPF black	20
Activated CaCo3	40
Ground whiting	30
Stearic acid	1
Coumarone resin	0.5
Paraffin wax	0.5
Antioxidant	0.5
MBT	1
TMTD	0.15
HMT	0.3
Sulphur	8.5

The soling stock formulas vary widely depending on quality and the building process used. The basic general pattern of formulation is as follows:

Rubber (natural and synthetic)	50 to 100
Reclaimed rubber	100 to 0
Zinc oxide	3 to 5
Stearic acid	0.5 to 2.5
Antioxidant	0 to 1
Sulphur	2 to 4
Pigments, carbon black, clay, whiting talc, cork etc.	80 to 200
Resins or oils	5 to 30
Accelerators	0.5 to 1.5

Upper and Sole Formulations

	All Rubber		Cloth-Lined	
	Upper	Sole	Upper	Sole
Smoked sheets	100	100	100	100
Pptd. $CaCo^3$	40	40	40	40
China clay	40	100	40	100
GPF black	20	20	20	20
Zinc oxide	5	5	5	5
Stearic acid	0.75	0.75	0.75	0.75
Paraffin wax	0.5	0.5	0.5	0.5
Brown factice	2.5	—	2.5	—
Sulphur	2.5	2.5	2.5	2.5
MBT	0.5	0.6	0.5	0.5
MBTS	—	—	0.5	0.5
DPG	0.25	0.25	—	—
TMT	—	—	0.2	0.2
A.O.PAN	1	1	1	1

In case of all rubber formulation curing is done for 30 minutes in open steam at 4 kg/cm² and in the case of the cloth-lined shoes curing is done for 1 hour at 120°C in autoclave with air pressure of about of 4 kg/cm2.

Soles and Foxings for Canvas Shoes (Good quality)

	Translucent	White	Brown	Black
Smoked sheets	—	—	100	100
Pale crepe	100	100	—	—
Whiting	—	70	250	250
Magnesium carbonate	20	25	25	25
Active zinc oxide	2	—	—	—
Zinc oxide	—	10	10	5
Stearic acid	0.5	0.5	0.5	0.5
Light mineral oil	2	2	2.5	2.5
Paraffin wax	—	0.5	1	1
GPF black	—	—	—	15
Mexphalte	—	—	—	5

	Translucent	White	Brown	Black
Titanium dioxide	—	10	—	—
Antioxidant	1	1	1	1
MBT	0.25	0.4	0.5	0.5
MBTS	0.3	0.4	0.5	0.5
TMT	0.15	0.2	0.25	2
Sulphur	2	2	2.7	2.7

In the case of translucent soles precipitated silica may also be used in the place of magnesium carbonate. For white foxing formulation of white soling formulations may be used. For brown and black foxings brown and black soling formulations may be used and quantity of sulphur is reduced somewhat. Curing at 120°C in autoclave at air pressure of about 3.5. kg/cm2 takes about 1 hour.

Solutions for Canvas Upper

Smoked sheet	100 Parts
Zinc oxide	10
Stearic acid	0.5
Whiting	75
MBT	0.4
MBTS	0.4
TMT	0.2
Sulphur	3
Antioxidant	1

A 20% solution in a solvent is prepared.

20

TYRES AND TUBES

(Cycle, Rickshaw & Auto)

Introduction

Cycle, Rickshaw and Automotive tyres are used in vehicles for comfortable ride and low power consumption. Various types of tyres are available namely, pneumatic and solid tyres. Pneumatic tyres protect the tube which contain the air filled at pressure. Pneumatic tyres may be classified into various categories according to use e.g. Scooter tyres, Tractor tyre, aeroplane tyres, cycle and rickshaw tyres, truck and car tyres etc. Solid tyres which do not contain any tube are also available which have special applications e.g. prams and children's cycles etc. The detailed process and formulations of these tyres and tubes are undermentioned :

Cycle Tyres

Cycle tyre, like any other pneumatic tyre has the following essential components:

1. Bead ring
2. Rubberised Cord fabric, the reinforcing member
3. Tread

The head ring is made from high tensile steel wire coated either with copper or zinc to prevent rusting during storage and use. It provides firm support to the rim and holds the tyre in its place. Wire should have good joint strength, bend resistance and should be able to bear the load under service conditions. Rubberised fabric consists of a number of warp threads held together by a few weft threads; so that the fabric has maximum flexibility. Cotton warp fabric finds the widest use. Carcass is composed of a number of plies of cord fabric, it gives real strength to the tyre preventing its ballooning or bursting. Tread is the outer grooved or patterned portion of the tyre. It has to stand traction against the road surface and protects the carcass from damage. Sidewall is quite thin. Side wall and tread donot have much of strength of their own. Tread designs are plain or patterned to prevent skidding.

Cycle tyres are made in standard sizes of 28 x 1 - 1/2", 28 x 1-3/4", 26 x 1-3/8", 26 x 1-1/2" and 26 x 1-3/4", the most popular size being 28 x 1-1/2". The first figure of the size is the outside inflated diameter of the tyre in inches, while the second figure indicates the cross-sectional outside width of the inflated tyre. The carcass is made of two piles of rubberised cord fabric. The cord usually employed is 4/14 *i.e.* 4 ply yarn of 14 counts. With a minimum breaking strength of 2.5 kg/cord with 30 ends/inch. In the case of rickshaw tyres a two stage plied yarn of 2/4/14 construction is used, to carry a heavier load. The bead wire usually 1 mm in diameter. If the bead is to be made of multistrand wires, then 4 strands of 0.9 mm wire are used.

Essential Parts of Cycle Tyres

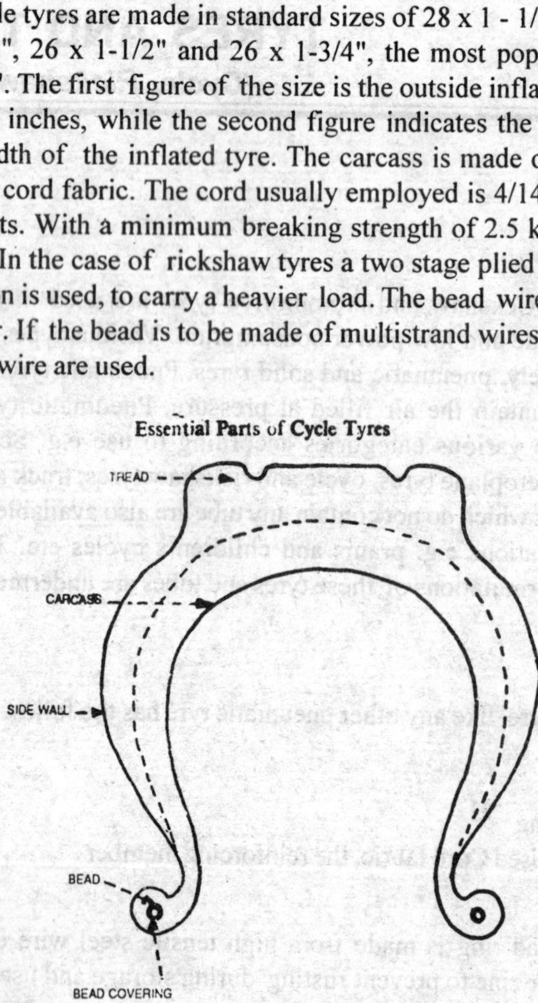

Manufacture of Cycle Tyres

In the manufacture of cycle tyres, first tread is prepared, followed by preparation of cord fabric. The tyre is then built using various components. The tread has the following shape. There are two methods by which the tread can be prepared *viz.* by extrusion and by profile calendering. In the extrusion method the control of dimensions is rather difficult. Therefore, popular method is that of calendering, using a profile calender with 3 or 4 grooves in the bottom roll and 3 or 4 treads can thus be obtained simultaneously. The calendered treads are cooled by immersion in cold water and stored with interleaving cotton liners.

Tread for Cycle Tyre.

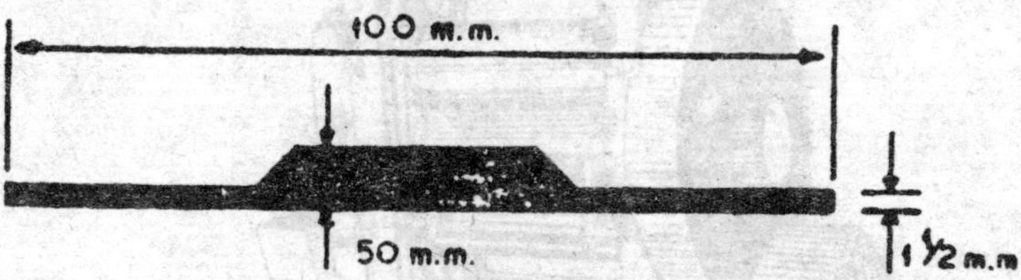

Fig. 58

The cord fabric may be rubberised by spreading or by calendering. The spreading process is as usual. Doctor blade is used for controlling the coat thickness. A number of coats are necessary to get the required coat thickness. The solid content in the rubber dough is normally between 30% to 40%. It is also important to control the viscosity of solution so that consistent deposit is obtained in each pass. Too thick a coating in one pass should be avoided; otherwise sponginess and porosity will occur. The spreading room should be well ventilated, machine should be earthed and room humidity should be kept high so as to reduce fire hazards. Spreading process requires low investment and gives uniform thickness together with better tack. Instead of spreading, calendering may also be used. In calendering 3-bowl calender is used, giving one coat on either side. Calendering operation gives faster production, cheaper products (no solvent required) and freedom from hazards, but is capital intensive and accurate control is a must. The pick up of rubber compound on the weight of the fabric is about 100%. The rubberised fabric is bias cut, at the angle of 45° and the width of the cut sheet is equal to the width of two plies plus overlap. For a 26 x 1-1/2 tyre, the width necessary for two plies is about 7-1/2".

Profile Calender

The bead wire is cut to size and the ends are butt welded and covered with a metal ferule to obtain the finished ring.

The most important step, now, is the building or forming of green tyre, carried out either on collapsible drums or on monoband machines.

Collapsible Drum Method

In this method the bias cut fabric, as above, is laid over a collapsible tyre building drum. The ends of the cut pieces are joined with an overlap of about 1-1/2". The bead rings are put over the fabric layer in the grooves which are about 3-1/2" apart. The fabric is folded back towards the centre giving an overlap joint. The assembly is rolled with hand rollers to remove air pockets. The tread is now applied and rolled on it; ends are joined and stitched with stitching wheels. A solvent brush on the underside of the tread gives a good bond with the casing. The drum is now collapsed allowing the green tyre to be removed easily.

Monoband Machine Method

In this method, the fabric is first cut longitudinally and rolled on a spool. The bead rings are mounted on two grooved pulleys and tensioned. The fabric is bias wrapped and pressed around bead rings mechanically. The process is repeated for applying tread rubber. This machine offers faster production and more uniform product; though skilled operators are required.

Curing

Vulcanisation of cycle tyres is carried out in multiday light hydraulic pressses, or single cavity Bag-o-Matic type presses, the latter being much faster and more efficient but capital incentive. Unvulcanised tyre is lightly dusted with a mould lubricant or wetting agent or glycerine or a combination of those and the air bag is inserted. This assembly is now placed in the mould, the press is closed, and compressed air is passed through a nozzle of the air bag. The air in the bag is at about 7 to 10 kg/cm. Curing is done for about 6 to 8 minutes, with steam pressure in the mould at about 4.5-5 kg/cm^2. After cure the air is released; bags are removed and used again. The flash on tyre is trimmed and the tyre are finished.

Compounding

The tread compound should be so formulated that it has reasonably good tear and flex resistance. It should have uniform plasticity, good processing safety and the ability to be vulcanised at high temperatures without reversion for faster economic production. The carcass compound should be tacky and its curing properties should be compatible with those of tread compound. Normally, curing rate of carcass compound is slightly faster than that of the tread compound since heating is done from one side only, that is, the tread side. In cycle tyres usually natural rubber is used, sometimes partly replaced by SBR. Some reclaimed rubber may also replace the natural rubber. GPF black and clay fillers are added. Precipitated silica also may used as a reinforcing agent in coloured tyres. HBS/TMT combination gives fast cure with sufficient process safety. Buffed dust is sometimes added to make the tread rough for good mouldability and to reduce cost. Polybutadiene may also replace a part of natural rubber, thereby improving the wearing qualities. Cycle tyre is in service intermittenly only, therefore addition of paraffin wax is beneficial, to protect against oxidative degradation.

Some Tread Compounds

	Good quality		Economic Quality	
	1	2	3	4
Smoked sheet	65	40	60	30
SBR-1712	—	40	—	30
Whole tyre reclaim	70	40	80	80
HAF black	15	25	15	25
Clay	40	50	50	50
Pine tar or aromatic mineral oil	3	10	4	10
Zinc oxide	5	4	5	4
Stearic acid	1.2	1.2	1.2	1.2
Paraffin wax	1.25	1.25	1.25	1.25
Vulkacit F	1.3	1	1	1
TMT	0.2	0.4	0.2	0.3
Vulkacit A	0.5	—	—	—
Sulphur	2.4	2.4	2.4	2.4
A.O.IPPD (401 ONA)	0.6	1	0.6	1
Vulcanox EC	0.6	—	0.6	—

The first compound takes about 4 minutes while the other three take 6 minutes to cure at a steam pressure of about 4 kg/cm^2.

	5	6	7
Smoked sheet	75	70	70
WTR	50	60	60
GPF black	30	20	30
HAF black	—	20	—
Hard clay	30	20	30
Tread crumb—20 mesh	30	20	20
Zinc oxide	5	5	5
Stearic acid	1	1	1
Process oil	1	1	1
Paraffin wax	0.5	0.5	0.5
A.O.HSL	1	1	1
A.O.4010NA	0.5	0.25	0.25
HBS	1	1	1
TMT	0.15	0.15	0.15
Sulphur	2.5	2.5	2.5

Curing at 150°C takes about 6 minutes.

Carcass Compound

	1	2
Smoked sheet	75	70
SBR-1712	—	30
WTR	50	—
SRF black	—	10
Whiting	75	60
Process oil	2	2
Rosin	0.5	—
Coumarone resin	—	4
Zinc oxide	5	4
Stearic acid	1	1
A.O.PBN	—	1
A.O.HSL	1	—
CBS	—	0.8
HBS	1	—
TMT	0.2	—
DPG	—	0.2
Sulphur	2.5	2.25

Formula 1 takes 6 minutes to cure at 150°C and the latter one takes 3 minutes at 162°C.

Curing Bags

Curing bags are usually made from butyl rubber compound. The butyl bag stands as much as 1000 to 1500 cures compared to the 100 cures with the natural rubber bags. Apart from the short life, the natural rubber bags start cracking after a few cures giving a bad appearance and rough surface to the inside of the tyres. The curing bag is made by extruding into a tube of the shape of the final bag, cut to length, valve inserted and the ends joined up. Usually a rubberised fabric reinforcement at the valve base is provided. The assembly is cured in a mould, with simultaneous air pressure inside the bag.

A few formulations for curing bags are given below :

	1	2	3	4	5
Smoked sheet	90	—	—	—	—
Butyl-400	—	100	100	90	—
Butyl - 301	—	—	—	—	100
Neoprene	—	—	—	10	5
WTR	20	—	—	—	—
Zinc oxide	25	25	25	5	5
Stearic acid	1	1	1	1	0.5
GPF black	25	25	25	20	—
HAF black	—	25	25	50	55
China clay	25	—	—	—	—
Paraffin wax	1	5	5	2	—
Castor oil	—	—	—	5	—
Naphthenic oil	2.5	—	—	—	7
TMT	—	1.5	—	—	—
HBS	2.5	—	—	—	—
MBT	—	1	—	1	—
Dibenzo GMF	—	—	4	—	—
Red lead	—	—	10	—	—
SP-1045 resin	—	—	—	10	10
Sulphur	1	—	—	—	—
A.O.HSL;	2	—	—	—	—

Formulations, 1,2,3 take about 30 minutes to cure at 150°C while the fourth formulation takes that much time at 180°C.

Cycle Tubes

Cycle tubes are manufactured by the moulding method or by the mandrel method. In the first method the mixed compound is extruded to the desired diameter and wall thickness, cut to the correct length, the valve is inserted and positioned and joint is made by splicing or overlapping. The assembly is cured in individual moulds, giving air pressure inside the tube during cure. The moulded tubes have a very smooth appearance with an invisible joint; but the production is low as each tube has to be moulded individually. The mandrel method is more popular as the production rate is higher. In one type of mandrel method, a cross-head extruder is used for extrusion of the tube directly on the mandrel. These are assembled in trolleys and cured in steam. In the second type mandrel method, the tubes are extruded to the desired cross-section and carried through a cooling tank and conveyer. A chalking device is provided to blow chalk through the inside of the tube during extrusion to prevent sticking of the walls. On the conveyor, the tubes are cut to length, and mounted over aluminium mandrels, by slipping one end of the mandrel in one end of the tube. The mandrels are stacked in trolleys and assembly cured in open steam. 300 to 400 tubes may be cured at a time.

The cured tubes are pulled off the mandrels, the tubes thus get reversed. The cured tubes are then cut to correct length plus 1 for the joint. The valves are inserted by punching holes in the tube and positioned. The ends are buffed and joined with self curing cement, or a hot vulcanised cure also could be given for the joints. The tubes are inflated and left for 24 hours to detect any leaks etc.

Compounding

Usually tube compounds are based on natural rubber. Some SR may also be incorporated. China clay and precipitated calcium carbonate are used as fillers in coloured tubes while SRF or GPF black is used for black tubes. In red coloured tubing compound antimony sulphide is used.

Black Tube Compounds

	1	2	3	4
Natural rubber	100	—	—	40
SBR-1712	—	100	60	60
SBR-1502	—	—	40	—
Zinc oxide	5	4	4	4
Stearic acid	2	1.5	1.5	1.5
Paraffin wax	2	1	1	1
SRF black	20	60	60	60
Fine china clay	25	—	—	—
Magnesium carbonate	5	—	—	—
Naphthenic oil	4	20	20	20
A.O.HSL	1	—	—	—
A.O.DPPD	—	1	1	1
A.O.PBN	—	1	1	1
MBTS	0.9	0.5	0.5	0.5
MBT	—	0.7	0.7	0.5
Sulphur	2.4	1.4	1.4	1.4

The first formula is cured in open steam 15 min. at 4.5 kg/cm^2 and the others are cured at 10 min. at 150°C.

Red Cycle Tubes

	1	2	3
Natural rubber	100	80	70
SBR-1500	—	20	30
Zinc oxide	5	5	4
Stearic acid	2	2	1.5
Paraffin wax	2	2	0.5
Precipitated Cal. Carbonate	20	20	80
Fine china clay	25	25	—
Magnesium carbonate	5	5	—
Brown factice	—	2	—
Naphthenic oil	4	4	10
TIO_2	5	5	5

	1	2	3
A.O.SP	1	1	1.5
MBS	—	1	—
MBTS	0.9	—	1
TMTD	—	—	0.2
Sulphur	2.4	2.2	1.3
Red/orange rubber colour		As required	

The first two formulations are cured in open steam for 15 min. at 4.5 kg/cm^2 whereas the third compound is cured for about 8 min. at 150°C.

Butyl Based Tube Formulations

	1	2	3
Butyl-301	100	100	—
Bromobutyl X-2	—	—	75
Natural tube	—	—	25
Stearic acid	1.5	1.5	2
Zinc oxide	5	5	4
SRF black	100	95	80
Paraffin oil	30	30	—
Naphthenic oil	—	—	25
Soft clay	—	40	—
Treated whiting	—	—	12.5
Aminox	—	—	1
MBT	0.75	0.75	—
MBTS	—	—	0.75
TMTD	1.75	1.75	0.2
Sulphur	1.75	1.75	0.55
Methyl zimate	0.5	0.5	—

Butyl compounds are cured at about 160-165°C for 6 to 7 minutes. They have better impermeability and heat resistance. Bromobutyl rubber is even better in this aspect.

Rickshaw Tyres

Rickshaw tyres are similar to cycle tyres, but are stronger, so better fabric reinforcement is given. Weight of rickshaw tyre varies from 800 to 900 gms. as compared to that of cycle tyre which varies between 725 to 850 gms. The total weight is more due to higher tread thickness. The rubber compounds used are similar to those of cycle tyres.

Auto Tubes and Tyres

The manufacture of auto tyres and tubes is rather a complex operation. The scooter or motorcycle tube should have very high air retention capacity, low modulus and high elongation with low hardness. Some such formulations are given below :

	1	2
Natural rubber	70	70
SBR-1712	30	—
SBR-1513	—	30
FEF black	20	20
SRF black	20	20
Proces oil	7	10
Coumarone resin	3	3
Zinc oxide	4	4
Stearic acid	1.5	1.5
A.O.PBN	1	1
A.O.IPPD	1	1
Paraffin wax	0.5	0.5
TBBS	0.6	0.6
MBTS	0.6	0.6
Sulphur	1.5	1.6

Curing at 150°C takes about 10 minutes.

Automotive Tubes

	Bias Ply	Radial Ply
Butyl-301	100	100
GPF black	70	—
FEF black	—	48
Paraffinic oil	25	20
Zinc oxide	5	5
Stearic acid	1	1.5
TMTD	1	1
MBT	0.5	—
Sulphur	2	1.75
Polyac, promotor	—	0.2

Very Big Size Tube

Bromobutyl-X2	50 Parts
Natural rubber	50
Stearic acid	2
Aminox	1
SRF black	60
Naphthenic oil	17.5
Treated whiting	12.5
Zinc oxide	4
MBTS	0.75
TMTD	0.2
Sulphur	1.1

Note : All formulaes are given in parts by weight.

Bromobutyl imparts heat resistance and impermeability while natural rubber imparts the green strength required for producing giant size tubes. A butyl truck inner tube is cured at 165-175°C for 7-10 minutes depending on its size.

21

Rubber Gaskets, Seals & Washers

Introduction

Rubber seal is a device for closing a gap or making a joint 'fluid-tight'. Seal is sometimes called packing or gland packing. The difference between seal and joint is that seal seals the gap between two components usually of metal which are subjected to relative motion. A joint is used to seal between two static components and is known as gasket. Thus seal is used in dynamic conditions and a gasket is used for static conditions. Rubber seals are used to seal anything from a wrist watch to the freight door on an aircraft. The former may be an O-ring of bore 8 mm and cross-sectional diameter 0.5 mm and the latter may have a section more than 40 mm across and a circumferential length of 15 metres.

Selection of Rubber for Oil Seals

Nitrile rubbers are the most important elastomers for use in seals. The resistance of nitrile rubbers to oils increases with increase in acrylonitrile content. They are particularly suitable for seals for petroleum oils, water, silicon oils, greases and glycol based fire resistant fluids but are not suitable for use with nitrocarbons, phosphates, ester fluids, ketones or strong acids and certain automobile brake fluids. Degree of swelling in petroleum oil depends on the aniline point of the oil. Lower the aniline point, higher will be the aromaticity of the oil, higher will be the swell. For usage in highly aromatic oil, nitrile rubber with high acrylonitrile is preferred. For low temperature use nitrile rubber with low acrylonitrile content is preferred. Low temperature resistance can be improved by using special plasticisers *e.g.* sebacates and adipate. For oil seals requiring ozone, weather, salt water resistance and resistance to gases *e.g.* freon, nitrile-PVC blend or polycelloroprene is used. For low premeability to gases butyl rubber may be used. Ethylene propylene rubber is used for seals used in hydraulic systems based on phosphate ester non-fllame fluids and silicon fluids and also with steam and hot water.

Polyurethane oil seals are used for applications requiring resistance to low temperatures, weather and ozone but cannot be used with aqueous solutions of acids and alkalies, chlorinated hydrocarbons, ketones, hot water, steam or glycols. Silicone rubbers have the chief advantage of retaining flexibility down to very low temperatures without hardening. Silicone has good resistance to alkalies, acids and ozone but only moderate as regards oils. They are not recommended for use with hydrocarbons *e.g.* petrol and paraffins or steam about 3 kg/cm^2 as otherwise considerable swelling and softening may take place.

Types of Seals

Seals may be divided into two broad categories namely, static and dynamic. Static seals are used to seal between two permanently or relatively static components. These are known as gaskets. Dynamic seals are required to seal the annular gap between two components which are subject to relative motion. These are further divided into two groups. Compression seals function under pressure, therefore they are reinforced by strong material like metal or rubber. Flexible seals function under zero or normal pressure and are therefore reinforced by a material which is incompressible but is flexible enough with a low shape rigidity *e.g.* fabrics.

Manufacturing Process

There are various methods of manufacture of seals. These may be made by cutting from calendered or proofed fabric sheets, cutting and joining of extruded material and by moulding.

Gaskets from sheets

There are several methods of cutting gaskets and other articles from sheet rubber or rubber bonded sheet materials. The Template and Hand Knife method is used for large gaskets. Knife must be sharp and water may be used as lubricant. Thin stock (about 0.045) is most difficult to cut because of its tendency to stretch and fold. The vibrating knife method employs a knife operating at about 7200 strokes per minute on 60 cycles/sec. and gives rapid, clean cutting of thin gaskets. Now wetting is required. A metal template is used as a guide.

When rubber rings to be made holes in the middle, the original unvulcanised rubber sheet is rolled round a cylindrical core of metal or wood having a round or square cross-section. The core surface is smoothed and dusted with talc. The core diameter is equal to the required internal diameter or cross-section of the rubber ring. This is now wrapped tightly with a narrow strip of cotton cloth. The tube is then vulcanised. The wrapping cloth is removed. It is now cut into small sections with the aid of lathe.

Formulations of Rubber Gaskets, Washers & Seals

Formulations

	Gaskets Rubber Fastener	Ventilator Window Seal
SBR-1502	—	45
SBR-1712	70	—
SBR-1958	—	10
Natural rubber	30	45
FEF black	30	30
Soft clay	50	50
Naphthenic oil	15	15
Coumarone resin	—	10
Zinc oxide	4	4
Stearic acid	1.5	1.5
A.O.PBN	1	1
Paraffin wax	1	1

CBS	1		1
TMTD	0.2		0.1
Sulphur	1.8		2.2

Curing takes about 10 minutes at about 150°C.

Pressure Cooker Gasket

Nitrile rubber (high ACN)	40
SBR-1502	60
FEF black	50
Precipitated calcium carbonate	30
Paraffin oil	5
Coumarone resin	4
Zinc oxide	5
Stearic acid	1
A.O.Ketone amine type	1.5
Paraffin wax	2
TMTD	0.75
TETD	0.75
ZDC	0.3
Sulphur	0.5

Curing takes about 8 minutes at about 150°C.

More formulae of Seals and Cords

	Trunk Lid Seal	**Door Seal**	**Weather Strip**	**Filler Cord**
SBR-1502	60	50	50	—
SBR-1513/1514	—	—	—	70
Natural rubber	40	50	50	30
FEF black	20	30	25	30
Soft clay	30	—	60	200
Whiting	30	40	60	200
Naphthenic oil	20	20	20	40

Brown factice	15	20	15	10
Zinc oxide	4	4	4	4
Stearic acid	1.5	1.5	1.5	1.5
CBS	1.2	1.2	1.2	1.3
TMTD	0.2	—	0.2	0.3
DPG	0.2	0.4	—	—
Sulphur	1.8	2.2	2	2.2
A.O.SP	1	1	1	1
Paraffin wax	1	1	1	1

Curing take about 8 to 10 min. at about 150° C

"Q" Channel and Refrigerator Gasket

	"Q" Channel	Refrigerator Gasket
SBR-1502	—	50
SBR-1712	70	—
Natural rubber	30	50
FEF black	30	—
China clay	100	40
Pptd. $CaCo^3$	20	60
Naphthenic oil	20	15
Coumarone resin	3	3
Brown factice	10	15
Zinc oxide	4	4
Stearic acid	1.5	1
CBS	1	1.25
DPG	0.5	0.4
Sulphur	2	2
A.O.SP	1	1
Paraffin wax	1	1
TiO^2 and colour	—	As required

Curing takes about 10 minutes at about 150°C.

Automotive, Seals, Rings and Gaskets

	Carburetter Pipe Seals	Suspension Sealing Rings	Dust Seals on Suspension	Radiator Pressure Filler Cap Wash
Chemaprene-3309	30	70	100	—
Synaprene-1502	70	30	—	100
FEF black	50	50	60	60
Whiting	60	60	80	75
Rosin	5	5	5	—
Di Octyl Phthalate	15	35	40	—
Naphthenic oil	—	—	—	25
Zinc oxide	4	4	4	4
Stearic acid	1.5	1.5	1.5	1.5
MBTS	1.5	1.5	1.5	1.5
TMTD	0.3	0.3	0.3	0.3
Paraffin wax	2	2	2	2
Sulphur	1.5	1.5	1.5	2
PBN	1	1	1	1

Curing takes about 15 minutes at 150°C.

Their hardness ranges between 55 to 65 shore A.

Elastic Rubber Bands

Most elastic rubber bands have to withstand considerable stretching. They may be manufactured from extruded rubber tubes or from calendered sheets made into tubes. The tubes are cut on automatic lathes. The mix should not be overworked. A suitable mix is as follows:

RMA IX	100 parts
Antimony sulphide	25
Vermilion	5

The sheet is run on a 3-roll calender and doubled from 0.5 mm sheet and finally rolled up tightly on the roller and allowed a whole day to cool down to obtain tougher and blisterless sheets. When the sheet has been unrolled, the separate pieces are gently warmed and pressed between zinc plates. The polished sheets are put through a cutting machine which cuts them into bands of a definite width and lays the ends together to form a tube. The tubes are vulcanised on glass mandrels on which they fit tightly and the heat is applied by means of a water bath preferably to lay the goods in chalk, the temperature being raised rapidly and the cure completed at a pretty high temperature. The bands are obtained by automatic cutting from the tubes.

O-Rings & Gaskets

Medium nitrile, nitrile rubber is used in oil resistant O-rings and gaskets. They have good resistance to oils, solvents and fuels. Moderate chemical resistance and heat resistance are also present. O-rings and gaskets of various hardness ranges are required in the industry. 45±5, 55±5, 65±5, 75±5, and 85±5 hardness ranges are commonly employed. The following compounds are suitable for compression or transfer moulding.

Hardness	45±5	55±5	65±5	75±5	85±5
Nitrile (Medium Nitrile)	100	100	100	100	100
Coumarone resin	3	4	5	5	—
P/F resin	—	—	—	—	15
Hexa	—	—	—	—	1
SRF black	35	45	30	40	40
FEF black	—	—	25	35	40

DBP	15	10	10	15	10
Zinc oxide	5	5	5	5	5
CBS	1.5	1.5	1.5	1.5	1.5
Stearic acid	1.5	1.5	1.5	1.5	1.5
TMTD	1..5	1.5	1.5	1.5	1.5
Sulphur	0.33	0.33	0.33	0.33	0.33
A.O.PBN	0.75	0.75	0.75	0.75	0.75
A.O.BL	0.75	0.75	0.75	0.75	0.75
Paraffin wax	1	1	1	1	1

Curing at about 160°C takes 10 minutes.

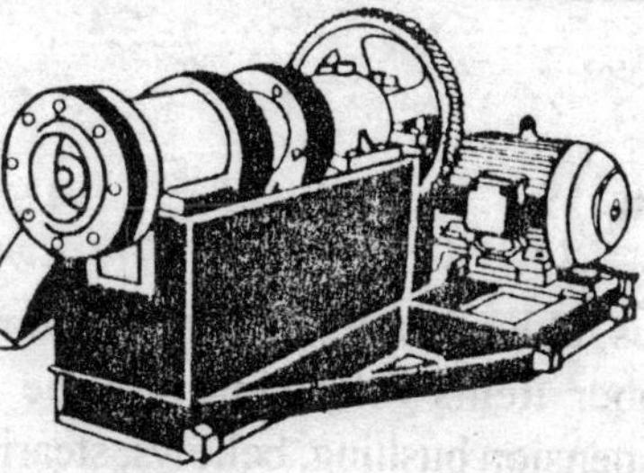

EXTRUDER MACHINE

CALENDER MACHINE

22

Rubber Auto Parts

Introduction

Various rubber items are used in automobile industry. To name a few of these rubber items following may be mentioned : shock absorber bushings, suspension bushing, bellows, stearing wheel boot, dustcover boot, foot pedal pads, gasket rubber fastener, ventilator window seal, buffer spring, cables, sponge arm rest, padding for door handle, mats and mattings, door stop, battery tray, door seal, weather strip, filler cord, Q-channel, V-belt for fan, hoses and tubes, latex treated upholstry for furnishing, brake lining etc. Tyres & tubes are the major items consuming rubber to a major extent.

These various items are manufactured by different methods namely, extrusion, calendering and moulding etc. and also some of these items *e.g.* belts, hoses, seals, tyres, and tubes etc. are important industries by themselves; hence many items of rubber finding application in automobiles have been given elsewhere. We are providing various formulations related with rubber items which are not available elsewhere.

Automotive Brake Linings

Friction brakes are used for almost all automotive vehicles. The flexible lining is adaptable to brake drums of different diameters. Moulded lining is made using asbestos fibre mixed with suitable fillers and bonding agents and appropriately processed. Rigid lining is formed to fit a specific drum diameter, the woven lining is made using woven fabric as a base, the principal ingredient of the fabric is asbestos. The brake lining material should not create noise during breaking, should be able to withstand the heat and moisture, it should have adequate mechanical strength to withstand rivetting during fitting to the brake shoe without cracking. Its life should be long with minimum of maintenance cost.

Recipe of Brake Lining (NBR Based)

NBR (high ACN grade)	75 Parts
SBR-1958	75
Phenolic resin	20
Asbestos	150
Clay	50
Naphthenic oil	5
Zinc oxide	5
Stearic acid	1.5
TMT	1.2
DPG	0.3
Sulphur	1
Curing at 150°C takes about 20 minutes.	

Brake Lining

Rubber from 30% latex	100 parts
Short fibre asbestos	600
Sulphur	30
Graphite	10
Powdered lead	7
Butyral dehyde aniline (Accelerator)	2
Carbon black	15

The asbestos is made into a water slurry containing a small amount of sodium hydroxide. The sulphur, graphite, powdered lead and carbon black are made into a water paste and mixed with the asbestos slurry, the water present being removed by filteration to give a 10% solids concentration. The latex 30% rubber cement to which emulsified accelerators has been added is then mixed with the slurry. This mixture is then moulded to shape, dried and set, and vulcanised in open steam for about 2 hours at 140°C.

Brake Cylinder Cu

For castor oil based fluid system.

Smoked sheet	50 parts
SBR-1500	50
GPF black	30
HAF-LS black	30
Zinc oxide	5
Stearic acid	1
A.O.PAN	1
A.O.401 ONA	1
HBS	0.3
TMT	2.5

One more formula for brake cylinder cup is as follows:

SBR-1502	100
FEF black	60
Mineral oil	3
Zinc oxide	4
Stearic acid	2.5
Paraffin wax	1
MBT	1
TMT	2
Sulphur	0.75
Nonox BL	1
A.O.PBN	1

Curing at 140°C takes about 15 minutes.

Brake Chamber Diaphragm

Diaphragms are made from simple flat or slightly convulated diaphragms from unsupported and supported spread or calender proofed material. Diaphragms with peripheral or centre beads and bosses for assembling and sealing purposes, and with deep convolutions. are also made by moulding. For these accurate blanks are required for the reinforced diaphragms to ensure that during moulding the fabric is not damaged or distorted by the flow of rubber. Simple two-plate compression moulds with accurate dowelling or trapper location are commonly used. Diaphragms are usually made with rubber coating on only one side of the fabric. The following formulation is for the rubber coating in case of air brake systems.

Smoked sheet	100 parts
HAF-LS Black	45
Zinc oxide	5
Stearic acid	2
A.O.PAN	2
A.O.401 ONA	1
A.O.EC	1
DCS	0.6
Sulphur	2.4

The above formulations take about 10 minutes to presscure at 150°C.

Brake Pedal Pads

SBR-1712	70 parts
Smoked sheet	30
FEF black	25
Hard clay	100
Naphthenic oil	15
Zinc oxide	4
Stearic acid	1.5
A.O.PBN	1
Paraffin wax	1
CBS	1
TMTD	0.2
Sulphur	1.8

Curing at 152°C takes about 10 minutes.

	Shock Absorber Bushing	Suspension Bushing 1	Suspension Bushing 2	Grommets
SBR-1502	50	—	—	—
SBR-1712	—	70	70	100
Smoked sheets	50	30	30	—
HAF Black	—	30	25	55
FEF black	40	—	—	—
Naphthenic oil	8	15	15	5
Hard clay	—	50	100	50
Zinc oxide	4	4	4	4
Stearic acid	1.5	1.5	1.5	1
A.O.PBN	—	1	1	1
A.O.Ketone/amine	1	—	—	—
A.O.ETDQ	1	—	—	—
Paraffin wax	—	1	1	1
CBS	1	1.2	1.25	1.25
TMTD	0.1	0.2	0.25	0.25
Sulphur	2.2	1.8	1.9	1.8

Curing at 150°C takes about 10 minutes.

	Bellows	Steering Wheel Boot	Dust Cover Boot
SBR-1712	100	100	100
HAF black	40	25	—
SRP black	—	—	50
Whiting	60	75	—
Naphthenic oil	30	15	20
Zinc oxide	4	4	4
Stearic acid	1	1	1
A.O.PBN	1	1	1
Paraffin wax	1	1	1
CBS	1.2	1.2	1.2
TMTD	0.2	0.2	0.2
Sulphur	1.7	1.7	1.6

Curing at 150°C takes about 10 minutes.

Compounds of Various Hardness

Suitable for automobile applications. Based on natural rubber.

	1	2	3	4	5	6
Smoked sheet	70	60	60	60	60	60
Whole tyre reclaim	60	80	80	80	80	80
Zinc oxide	5	5	5	5	5	5
Stearic acid	2	2.5	2.5	2.5	2.5	2.5
GPF black	—	—	—	—	30	40
SRF black	—	—	5	15	15	40
Whiting	10	15	20	30	40	30
China clay	—	5	10	10	—	—
Blown asphalt	—	5	5	5	5	5
Process oil	15	10	10	5	5	5
Brown factice	10	—	—	—	—	—
Antioxidant	1	1	1	1	1	1
MBTS	1	1	1	1.1	1.1	1.1
TMT	—	0.1	0.1	0.1	0.1	0.1
Sulphur	2.5	2.75	3	3	3	3.5
Shore hardness	**30**	**40**	**50**	**60**	**70**	**80**

Curing at 150°C takes about 20 minutes

SBR base compounds for miscellaneous automotive applications.

	Hardness Shore	
	70	**80**
SBR-1500	70	60
Whole tyre reclaim	60	80
Zinc oxide	5	5
Stearic acid	1	1
GPF black	30	40
SRF black	15	30
Whiting	40	40
Process oil	5	5

Blown asphalt	5	5
Antioxidant	1	1
MBTS	1.25	1.25
TMT	0.1	0.1
Sulphur	2.5	3

Curing at 150°C takes about 20 minutes.

Recipe for Grommets

Smoked sheets	50 Parts
SBR-1712	50
HAF black	60
Naphthenic oil	10
Hard clay	50
Zinc oxide	4
Stearic acid	1
A.O.PBN	1
Paraffin wax	1
CBS	1
TMTM	0.2
Sulphur	2.2

Curing at 150°C takes about 8 to 10 minutes.

Formulations Based on Nitrile Rubber

Recipe for Clutch Plate

Nitrile rubber	80 parts
SBR-1502	20
SRF black	40
GPF black	20
Naphthenic oil	8
Zinc oxide	4.5
Stearic acid	1.5
A.O.PBN	1
TMT	1.2
DPG	0.3
Sulphur	2

Curing at 150°C takes about 15 minutes.

	Carburettor Pipe Seals	Suspension	
		Sealing Rings	Dust Seals
Nitrile Rubber	30	70	100
SBR-1502	70	30	—
FEF black	50	50	60
Whiting	60	60	80
Rosin	5	5	5
D.O.P	15	35	40
Zinc oxide	4	4	4
Stearic acid	1.5	1.5	1.5
MBTS	1.5	1.5	1.5
TMTD	0.3	0.3	0.3
Paraffin wax	2	2	2
Sulphur	1.5	1.5	1.5
A.O.PBN	1	1	1

Some more formulation of lip seals suitable for hub bearings, engine and gear box are given below. Medium nitrile rubber is suitable for this purpose for good service.

Hardness (Shore A_2)	90±3	82±5	70±5
Nitrile rubber (medium)	90	90	90
SBR-1958	10	—	—
SBR-1502	—	10	10
SRF black	40	40	40
FEF black	40	40	30
DOP	10	10	10
PF resin (Thermosetting)	15	15	15
Hexa	1	1	1
Zinc oxide	4	4	4
Stearic acid	1.5	1.5	1.5
MBTS	1.5	1.5.	1.5
TMTD	0.3	0.3	0.3
Sulphur	1.6	1.6	1.6
PBN A.O.	0.5	0.5	0.5
Paraffin wax	1	1	1

Curing at 150°C takes about 15 minutes.

Sponge Based Items

	Black Sponge	Coloured Sponge	Sponge Armrest	Padding for Door Handle
SBR-1502	—	—	100	100
SBR-1513	100	100	—	—
FEF black	—	—	40	30
SRF black	30	—	—	—
Calcium silicate	—	15	—	—
Whiting	80	80	100	100
Naphthenic oil	70	70	60	75
Zinc oxide	5	5	4	4
Stearic acid	2	2	3.5	4
A.O.SP	—	1	1	1
A.O.PBN	1	—	—	—
Paraffin wax	—	—	3	3
MBTS	3	3	—	—
CBS	—	—	1.5	1.5
Sulphur	4.5	4.5	3	3
Sodium bicarbonate	14	14	—	—
DPT	3	3	3	3
Retarder TSA	—	—	0.5	0.5
Startch	2.5	2.5	—	—
TiO_2 and colour	—	As required	—	—
Curing time at 150°C, minutes	**25**	**25**	**15**	**20**

Automobile seats are based on microcellular and foam rubber cushions and is an important outlet for rubber.

Oil Seals for High Temperature

Oil seals are required to have good compression set resistance. When it is also required to be used at high temperature along with retention of other vulcanisation properties at these temperatures, retention of compression set characteristics is also important. Higher doses of accelerators and low sulphur is required.

	Formula with Blooming	Formula free from Blooming
Nitrile rubber (medium)	100	100
SRF black	50	50
D.O.P	5	5
Zinc oxide	5	5
Stearic acid	1	1
A.O.PBNA	1.5	1.5
TMTD	3.5	2
CBS	—	2
Sulphur	0.5	0.5

Bellows and Dust Seal

Bellows requires properties of high tear resistance and elogation. These are achieved by using MBTS along with sulphur. Dust seal has low thickness and is required to have resistance to only moderately high temperature. Hence normal curing system with quick curing can be used. The following formulations are based on nitrile rubber of medium nitrile content.

	Oil resistant Bellow	Dust Seal for Suspension
Nitrile rubber	100	100
SRF black	40	—
FEF black	—	50
DOP	10	20
Coumaron inden resine	5	5
Zinc oxide	5	5
Stearic acid	1	1
A.O.PBNA	1	1
MBTS	2	—
CBS	—	1
TMTD	—	0.25
Sulphur	1.5	1.5

Curing at 155°C takes 15 minutes.

23

Various Other Important Formulations

Household Rubber Gloves

Formulation

60% NR latex, LA -TZ Type	167
10% Potassium hydroxide	4
20% Potassium laurate	2
50% Sulphur dispersion	2.5
50% Zinc diethyldithiocarbamate	2
50% Antioxidant	2
50% Zinc oxide	2
Colour dispersion	as required

Processing

The latex mix is matured, strained and transferred to a dipping tank. Porcelain or aluminium formers at 40-50°C are dipped into a calcium nitrate coagulant and then into the latex. After the required thickness of latex deposit has been obtained, the formers are withdrawn and dried. The gloves are then stripped, leached and vulcanized. Immersion in dilute chlorine solution for a few seconds reduces the surface friction; this should be followed by washing and drying.

Surgeon's Gloves

Formulation

	Sterlization	*Disposable*
60% NR latex, LA -TZ Type	167	167
10% Potassium hydroxide solution	3	3
20% Potassium laurate solution[1]	1	1
50% Sulphur	0.4	1
50% Antioxidant[2]	2	1
50% TMTD	1	
50% ZDBC	2	1.5
Zinc Oxide	0.5	0.5

1. Potassium caprylate is a subsitute
2. Non-staining phenolic type, *e.g.* Antioxidant 2246 (Cyanamid) or Permanax WSL (Vulnax)

Processing : The coagulant is calcium nitrate in aqueous methylated spirit.

Curing : Dry and cure - 15 min at 120°C.

Contraceptives :

1. Stripping in the dry using rotating bushes
2. Stripping in the wet using air and pressurized water sprays.

Formulation

	1	**2**
60% NR latex, LA -TZ Type	167	167
10% Potassium hydroxide	2	2
20% Potassium laurate	0.5	10
50% Sulphur	1.8	1.5
50% Zinc oxide	0.5	0.5
50% Antioxidant[1]	1	1
50% ZDBC	2.5	1.5
50% ZMBT	2.5	2.5
Water	24	15

1. Non-toxic non-staining phenolic type

Processing

Maturing condition 36h at 25°C for (1) 4h at 55°C for (2). The formers are rotated after withdrawl from the mix and partially dried at 60-80°C before being given a second mix.

Curing : 20 min at 110°C prior to stripping.

Transparent Teats/Nipples

Formulation

60% NR Latex, LA-TZ type	167
10% Potassium hydroxide	2
70% Potassium laurate	2
50% ZDBC	2
50% Sulphur	2

Processing

Prevulcanize for 2h at 60°C. Dip, dry at 70°C and leach thoroughly.

Latex Thread (General Purpose)

Formulated to minimize Copper-staining

Formulation

60% Nr latex, LA-TZ type[1]	167
10% Potassium hydroxide	4
20% Potassium laurate	2.5
50% Sulphur	3.5
50% ZMBT	3
50% ZDBC	0.5
50% Antioxidant[2]	3
50% Titanium dioxide	10
50% Zinc oxide	5

1. Substitute : 152 parts of 66% creamed latex.
2. Non-staining phenolic type, *e.g.* Antioxidant 2246 or 425 (Cynamid), Permanax WSP (Vulnax), Naugard 445 (Uniroyal).

Processing :

All dispersion must be free of coarse particles; particle size of less than 5 microns is advised. The mix should be matured for 4 days at 25°C then homogenized, deaerated and filtered before use. Recommended drying and curing condition are 10-15 min. at 130°C. Alternatively the thread can be given sufficient cure to enable to be handled without distortion (3 min at 135°C) and then given a post cure often at a lower temperature (16h at 70°C).

Packaging Pressure-sensitive Adhesive

Formulation

NR[1]	100
Ester gum[2]	175
Lanolin	25
Antioxidant[3]	1
Zinc oxide[4]	50
Solvent	400

1. Pale crepe for lightest colours
2. Tackifier
3. Non-staining phenolic type *e.g.* permanax WSL (Vulnax)
4. Fillers such as calcium carbonate aluminimum hydrate or clay may be substituted for zinc oxide.
5. Toluene, naphtha or trychloroethylene.

Mix procedure :

Initial shredding or granulation of the rubber aids dissolution. Alternatively, lightly mill the rubber and zinc oxide, then add solvent. Blend the swollen mixture in a Z-blade mixer until homogenous, then add the ester gum, antioxidant and finally lanolin.

Tubing , Laboratory

Formulation

SP 50[1]	100
Soft Clay[2]	30
Whiting	30
Process oil[3]	15
Zinc oxide	3
Stearic acid	1.5
Phenolic anti-oxidant[4]	1.5
Sulphur	2
MBTS	0.5
TMTD	0.15
Red ochre pigment	5

1. Superior processing rubber.
2. Devolite (English China Clays)
3. Naphthenic oil, *e.g.* Circosol 380 Sun oil
4. Permanax WSP (Vulnax)

Water Tubing

Formulation (Synaprene based)

Synaprene 1712	100
FEF	20
China clay	200
Precipitated $CaCO_3$	40
Paraffin oil	25
Cumar	5
Zinc oxide	4
Stearic acid	1
CBS	1.2
DPG	0.3
TMTD	0.3
Sulphur	2.5
PBN	1
Paraffin wax	1

Seals, LCM vulcanization (Vacuum extrusion)

Formulation

SMR 20[1]	100	100	100
N990, MT	100		
N330, HAF		40	
N550, FEF			50
Whiting[2]		100	
Coated calcium carbonate[3]			110
Paraffin oil[4]	5	5	5
Process acid[5]	4	4	4
Zinc oxide	5	5	5
Stearic acid	1	1	1
Antioxidant[6]	2.5	2.5	2.5
Wax blend[7]	7	7	7
Sulphur	1.2	1.2	1.2
MBTS	2	2	2
BIDMC	0.5	0.5	0.5
Desiccant[8]	6	6	6

1. Premasticated to 60-65 mooney
2. Fine ground, *e.g.* Britomya Violet (Croxton and Garry)
3. Winnofil S (ICI)
4. Sunpar 2280 (Sun Oil)
5. Struktol WB212 (Schill and Seilacher)
6. Blend of 2 parts phr TMQ *e.g.* Flectol H (Monsanto) and 0.5 parts phr diaryl-p-phenylenediamine, Wingstay 100 (Goodyear)
7. Sunproof improved (Uniroyal)
8. Caloxol CP2 John & E Sturge.

Cable insulation

White colour; nominal hardness Shore D 35

Formulation

SMR L	70
Pelletized polypropylene[1]	30
Oil[2]	15
Precipitated silica[3]	15
Zinc oxide	4
Stearic acid	1
TMTD	1
Titanium dioxide	1
Antioxidant blend[4]	0.5

1. Propathane GWM 101 (ICI)
2. Sunpar 2280 (Sun Oil)
3. Ultrasil VN3 (Degussa)
4. Permanax CNS (Vulnax)

Rubber-coated Fabric

Highly flexible and abrasion resistant

Formulation

SMR 5	80
Polybutadiene[1]	20
N330, HAF black	25
Precipitated silica[2]	15
Process oil[3]	4
Zinc oxide	5
Stearic acid	2
Antidegradant, HPPD[4]	3
Wax blend[5]	1
Bonding agent[6]	5
Sulphur	2.25
TBBS	1.2
TETD	0.1

1. Solution-polymerised low-cis polybutadiene, Intene 55NF (Enichem)
2. Ultrasit VN3 (Degussa),
3. Dultrex 729 UK (Shell),
4. Santoflex 13 (Monsanto),
5. Sunproof Improved (Uniroyal),
6. Solution of resorcinol in formaldehyde donor, Cohedur RL (Bayer).

Mouldings (20-25 IRHD)

PA 57 enhances mix viscosity. Oil is conveniently added to reduce hardness as OENR and PA-57 are in use. Carbon black may be added as a pigment.

Formulation

Nominal hardness	25	20	20
OENR 75/25 N[1]	50		100
PA 57[2]	50	80	
Process oil[3]		20	
Zinc oxide	3	3	3
Stearic acid	1	1	1
Antioxidant[4]	1	1	1
Sulphur	1	0.5	1
CBS	0.2	0.1	0.2

1. Oil extended natural rubber, 25% naphthenic oil,
2. Superior processing rubber,
3. Fina Process Oil 2059 (Petrofina),
4. Amine or non-staining phenolic.

Erasers

Erasers may be either individually moulded or cut to size from sheet. Cured in simple clamped moulds in a steam pan or extruded and steam cured.

Formulation

	Pencil	Ink
SMR L	100	100
White factice[1]	100	50
Magnesia[2]	30	30
Lithopone	100	20
Barytes	80	
Whiting	150	
Titanium dioxide	10	5
Pumice		150
Light oil[3]	30	
Zinc oxide	10	10
Stearic acid	2	2
Sulphur	8	6
MBTS	1	1
DPG	2	1.5
Pigment	as required	

1. White factice (Anchor),
2. Maglite D (Merck)
3. Fina Process Oil 2059 (Petrofina)

Erasers for typewriter

Formulation

NR latex, LA-TZ type	100
Lithopone	10
Pumice Powder	60
Whiting	100
Ground glass powder	100
Zinc oxide	10
Magnesium carbonate	10
Light mineral oil	10
Sulphur	2.5
MBTS	1.5

Stereo Rubbers

For printing purpose

Formulation

Nominal hardness-IRHD	60	50	30	20
SMR CV	100	100	20	
PA 57[1]			80	100
Barytes	40	40	30	30
Factice[2]		10		
Soft clay[3]	50	20		
Light oil[4]	2	5	30	30
Zinc oxide	5	5	3	3
Antioxidant, TMQ[5]	1	1	1	1
Sulphur	1.5	1.5	1	0.5
CBS	1.5	1.5		
ZDEC	0.2	0.2		
TMTD			0.2	0.3
MBTS			1	

1. Superior processing rubber,
2. Whitbro 844 (Anchor),
3. Devolite (English China clays),
4. Fina Process Oil 2059 (Petrofina),
5. Flectol H (Monsanto)

Conveyor belt covers - general purpose

The oil-extended formulation for use with moderately abrasive materials like sand, cement or coal.

Formulation

SMR 10	100	
OENR 75/25A[1]		133
N326, HAF-LS black	80	
HAF Improved[2]		75
Aromatic Oil[3]	27	21
Zinc oxide	6	6
Stearic acid	2	2
Antidegradant,HPPD[4]	2	2
Sulphur	2.5	3
CBS	0.5	0.6

1. Oil-extended natural rubber, 25% aromatic oil,
2. Vulcan J N375 black (Cabot Carbon),
3. Dutrex 729 UK (Shell),
4. Santoflex 13 (Monsanto).

Conveyor belts - friction formulation

For use with natural or synthetic fabric

Formulation

	Heat-Resistant	General Purpose
SMR20	100	100
N762,SRF-LM-NS black	20	18
Coated calcium carbonate[1]	10	12
Coal tar oil		9
Coumarone resin		15
Pine tar	7.5	
Zinc oxide	15	10
Stearic acid	2	1
Antioxidant[2]	1	1
Sulphur	0.5	2.5
CBS	0.5	1
TMTD	0.5	

1. Calofer S (John & E Sturge),
2. Flectol H (Monsanto)

Ebonite lining adhesive (Vulcanizable)

Formulation

SMR WF	95
Ebonite dust	25
SRF black	1
Litharge	5
China clay[1]	75
Heavy calcined magnesium oxide	10
Linseed oil	3
MC Sulphur[2]	45
DPG	1
Petroleum solvent	For 30% solution

1. Devolite (English China Clays)
2. Sulphur surface treated with magnesium carbonate

Automotive hose lining

For application in which resistance to hydrocarbon oils is not required.

Formulation

SMR-20	100
N762,SRF-LM-NS black	65
Whiting	100
Process oil	20
Zinc oxide	5
Stearic acid	.2
Antioxidant, TMQ[2]	2
DTDM	0.75
TMTD	1.5
MBTS	1.8

1. Dutrex 729 UK (Shell)
2. Flectol H (Monsanto)

Expanded Rubber

Hardness and density depends upon on the time and temperature of curing stages. Curing stage 1 : partial cure under pressure; gives adequate cross linking to avoid rupture of the cell walls as the product expands out of the mould. Curing stage 2: Inserts crosslinks in the expanded state improving dimensional stability.

Formulation

Cell dia	0.1-0.4 mm	0.1mm or less
OENR 75/25[1]	100	100
Talc[2]	100	100
Process aid[3]		3
Zinc oxide	5	5
Stearic acid	2	2
Antioxidant[4]	1	1
Sulphur	2	3
MBTS	1	1
BSH [5]	7	
OBSH [6]		7
Desiccant[7]	1	1
Pigment	— as required	—

1. Oil-extended natural rubber, 25% naphthenic oil,
2. Steamic OOS (Talc de Luzanac)
3. Struktol W33 (Schill & Seilacher),
4. Permanax EXP (Vulnax)
5. Genitron BSH (Fisons),
6. Celgon OT (Uniroyal),
7. Caloxol CP2 (John & E Sturge)

Shoe soles (High quality)

Formulation for injection moulding

Formulation

SMR L	90	100
High-styrene resin[1]	20	
Light oil[2]	10	10
Aluminium silicate[3]	30	35
Coated calcium carbonate[4]	70	80
Titanium dioxide	10	10
Zinc oxide	5	5
Stearic acid	1	1
Antioxidant[5]	0.7	0.7
Paraffin wax	1	1
Sulphur	1.3	1.3
CBS		2.2
MBTS		2.4
Hexamine[6]	0.5	
TMTD	0.3	

1. Polysar SS 250, 50% styrene masterbatch (polysar),
2. Fina Process Oil 2059 (Petrofina),
3. Silteg AS7 (Degussa),
4. Winnofil S (ICI)
5. Wingstay L (Goodyear)
6. Vulkacit H30 (Bayer)

Shoe soles (Low quality)

Formulations

SMR L	90
High-styrene resin[1]	20
Light oil[2]	10
Hard clay[3]	75
Whiting[4]	80
Zinc oxide	5
Titanium dioxide	5
Stearic acid	2
Antioxidant[5]	0.5
Antioxidant[6]	0.5
Paraffin wax	1
Sulphur	2.5
MBTS	1.3
TMTM	0.5

1. Polysar SS250, 50% styrene masterbatch (Polysår),
2. Fina Process oil 2059 (petrofina),
3. Hexafil (English China Clays)
4. Britomya Violet (Croxton & garry)
5. Wingstay L (Goodyear),
6. Polygard (Uniroyal)

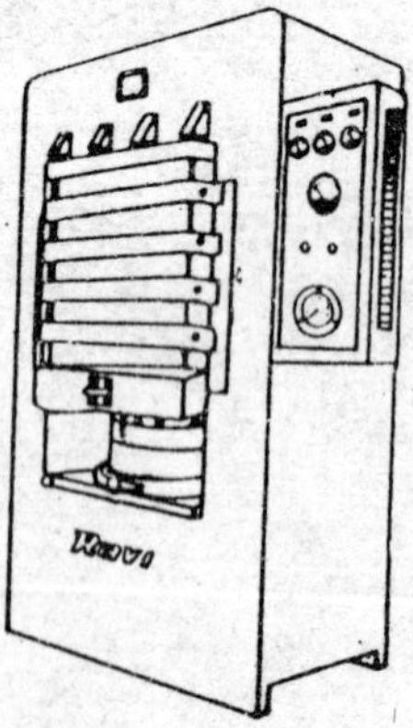

HYDRAULIC PRESS

Moulded shoe sole

Formulation

Synaprene 1502	100	100
HAF	30	
Hard clay	100	150
Naphthenic oil	30	10
Cumar	7	10
Zinc oxide	4	4
Stearic acid	1.5	1.5
Antioxidant PBN		1
Antioxidant DPPD	1	
Paraffin wax	2	
MBTS	1	1
DPG	1	1
DEG		2
Sulphur	2	2
TiO_2 & Colour	as required	

Battery plate separators

Formulation

SMR WF	100
Ebonite dust	200
Paraffin wax	2
Stearic acid	1
Sulphur	50
DPG	1

Press cure: 25 min. at 153°C followed by 2h at 153°C in steam or 4h at 153°C in a steam pan.

Truck tyre retreads

OENR gives wear resistance, grip and resistance to groove cracking and lowest heat generation.

Formulations

	Heavy-duty	Light-duty
OENR 75/25A		107
SMR 20	80	
N220, FEF black		70
N375,HAF black	45	
Low-cis polybutadiene	20	20
Process oil	5	
Zinc oxide	5	5
Stearic acid	2	2
Antidegradant	2	2
Wax blend	1	1
Sulphur	1.5	1.5
TBBS	1.5	1.5

1. Oil-extended natural rubber, 25% aromatic oil.
2. Premasticated to 60 Mooney.
3. Intene 50 (Enichem).
4. Vulcan J (Cabot Carbon).
5. Dutrex 729 UK (Shell).
6. Santoflex 13 (Monsanto).
7. Sunproof Improved (Uniroyal).

Winter Passenger tyre retreads

For grip in temperature and cold winter conditions. Good wear resistance, Hardness : 70-60 IRHD.

Formulation

SMR premasticated	80	80
N220, ISAF black	28	70
High-cis polybutadiene[1]	20	20
Precipitated silica[2]	42	
Process oil[3]	15	15
Zinc oxide	6	6
Stearic acid	2.5	2.5
Antioxidant, IPPD[4]	2.5	2.5
Silane coupling agent[5]	5.6	
Sulphur	1.5	1.5
CBS	1.5	1.5

1. Europene Cis (Enichem).
2. Ultrasit VN3 (Degussa)
3. Dutrex 729 UK (Shell).
4. Permanax IPPD (Vulnax).
5. Si 69 (Degussa).

Motor cycle/Scooter treads

Formulation (Synaprene based)

Synaprene 1712	80	100
RMA IX	20	
HAF	50	50
Zinc oxide	4	4
Stearic acid	2	2
H.Ar.Oil	3	3
Antiozonant PBN	1	1
Antiozonant IPPD	1	1
Paraffin wax	1	1
TBBS	0.9	1
DPG	0.2	0.2
Sulphur	1.9	1.75

Brake seals

For brake seals operating at low to moderate temperature.

Nominal hardness : 70-65 IRHD

Formulation

SMR CV	100	100
N326, HAF-LS black	50	50
Zinc oxide	5	5
Stearic acid	1	1
Antioxidant, TMQ[1]	1	1
Antioxidant[2]	1	1
ZMBI[3]	1	
Sulphur	0.5	0.5
CBS	1.5	1
DTDM	1	1
TETD	0.3	0.3

1. Flectol H (Monsanto),
2. Permanax BL (Vulnax),
3. Vulkanox ZMB 2 (Bayer)

Detergent resistant washing machine seal

Hardness : 45 IRHD

Resistance to leaching is attained by using high levels of antioxidants

Formulation

SMR 10	100	100
Coated calcium carbonate[1]	20	20
Titanium dioxide	10	10
Zinc oxide	4	4
Stearic acid	2	2
Antioxidant, TMQ[2]	1	1
Antioxidant[3]	2.5	6
Antioxidant[4]	1	
Sulphur	1	1
MBS	1.2	1.2
TMTD	0.3	0.3

1. Winnofil S (ICI)
2. Flectol H (Monsanto)
3. Perkanox P15/60 (Akzo Chemie)
4. Wingstay L (Goodyear)

Refrigerator gasket

Formulation (Synaprene based)

Synaprene 1502	50
NR	50
China clay	40
Precipitated $CaCo_3$	60
Naphthenic oil	15
Cumar	3
Br. Factice	15
Zinc oxide	4
Stearic acid	1
CBS	1.25
DPG	0.4
Sulphur	2
A.O.SP	1
TiO_2	as required

Pressure cooker gasket

Formulation (Synaprene based)

NBR	40
Synaprene 1502	60
FEF	50
Precipitated $CaCo_3$	30
Paraffin oil	5
Cumar	4
Zinc oxide	5
Stearic acid	1
Antioxidant-Ketone-amine	1.5
Paraffin wax	2
TMTD	0.75
TETD	0.75
ZDC	0.3
Sulphur	0.5

Flame-retardant foam

Formulation

60% NR latex, LA-TZ type	167
20% Potassium oleate	7.5
50% Sulphur	5
50% ZDEC	2
50% ZMBT	2
50% Antioxidant[1]	2
50% Chlorinated wax[2]	5
50% Tetrabromobisphenol A[3]	10
50% Hydrated alumina	20
50% Secondry Jelling agent[4]	2
50% Zinc oxide	6
20% Sodium silicofluoride	5

Dry & cure : 30 min at 100°C in steam

1. Polymerized 2,2,4-trimethyl-1, 2-dihydroquinoline
2. Solid chlorinated paraffin wax containing 70% chlorine, *e.g.* Cereclor 70 (ICI).
3. Great Lakes Chemical Co.
4. Baco FRFS or Baco FRF 40 (British Aluminium Co.)
5. Ethyl chloride-formaldehyde-ammonia reaction product, *e.g.* Trimene Base (Uniroyal) or Vulcafor EFA (Vulnax)

Moulded foam

For articles of thin section

Formulation

60% NR latex, LA-TZ type	167
20% Potassium ricinolcate[1]	1
50% Antioxidant[2]	2
50% ZDEC	2
50% ZMBT	2
50% Sulphur	2
50% Filler slurry[3]	5
50% Colour	as required
25% Polypropylene glycol[4]	as required
10% Secondry Jelling agent[5]	10
50% Zinc oxide	6

Cure : 30 min at 100°C in steam or hot water

1. Castor oil soap
2. Non-staining phenolic type
3. Whiting, clay, talc, lithopone etc.
4. Propylan D702(Lankro Chemicals)
5. Cetyl trimethylammonium bromide or similar cationic surfactant.

Processing :

Add ricinolate, antioxidant, accelerators and sulphur to the latex and mix. Foam to the required volume before adding the mixture of the other ingredients. Preheat the mould to 55-65°C and pour the mould into it. Allow to gel for 5-10 min.

For curing : Heat the mould in steam or hot air at 100°C for ca 30 min.

Moulded foam (Dunlop method)

Formulation

60% NR latex, LA-TZ type	167
20% Potassium oleate	7.5
50% Sulphur	4
50% ZDEC	2
50% ZMBT	2
50% Antioxidant[1]	2
50% Secondry Jelling agent[2]	1.6
50% Zinc oxide	10
20% Sodium silicofluoride	6

1. Non-staining phenolic type
2. Ethyl chloride-formaldehyde-ammonia reaction product, *e.g.* Trimene Base (Uniroyal or Vulcafor EFA (Vulnax)

Spread foam

Suitable for carpet backing and underlays

Formulation

60% NR latex, LA-TZ type	167
20% Potassium ricinoleate[1]	6
50% Antioxidant[2]	2
10% Casein	10
50% ZDEC	2
50% ZMBT	2
50% Sulphur	5
China clay	70-100
25% Polypropylene glycol[3]	4
10% Secondry Jelling agent[4]	6
50% Zinc oxide	6
50% Colour	as required

1. Castor oil soap
2. Non-staining phenolic type
3. Propylan D702 (Lankro Chemicals)
4. Cetyl trimethyl ammonium bromide or similar cationic surfactant.

Processing :

Add ricinolate, antioxidant, casein, accelerators and sulphur to the latex and mix. Foam to approximately six times its original volume. Add the mixture of the remaining ingredient. Allow to gel in hot-air stream at 90°C or using an infrared heating unit. Dry and cure in a hot-air oven at 100-130°C.

Baby-bottle teat

Formulation

NR-pale crepe	100	100
Zinc oxide	0.6	0.6
Stearic acid	0.6	0.6
Sulphur	2	2
ZDED[1]	0.4	0.6
MBTS[2]	0.05	

1. Zinc dibenzyldithiocarbamate, Robac Zded (Robinson Brothers Ltd.)
2. Dibenzthiaazyl disulphide.

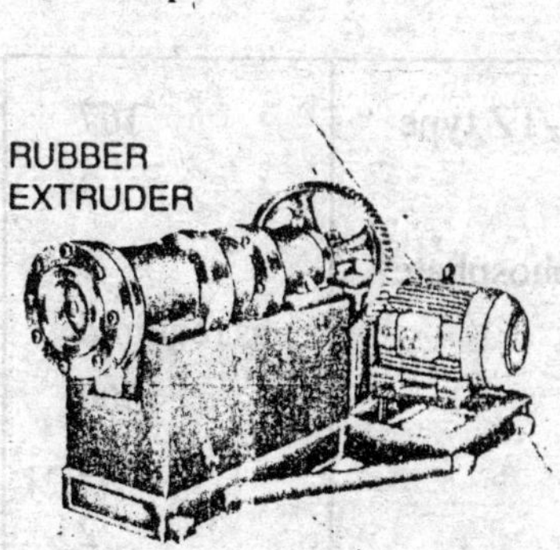

Rug anchor backing (washing)

Formulation

Ingredient	Parts
60% NR latex, LA-TZ type	167
25% Surfactant[1]	3
Filler[2]	50
Zinc oxide	6
50% Antioxidant[3]	2
50% ZDEC	2
50% ZMBT	2
50% Sulphur	4
10% Thickener[4]	10

1. Sulphated alkyl phenol-ethylene oxide condensate, *e.g.* Solumin FX 85SD (ABM Chemicals)
2. Whiting, limestone or clay
3. Non-staining phenolic type, *e.g.* Antioxidant 2246 or 425 (Cynamid) Permanax WSP (Vulnax)
4. Polyacrylate or cellulosic type.

Dry and cure : 15 min at 130°C. Maximum oven temp. 150°C.

Woven carpet backing

Formulation

Ingredient	Parts
60% NR latex, LA-TZ type	167
25% Surfactant[1]	3
Tetrasodium pyrophosphate[2]	1
Water	as required
Filler[3]	300
50% ZDEC	2
50% Antioxidant[4]	2
10% Potasium hydroxide	1
10% Thickener[5]	5

1. Sulphated alkyl phenol-ethylene oxide condensate, *e.g.* Solumin FX 85SD (ABM Chemicals)
2. Tetron (Albright and Wilson)
3. Whiting, limestone and clay
4. Phenolic amine types
5. Polyacrylate type, *e.g.* Rohagit S-MV (Rohmn and Hass)

Drying curing : 5-10 min at 130°C.

Automotive bushings

Formulation (Synaprene based)

	Suspension	Shock absorber
Synaprene 1503		50
Synaprene 1712	70	
NR	30	50
HAF		25
FEF	40	
Naphthenic oil	15	8
Hard clay	100	
Zinc oxide	4	4
Stearic acid	1.5	1.5
Antioxidant PBN	1	
AO Ketone-amine		1
AO ETDQ	1	
Paraffin wax	1	
CBS	1.25	1
TMTD	0.25	0.1
Sulphur	1.9	2.2

Automotive Bumpers

Formulation (Synaprene based)

Synaprene 1514	100
FEF	40
Hard clay	60
Aromatic oil	30
Zinc oxide	3
Stearic acid	1.5
Antioxidant ETDQ	1.5
Paraffin wax	1
PBN	1
CBS	0.75
MBT & DPG	0.75
Sulphur	1.8

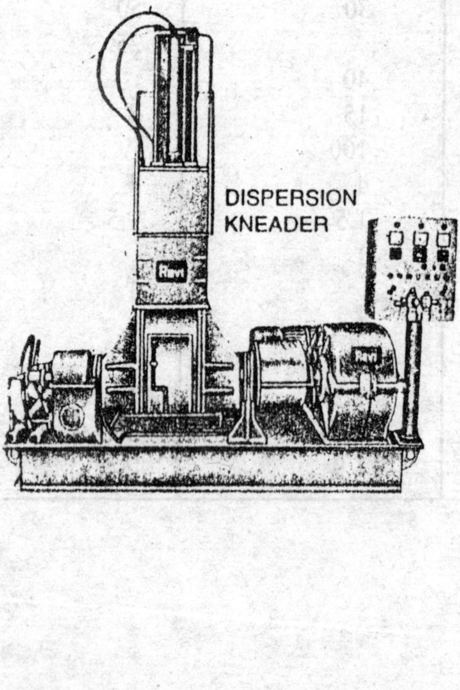

24

Polymers Related To Rubbers

Polythylene

Ethylene can be manufactured by the thermal and catalytic cracking of a variety of hydrocarbons such as ethane derived from natural gas to fuel oil. About half of it is used to produce ethylene polymers and copoylmers. The consumption of polyethylene exceeds any other plastic material in the world. Polyethylene can be obtained using two methods :

(i) By high pressure which yields low density material
(ii) By low pressure which gives high density material

High Pressure Polyethylene

The high pressure technique uses pressures, between 1,000-3,000 atmosphere and temperature upto 250 to 15°C. Free radical initators such as benzoyl or diethyl peroxides and hydroperoxides or traces of oxygen (0.01%) can start the reaction. Ethylene must be pure and impurities *viz.*, hydrogen and acetylene should be absent otherwise they act as chain transfer agents and it is difficult to get high-molecular weight products.

Properties

Low-density polyethylene is partially crystalline (50-60%) having melting point 105-115°C and density 0.91-0.94. It does not dissolve in any solvent at room temperature but it is soluble in many solvents at temperatures above 100°C. The polymer has both long and short branches.

It is inert chemically and has good resistance to acids and alkalies. It is used in containers for acids including hydrofluoric.

The electrical properties of polyethylene are exceedingly good. It ages on exposure to light or oxygen with loss of strength and other properties.

It has weight average molecular weight of 50,000-2,50,000 and number average molecular-weight 5,000-20,000.

Applications

The main use of low density polyethylene is in film) less than 0.01 inch thickness) and sheeting. This is because of its unique combinations of properties such as flexibilty (even without a plasticiser), high tear strength, moisture and chemical resistance. Nearly three-fourth of polyethylene manufactured is used in packaging, while a good portion goes for application in agriculture in canal or tank liners.

The other major use of polyethylene is in electric insulation because of its chemical inertness and light weight. About 10% of the material is used for toys, pipe, containers etc.

High-Density (Linear) Polyethylene

There are two processes for manufacture of this material.

(i) Phillips Process
(ii) Ziegler Process

The Phillips process uses a chromium oxide catalyst on a silica support for polymerisation of ethylene at low pressure in paraffinic solvent. The pressure used is about 500 p.s.i and temperature 60-200°C. The product has density of 0.925-0.965 and molecular weight 25,000-1,00,000.

The Ziegler process uses an oreganometal catalyst comprising of group IV to group VI metal halides such as titanium tetrachloride and an aluminimum alkyl such as triethylaluminimum for polumerisation of ethylene in a solvent such as heptane. A temperature of 50-70°C and slight pressure are used for polymerisation.

Linear polyethylenes are over 90% crystalline having melting point above 125°C and density in the range of 0.95-0.97. There is less than one side per 200 carbon atoms chain. The weight average molecular weights are in the range of 100,000—200,000..

Properties

A comparison of the properties of high & low density polyethylenes

Type	Crystallinity %	Melting Point°C	Density	Tensile strength	Elongation at break	Hardness shoreD
High Density	95	134-137	0.96	4,400	25	68
Low Density	65	114-116	0.92	2,000	500	52

Crystalline and molecular-weight determine the properties of polyethylene. High-density polyethylene of 95% crystallinity and 0.96 density exhibits higher melting point, tensile strength and hardness than low-density polyethylene of 65% crystallinity and 0.92 density. Chemical properties such as reisitance to oils, solvents and permeation by water vapour and gases are also superior in case of high density polyethylenes.

Applications

40% of linear polyethylene is used in the manufacture of bottles and other containers by blow moulding. About 25% of linear polyethylene finds use in the injection moulding of crates, tubes and house-wares.

Other uses of linear are in film and sheet, wire and cable insulation and pipe and conduct.

High Molecular Weight Polyethylenes

High-molecular-weight polyethylene has weight-average molecular weight of 300,000-500,000 and has high impact and tensile strength and crack reisitance. Ultra high-molecular-weight polyethyllene has weight-average molecular weight of 3000,000-6,000,000 and has exceptional abrasion and impact resistance. It finds use in bearings, gaskets, conveyer belt parts etc.

Fabrication Equipment

Extruders, Banbury Mixers and Injection Moulding Machines are used widely while Roll mills and Calenders are used in some cases. Extruders are used in some cases. Extruders are used for pellletising and for wire and cable coaring, Production od pipe, sheetand film and for feeding blow-moulding units in the production of bottles and other containers. Polyethylene must be extruded at a high temperature and because of high temperature requirement for a crystalline material, polyethylene extruders must be capable of high temperature operation and high-heat input.

The polyethylene extruders are mostly electrically heated. In general, their length to diameter ratios are 20/1 to30/1 compared to 8/1 to 10/1 for machines designed for rubber and non-crystalline plastics. Because of long barrel design, there is adequate melting, mastication and proper metering of the polymer, which is particularly important for high speed extrusion of high-density polyethylene. Stock temperatures range between 150-250°C. Screw diameters of 1-12 inches are common and output varies between a few kg to several tons per hour.

Injection moulding machines for polyethylene are similar to those used throughout the plastic industry. In this operation, the polymer is melted on the barrel of the machine and forced into a mould under pressure. Most machines have hydraulically operated rams and mould clamps. Ram pressures are in the range of 10,000-30,000 p.s.i. Injection moulding machines are used for making housewares such as waste paper baskets, garbage cans, dishes and automobile parts.

Roll mills, Banbury Mixers and calenders are similar to those used in the rubber industry. Banbury Mixers are used for homogenizing and for incorporation of pigments etc. Roll mills have provision of high temperature operation. Calenders are used for lamination and sheeting. In some cases special type of film or tape are derived from calendering. However, most laminating film or sheet production involves extruder-fed units.

Film and Sheeting

Material of less than 0.001 inch thickness is called as sheeting. The polyethylene film can be produced by tubular, chill-roll or water-quench process, an extruders feeds molten material to a heated die designed to give tubular shape. Air pressure is maintained to provide a bubble of the desired size. The melt is cooled in air. The tubing is pulled from the die and wound up on rolls. It may usd directly or may be slit to provide flat films up to 20 feet or more in width.

In the chill roll process the extruder feeds molten polymer to a slit-type of die from which the melt extrudes as a thin sheet or web. The die is placed near the polished chill roll and the polymer is pulled under and over a serves of rolls onto 500-1000 feet per minute are common and film clarity is excellent.

Fresh polyethylene film surfaces are non-receptive to printing ink and must be treated by flame or electric discharge to create a mild oxidation on the surface.

For production of sheet, the most common practice is to extrude molten web on a polished chill roll. Polyethylene of trays, boats, chairs etc.

Injection Moulding

Equipment of this type are expensive and the technique is economic only for continuous runs in which thousands of identical parts are manufactured.

High density resins are slowly gaining acceptance in this area as they provide greater stiffness and so thinner walls can be produced. However, low density polyethylene is also used in great quantity for house-ware and for general purpose containers. If pigments are added, coloured items are obtained. Concentrates of pigments and polymer are included along with pellets fed to the machine.

Blow Moulding

Blow moulding is an important application for high density polyethylene. Bottles, cans and containers can be produced using this technique. Large tanks, box containers, large toy cars and animals can also be manufactured with its help.

A molten tubing (parsion) is extruded into an open mould. By means of compressed air or steam, the plastic is then blown into the configuration of the mould. The solidifierd part is ejected from the mould and trimmed if needed.

Blow moulding is one of the fastest growing field of the polyethylene industry.

Wire and Cable

Polyethylene wire and cable coatings are applied by means of crosshead dies which are fed by extruders placed at right angles to the path of the wire. The wire is cleaned, preheated and straightened before entering the die. It is coated by molten polymer at speeds upto 2000 ft. per minute. As the wire comes out of the die, it is cooled and electrically tested for the integerity of the coating. In the case of the cable coating, the principle is applied but the diameter and thickness are greater and linear rates arev lower.

Pipe

Recently the trend has been towards the use of medium and high densityb polyethylene for this product, although previously loe-density polyethylene was the chief material for its production. Low density polymer has lower cost while high density polymer gives better performance withstand high pressure are produced from high density polymer having high molecular weight.

The main outlet for polyethylene pipe is in farm and outdoor applications such as sprinkler system. Usuallly pipe having 1-2 inch diameter is manufactured in coils of 100 feet in length. Pipes of diameter more than 2 inches are too rigid and cannot be coiled easily and are usually marketed in

20-40 feet length. They are mostly used in industry and in drain lines.

The polyethylene pipe can be produced by many techniques such as external-sizing tube, internal sizing, positive-pressure dues and biaxial orientation. The molten polymer is fed through a suitable die with the help of an extruder in all these techbiques.

Polyvinyl Chloride

Polyethylene, polyvinyl chloride (PVC) and polystyrene are the three major plastic materialls produced in the world today. PVC is unique among them because of its excellent range of properties and low cost.

Monomer

PVC is produced by the polymerisation of vinyl chloride monomer which is a gas boiling at 14°C. Vinyl chloride is manufactured by the chlorination of ethylene to 1,2 dichloroethane followed by its pyrolysis. The pyrolysis creates HCL as a by-product. Oxychlorination uses the HCI along with oxygen to react with ethylene to produce more dichloroethane. Following reactions are involved :

$$CH_2{=}CH_2 + Cl_2 \; 2 \; Cl\,CH_2\,CH_2\,Cl$$

$$[Cl\,CH_2\,CH_2\,Cl \; 2 \; CH_2{=}CHCl + HCl] \times 2$$

$$CH_2{=}CH_2 + 2HCl + \tfrac{1}{2}\,O_2 \; 2 \; Cl\,CH_2\,CH_2\,Cl + H_2O$$

$$2CH_2{=}CH_2 + Cl_2 + \tfrac{1}{2}\,O_2 \; 2 \; Cl\,CH_2\,CH_2\,CH_2\,Cl + H_2O$$

Manufacture

PVC can be manufactured by four polymerisation techniques- suspension, bulk emulsion and solution. Suspension polymerisation is used for the production of 80% of PVC. Small amounts are made by other methods.The suspension method consists of polymerisding monomer droplets in water which also acts as the heat transfer medium to remove the large heat of polymerisation.

$$n\,CH_2{=}\underset{\displaystyle Cl}{\underset{|}{CH}} \;\xrightarrow[\text{40-70°C}]{\text{Free radical initation}}\; 2 \;\left[\,CH_2{-}\underset{\displaystyle Cl}{\underset{|}{CH}}{-}\,\right]_n$$

By vigrous agitation, vinyl chloride is dispersed into small droplets. Hydroxypropyl methyl cellulose, hydrolysed polyvinylacetate or gelation are used as suspension stablisers. Buffers are added to react with HCI liberated from vinyl chloride peroxide formed during the polymerisation reaction. Initators such as peroxidicarbonate or peroxyeser are used. The polymerisation takes 4-16 hours. Polymerisation temperature controls molecular-weight which can be between 20,000-120,000.

Structure

Crystalline in PVC is quite low because it is a partially syndiotactic material with sufficient irregularity of structure.

Stability

PVC is unstable to heat and light and stablisers are used to improve these properties. Oregno-metallic compounds and metallic salts of lead,barium.tin or cadium are some examples. Epoxy resin and fatty-acid salts are very effective stablisers. All these materials take up HCI formed during degradation of PVC or react with unstable sites along the polymer chain.

Plasticiation

PVC is a rigid plastic and needsa plasticiser to improve its properties. It lowers the glass-transition temperature. Tricresyl phosphate was the first important plasticiser to be used with it but has been replaced by other esters. Dibutyl phthalate, dibutyl sebacate and tributyl phosphate were also used with it but has been replaced. Now various low-molecular weight polymers such as polypropylene glycol esters, dioctyl phthalate, dioctyl sebacate and adipate and triocyl phosphate are used as plasticisers. A large proportion (nearly 30% by weight) of the plasticisers is added on hot rolls or in Banbury.

Applications

PVC has excellent range of properties such as (i) chemical, moisture and oxidative resistance (ii) transparency and ease of colouring (iii) flame mretardance (iv) strength and toughness (v) ease of fabrication. It has replaced many natural materials *viz*., wood, rubber, leather etc.

Nearly half of PVC is used as rigid resin while the rest is plasticised. In the rigid field, nearly 40% of the production is used as pipe for water supply, agricultural irrigation, drain and conduits for electrical and telephone cables.

Twenty percent of PVC production goes in building construction for purposes such as window frames, guttersand siding. the rest is used in wire and cable insulation, flooring, wall coverings, footwear, food packaging, bottles, phonograph records, toys etc.

Copolymers

Copolymerisation of small amounts of vinyl acetate with vinyl chloride results in improvements in many properties such as stability, lower softening point, higher solubility, colour clarity and flexibility. Compositions containing 5-40% of vinyl acetate are available in the market.Sound records (filler less), rain coat and watch strap are made out of copolymers of vinyl chloride and vinyl acetate.

Fabrication

Moulding, Organosols and plastisols (pastes) of PVC are applied by dip, slush, and rotational moulding. In moulding, an article such as at glove, wire rack, or tool handle is coated by dipping a heated form into a plastisol, gelling the required amount of compound, and then transferring this preformed article to a finishing oven set a higher temperature to complete fusion.

In Slush Moulding, organosols and plastisols are transferred to open moulds, and then heated to complcte the plasticisation of the PVC. The moulds are then cooled, and the articles removed. Products such as toys, shoes, vinyl boots, and traffic cones are formed by filling the mould with the proper compound, heating the mould to gel the outer layer emptying the mould of excess compound, fusion of the finihed object.

Rotocasting is a method of forming large, hollow parts or toys by rotation of the mould during the loading and fusing of the PVC plastisol. machines with a number of arms containing moulds spin the plastosol to form the desired shape while the mould is programmed through its heatingand cooling cycle. Boat bumpers, dolls and vinyl balls are all produced by this method. Below Table shows a representative recipe for a rotocasting operation. This may be compared to a rigid extrusion recipe for a pipe.

Rotocast Doll Formulation Using Dispersion Resin

Ingredient	Level (Parts per 100 parts Resin)
Geon 121	70
Geon 212	30
Di-2-cthyllhexyl phthalate	45
Butyl benzyl phthalate	15
Liquid Ba/Cd/Zn stabilizer	3

A PVC Compoundnd for Rigid Pipe

Ingredient	Parts per 100 parts Resin
Geon 103 EPF-76	100.0
MBS impact modifier	0.0-10.0
Acrylic processing aid	0.0-3.0
Sn stablizer	1.0-2.5
Ca stearate	1.0-2.0
Oxidized polyethylene	0.0-0.5
Paraffin wax	0.4-1.2
TiO_2	0.5-3.0
$CaCO_3$ — stearic coated	0.0-5.0

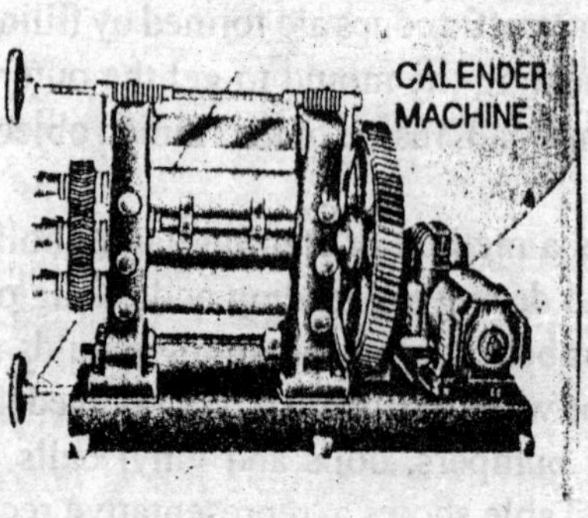

25

Compounding

Introduction

The term compounding in rubber technology is used for selection and incorporation of various additives into so as to give a homogeneous mix for processing. Every recipe contains a number of components, each having a particular function to perform either during processing, reinforcement or vulcanisation and ultimately in the end use of the product.

Ingredients

The material ised in compounding can be categorised under the following heads.

1. Elastomers

These form the backbone and are the basic components. They can be natural or any synthetic rubber or thermoplastic elastomer and are selected to give specific physical properties to the final product e.g., oil, heat or aging resistance.

2. Fillers

These are used for reinforcing or reducing the cost.

3. Processing Acids

As the same suggest, these materials help in a marked help during which may include mixing, extrusion, calendring or moulding.

4. Vulcanising Agents

These substance bring about cross-linking resulting in a marked improvements in the physical properties of the rubber products.

5. Accelerators

These ingredients reduce the time of vulcanisation by acccelerating the rate of vulcanisation

6. Activators

Then addition is essential for deriving the maximum benefit from vulcanisation.They form complexes with accelerates.

7. Antioxidants

They slow down the process of deterioration in service of the rubbercompounds by checking oxidation.

8. Antiozonants

These ingredients slow down the deterioration to attack by ozone.

9. Miscellanous Additives

These substances are not normally incoroporated in the rubber compounds but may be used for for specific purposes. Examples are blowing agents, colours, odotants, retraders etc.

We shall take up the ingredients in more detail now :

Elastomers or Rubbers-Classification

Rubbers are classified into following 3 major classes.

1. General Purpose

They are for general purpose where specific resistance to the action of petroleum or heat is not required. Examples are natural, SBR, polyisoprene polybutadiene, EDPM, butyl rubbers.

2. Heat resistance type

They are used where effect of exposure to high temps. can be tolerated. Examples are silicone and fluoro rubbers.

Table lists some of the physical and chemical properties 1+2 of important elastomers. The properties depend to a large extent on compounding, reinforcement and vulcanisation and the values assigned are for general guidance only.

Fillers & Others Additives

Fillers are used to reinforcement or reduce the cost of the product. There are 3 main types of fillers-Carbon black fillers and Oragnic fillers.

Carbon blacks are the most important fillers used for rubbers. They are named by the process by which they are produced e.g. thermal, furnance and acetylene balcks. Their incoroporation brings about marked improvement in properties such as hardness, tensile strength, tear and abrasion resistance.

The non-black fillers include clays (semireinforcing), precipitated silica (reinforcing), calcium carbonate(extending filler). Many other materials are used in rubbber compounding, those having small particle size are reinforcing while others are used to reduce the cost.

Organic fillers include high styrene resin, phenolic resin, cylised rubber, liginin etc. Their incoroporation brings about ease in processing of unvulcanised stocks and after vulcanisation incraese hardness & strength.

Property	Natural Rubber	SBR	Butyl	Chloro-sulp--honated Polyethylene	EDPM	Fluorinated Rubber
Tensile strength (psi)	4000	3500	3000	2800	3000	2400
Elongation (%)	700	700	700	500	300	400
Modulus (Psi at 300-400% elongation)	2500	2500	1000	—	—	250
Tear resistance	Excel	Good	Excel	Good	Good	Fair
Abrasion resistance	Fair	Good	Good	—	—	—
Adhesion	Excel	Excel	Good	Excel	Excel	Good
Electrical Properties	Excel	Fair	Excel	Fair	Excel	Excel
Gas permeability	High	High	Low	—	—	—
Upper use temp. (^oC)	80	110	100	120	150	230
Lower use temp. (^oC)	-50	-50	-50	-50	-40	-40
Weather resistance	Fair	Fair	Excel	Excel	Excel	Excel
Ozone resistance	Poor	Fair	Excel	Excel	Excel	Excel
Oil resistance	Poor	Poor	Good	Good	Poor	Excel
Water Swelling	Excel	Good	Excel	Excel	Excel	Excel

Property	Neoprene	Nitrile	Polybut-adiene (cis.1-4)	Polyisoprene (cis.1-4)	Poly-Sulphide	Silicone	Urethane
Tensile strength (psi)	4000	4000	3000	4000	1200	1500	8000
Elongation (%)	700	600	700	750	400	800	700
Modulus (Psi at 300-400% elongation)	1000	1500	—	2500	1400	—	1200
Tear resistance	Good	Good	Excel	Excel	Good	Poor	Excel
Abrasion resistance	Good	—	—	Fair	Poor	Poor	Excel
Adhesion	Excel	Excel	Excel	Excel	poor	Poor	Excel
Electrical Properties	Good	Fair	Good	Good	Excel	Excel	Fair
Gas permeability	Moder	Moder	—	High	Low	—	—
Upper use temp. (°C)	100	120	100	80	80	230	100
Lower use temp. (°C)	-50	-50	-60	-50	-50	-80	-50
Weather resistance.	Excel	Poor	Fair	Fair	Excel	Excel	Excel
Ozone resistance	Good	Fair	Poor	Poor	Good	Excel	Excel
Oil resistance	Fair	Excel	Poor	Poor	Excel	Fair	Excel
Water Swelling	Good	Excel	Excel	Excel	Excel	Excel	Fair

Vulcanising Agents

Sulphur is the most common vulcanising agent. General purpose rubbers which form the bulk of rubbers used contain unsaturation and vulcanisation with sulphur is possible. Sulphur brings about cross-linking and converts the rubberto form three-dimensional structure. Thus a weak material is transformed into a strong elastic product having many desirable properties properties. Usually 0.5-5.0 phr of sulphur is used.

The saturated rubbers cannot be crosslinked with sulphur and an organic peroxide is required for vulcanisation. Free radicals are generated when a peroxide decomposes and these make polymer chains to combine. Usually 2.5 phr of a peroxide is used. Dicumyl peroxide is most prominent.

Accelerators

The vulcanisation with sulphur is slow and can be speeded up many times by the addition of small amounts of organic or inorganic comounds known as accelerators (-0.5-2 phr.). Most common accelerators are listed in Table.

Type	Example	Properties
Amines	Hexamethylene tetramine	Delayed action
Aldehyde-amine	Butra alldehyde-aniline	In self curing adhesives
Guanidines	Diphenyl guanidine	Secondary accelerator
Thiazoles	2-mercapto Benzo-thiazole-MBT	Mediumspeed, scorchy.Most commonly used
	Benzothiazole disulphide-MBTS	Safe processing, General Purpose, Less scorchy, Expensive.

Type	Example	Properties
Thiourams	Tetramethylithuram Disulphide -TMTD	Safe,fast curing Give good ageing & heat resistance
Sulphenamides	N-cyclolexyl-2 benzothiozl sulphenamide-CBS	Safe processing, Delayed action, used for heavily loaded compounds e.g. tyres
Dithio-carbonates	Zinc dimethyl dithio-carbonate -ZDC	Fast, Used in latex
Xanthates	Dibutyl xanthogen disulphide	General purpose, Low temp. use 70°C, Used in latex

Activators

These compounds activate the accelerators to work more effectively and increase the cure rate.

Most common examples is of Zinc oxide which is used (3-5 phr.)

Antioxidant

Rubbers are effected by ageing process when in service resulting in lowering in physical properties. Antioxidant are added to slow down and improve the aging behaviour and to enhance the service life.

There are 3 types of compounds which can be used for protection.

Amines tend to discolour (staining) but are powerful antioxidants. Phenol are less powerful and less staining and are used in light coloured products. Phosphites are less effective in natural rubber and more in SBR. Used 2-3 phr.

Antiozonates

These compouds are effectively to check the action of ozone. They are mostly derivatives of paraphenyldiamene.

RNH NRH_2

R can be cyclohexyl

R_2 can be phenyl

Waxes are also used for this purpose.

Procesing Aids

These compounds are used usually 2-10 phr and help proper mixing. The processing aid must be completely compatible with the rubber sand other compounding ingredients. incompatibility will result in proper processing or bleeding in the final product.

The aids can be petroleum or coal tar products such as mineral oils, coal-tar pitch, cumar resins, vegetable oils, pine tar or resins such as coumarone-indene, phenol-formula-dehyde, shellac or waxes, fatty acids, esters etc.

Miscellaneous Ingredients

These substances are used for some specific effect in a vulcanisate.

Flame retardants

To reduce flammability, chlorinated hydrocarbons, phosphates and antimony compounds may be added.

Colourants

For increasing customer appeal, these ingredients are added. They should be stable and fast in colour.

Odorants

For masking odor of rubber compounds, these compounds (essential oils) are added generally in wearing apparel and drug sundries.

Retraders

These chemicals reduce the effect of accelerators and prevent scorching during processing and storage. These are generally organic acids *e.g.* salicycle acid.

Mixing Methods

For incorporation of compounding ingredients into rubber, either a mill or a banbury (internal) mixer is used. These are availble in many sizes *e.g.* mills having size from 6"/(D) x 13"(L) provided with motor of 250 H.P. capable of taking 150 Kg and banbury capablie of taking batch of 500 g (H.P.of motor 7.5) to 500 kgs. (H.P. of motor 1500).

The rolls of a mill rotate in opposite direction and can be heated or cooled. They are made of chilled cast iron which is very hard. The front roll rotates at a slower speed compared to the back roll, while it is kept at a cooler temperature. for safety, a safety fuse called breaker plate or breaker nut is provided which is a fragile member between bearing block and screw. The two roll mill has the advantages that there is ease of processing, temperaturedoes not rise to cause scorch and premature cross linking while the short comings are that it is slow in operation. Degree of dispersion depends on manual efforts and high temperature operation is difficult.

The internal mixer has an enclosed chamber in which two rotors turn in opposite direction. There is greater efficiency in carrying out shearing action, mixing is automatic, ther is reduction in mixing time, dispersion is better and it can produce highly compounded stock.

Cooling water or steam is circulated through the rotors.

The short comings are that cleaning is difficult and sliding door has tendency to jam.

Mixing Cycles

Following mixing cycles are recommended

Temp °C	Mill 70 ± 5	Banbury 120 ± 5
Mixing speed Slow roll	24 r.p.m.	11 r.p.m.
fast roll	33 r.p.m.	

No.	Step	Time-minutes (Mill)	Time-minutes (Banbury)
1.	Set mill opening at 1.4 min. temp 70 ± 5° C	0	—
	Close discharge gate of Banbury. Start rotor raise ram. Lower after each operation Temp 120 ± 5°C		
2.	Add rubber on front roll Make cuts	2	—
	Add Rubber	—	0.5
3.	Increase opening 1.6 mm Add stearic acid Make cuts	2.5	—
	Add accelerator	—	0.5
4.	Add sulphur, accelerator and zinc oxide Make cuts	20	—
	Add stearic acid	—	1.0
5.	Add filler Make cuts. Increase opening to 1.9 mm	7.5	—
	Add zinc oxide and half filler	—	1.5
6.	Set mill opening 0.8 mm Pass rolled stock 6 times	2.0	—
	Add rest of the filler	—	1.5

7.	Open the mill to give stock thickness 6 mm & pass stock 4 times.	1	—
	Add sulphur. Clean top of ram	—	1.0
8.	Dump at 7 mins. Maintain Banbury temp. 120 ± 5°C.	—	1.0
9.	Kep mill opening at 0.8 mm and temp. 70 ± 5°C. Pass rolled batch 6-times	—	2.0
10.	Increase mill opening 6 mm and pass stock through the mills 4 times	—	1.0
	Total time (minutes)	17	10.0

The above schedule is for natural rubber. Each rubber has a different optimum temp. range for dispersion of compounding ingredients.

The batch size for a laboratory mill is 4 times the recipe weight while for a Banbury, it is 6 times.

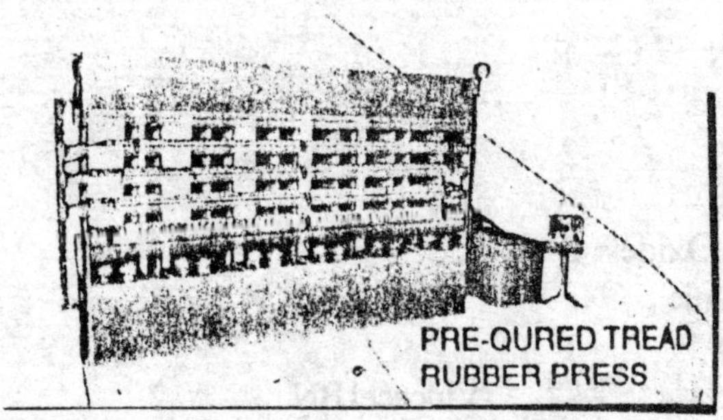

PRE-QURED TREAD RUBBER PRESS

Few Formulatuions

Recipe for a few rubber products are given on the following pages:

Formulations

	Beer House		Cellular Rubber		Cut Thread	
Polymer	N.R. SBR(OE)	60 40	Well masticated rubber	100	RSS	100
Biller	China clay	120	Grand crum	30	$MgCO_3$	10
Processing Aid	Micro crystalline Wax	1	Grand crum	20-25		—
Zinc oxide		3		15-20		3
Stearic Acid		1				1
Sulphur						
Accelerator	CBS	1.25	Dithiocarbonate	1.5	Butra-aldehyde amine	1
Antioxidant	PBN	1		—		1.5
Colouring Matter	TiO_2	2		—		—
	Iron Oxide	2				
	Organic Dye	1				
Special	—		Vulcacel BN (Blowing agent)	2		

Special	1. China clay used as filler as extrusion good with it. It is also not attacked by acetic acid.	1. Rubber should be will masticated to help blowing.	1. $MgCo_3$ gives high modulus
	2. Accelerator should be nontoxic and tasteless	2. Softner should be used more.	2. Filler low to resist chaff resistance.
	3. Do not use reclaim as it smells	3. Zno should be more to increase thermal	3. Mix in internal mixer
	4. Organic dye used as it insoluble in alcohol	4. Sulphur used more to put non X links	4. The accelerat -or selected gives high elongation

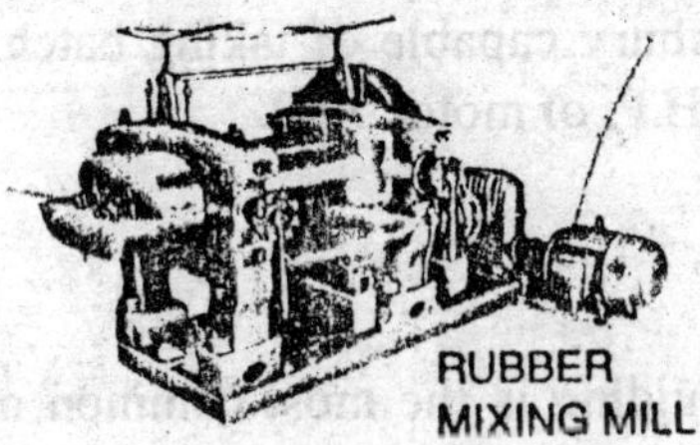

26

Processing Methods

Mixing

For incoroporation of compounding ingredients into rubber either a mill or a banbury (internal) mixer is used. These are available in many sizes e.g. mills having size from 6" x 8" provided with motor of 7.5 H.P. capable of taking 1 kg and banbury capable of taking batch of 500 g (H.P. of motor 7.5) to 500 kgs. (H.P. of motor 500).

Moulding

Compression moulding is the most common method used in the industry. Here the blank is placed in a 2 piece mould, one part of which is movable and other stationary. The mould is closed and heat and pressure are applied soo that the material flows to fill the mould. A little excess of the material is used that the mould is completely filled.

Extrusion

In the extrusion process1-2 polymer or rubber is propelled continuously along a screw through regions of high temperature and pressure where it is melted and compacted and finally forced through a die shaped to give the final product. several shapes can be given by extrusion such as rods, tubing, hose, sheeting and film.

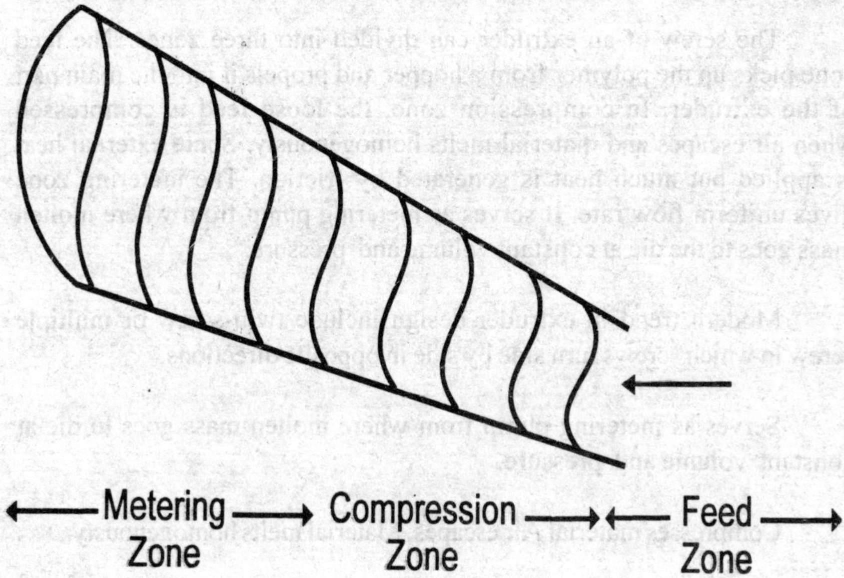

Metering Zone
Compression Zone
Feed Zone

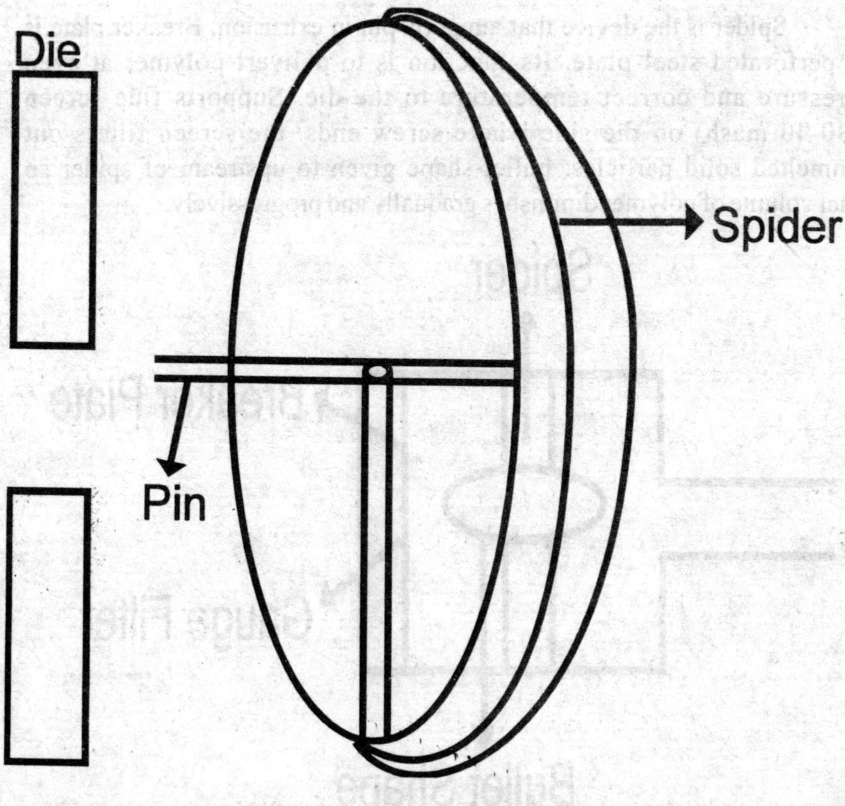

Die
Spider
Pin

The screw of an extruder can divided into three zones. The feed zone picks up the polymer from a hopper and propels it into the main part of the extruder. In compression zone, the loose feed is compressed when air escapes and material melts homogenously. Some external heat is applied but much heat is generated by friction. The metering zone gives uniform flow rate. It serves as metering pump from where molten mass goes to the die at constant volume and pressure.

Modern trend in extruder design include twin-screw or multiple screw in which screws turn side by side in opposite directions.

Serves as metering pump from where molten mass goes to die at constant volume and pressure.

Compresses material Air escapes, Material melts homogenously.

Angle material to compression zone

Spider is the device that aupports pin in extrusion. Breaker plate is a perforated steel plate. Its function is to delivert polymer at even pressure and correct temperature to the die. Supports fine screen (30-40 mash) on the side where screw ends. the screen filters out unmelted solid particles. bullet shape given to upstream of spider so that volume of polymer diminshes gradually and progressively.

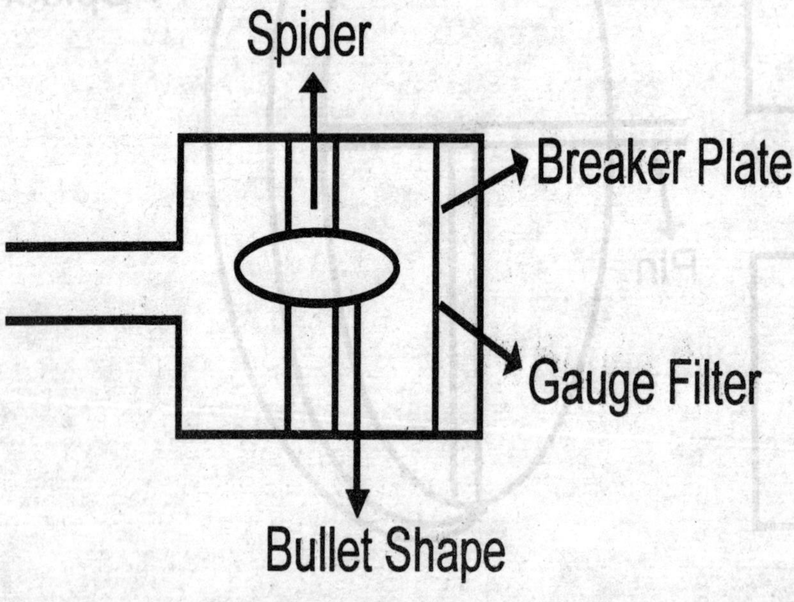

For good extrusion :

(i) Particles having flat plate like structure give good surface and easier flow *e.g.* china clay and mica.
(ii) Rubber content should be between 10-70%. Above 70% rough surface obtained.
(iii) S.P. (Superior rubber) rubber or high filler loading or high styrene resin gives better performance and speeds extrusion.
(iv) Factice increases rate of extrusion.
(v) Mixing in internal mixer is recomended. Tough stock is good.
(vi) There should be rest period between mixing and extrusion.
(vii) Water should be absent in the stock or porosity develops.
(viii) Die should not be too close to spider otherwise spider marks will come.
(ix) There should be no area where rubber can stay in head. It will vulcanise and cause trouble.
(x) The material should be supplied at constant temperature and rate.

Calendering

Calendering is a process used (i) for the manufacture of smooth sheet of uniform controlled thickness (ii) to apply rubber to textiles or (iii) embossing. Rubber in the process is passed between pairs of highly polished heated rolls under pressure.

Proper calendering requires precise control of roll temperature, Pressure and speed of rotation. By maintaining a slight speed differentiation between a roll pair, it is possible to impart an exceedingly high gloss to the film or sheet surface. it is also possible to produce an embossed design on the surface by means of a calender roll which is engraved.

The rolls are of chilled cast iron. Channels are built up inside so that steam or water can reach nearest to surface. The temperature control is accurate and it is nearly same inside and outside of rolls. The rolls can be considered as rotating beams under stress with resulting deflection. The rolls are cambered. The middle roll is grind cylindrically while the lower one is slightly concave. The upper roll has a tendency to go up while middle and bottom rolls have a tendency to deflect down so bottom roll is given concave shape. Top and bottom rolls can be moved independently to adjust thickness.

High rubber mixes are difficult to calender and require higher temperature. Incorporation of fillers ease calendering.

Calendering can be done single bank or double bank.

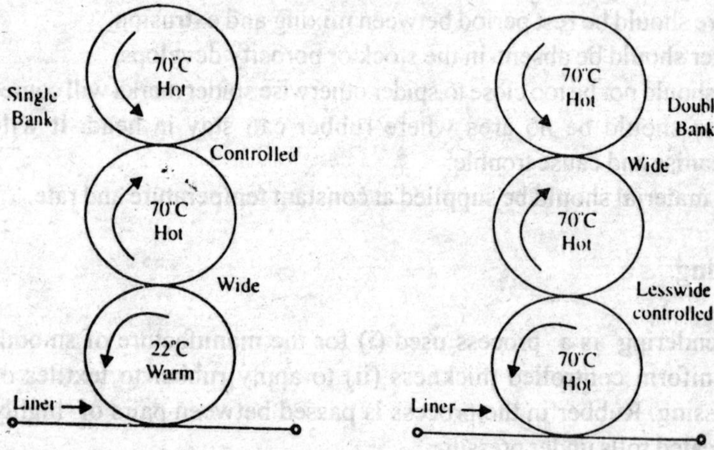

Typical Composition for Calendering Compounding

Rubber	100
Filler (winnofil)	85
Factice	20
Zno	5
Sulphur	2
MBT	0.8
Mineral oil	3
Antioxidant	1.5

Double bank calendering gives more uniform thickness as air blistering is reduced.

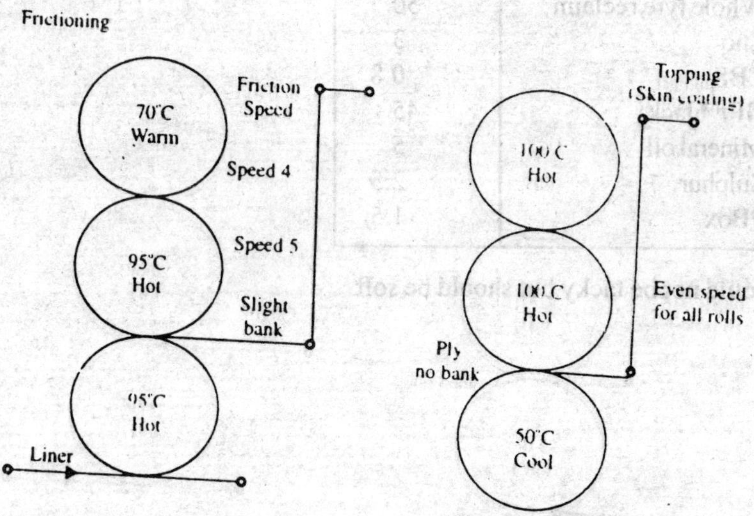

Typical Composition for Frictioning Compound

Masticated rubber	50
Whole tyre reclaim	40
Zno	8
MBTS	0.6
MRX	4
Pine Tar	3
Sulphur	2.5

Stock should be tacky. Pine tar added not be scorchy as temperature high.

Typical Compositions for Topping Compound

Masticated rubber	75
Whole tyre reclaim	50
Zno	3
CBS	0.8
GPF black	45
Mineral oil	5
Sulphur	2.5
PBox	1.5

Mix should not be tacky but should be soft

27

TESTING

For Processibility

In rubber industry, many operations such as milling and mixing have to be carried out for converting a tough and elastic raw materials into a soft and pliable state, incorporating various compounding additives such as fillers, sulphur, accelerator, activator, processing acid, antioxidants etc. to get a 'stock'. The prepared stock is then given shape by calendering or extruding. The ease with which all these operations can be carried out is called "processibility". and depends on its plasticity, temperature and applied force. A number of terms are used in the Industry and are described below :

Scorch

Scorch is permature vulcanisation or crosslinking. Scorch time is very important and denotes time available for processing.

Optimum Cure Time

Optimum cure time is time required for vulcanisation to yield best level of physical properties such as tensile strength or modulus. It must be remembered all these properties do not attain the optimum values at the same level of cure.

Plasticity Test

Various operations such as mixing, extrusion, calendering and moulding require different levels of shear. Tests to determine the processing characteristics of a compound should expose the test sample to shear level similar to one encountered in the actual operation. However it is not possible to do so.

The shearing disc viscometer developed by Melvin Mooney has become very popular in the rubber industry. In this instrument, a flat disc rotates in a mass of rubber contained in a grooved cavity under pressure. The torque required to rotate the disc at 2 rpm at a tmp. of 120°C is termed Mooney Viscosity..

Mooney Viscosity

Two discs of diameter 1.75" are cut from rubber sheet not less than 0.4" thick. A hole 0.5" in diameter is made in centre of one of the discs which is kept below the rotor. The other disc is kept above the rotor. The platens are electrically heated and the temperature is controlled at the desired level. The top platen is pneumatically lowered. The sample is allowed to warm up for one minute after the platens are closed. The motor is then started and the torque required to turn the rotor at 2 rpm is recorded after the prescribed time.

There are two rotors for the mooney viscosity test a large one (1-5" dia) for general use and a smaller one (1.2" dia) for tough rubbers. Reading taken after 4 minutes is called Mooney Plasticity. The result is expressed as follows :

40-ML 1+4 (120°C)

Where 40-M is the Mooney Plasticity number, L indicates that large rotor has been used, 1 is the time in minute for which the specimen has been preheated, 4 is the time in minutes after starting the motor at which the reading has been taken and 120°C is the temp. of the test. Scorch time is taken as the time when plasticity is 5 units higher than minimum value.

Evaluation of the State of Cure

As already mentioned, optimum cure is the one which optimises the properties desired in the product. Conventionally, tensile strength modulus and ultimate elongation data have been used to estimate the best state of cure. Often the time at which maximum tensile strength is obtained is taken as the optimum period for cure.

If the optimum cure time is to be based on modulus and the modulus shows either a peak or a plateau at its maximum value the cure time required to reach 90% of that value is taken as optimum.

Ultimate elongation is also taken into consideration along with tensile strength and modulus for deciding optimum cure time. Many times it reaches maximum at an early curing time which is taken as the optimum cure time as a vulcanisate which breaks at low elongation is undesirable. Besides tensile strength, modulus or elongation, any other property which is of greatest consequence may also be used for determining time for optimum cure.

Cure Meteres

Curing for separate ranges of temperature and carrying out separate tensile tests is a laborious business and so cure meteres have been developed. Modulus change is monitored in the instruments. Several useful properties such as maximum and minimum stiffness, scorch time, cure time are obtainable from the data.

The most popular cure meter used in the industry is oscilliating disk rheometer. Many versions of the instrument have been evolved.

Physical Testing of Vulcanisates

No tests should be performed until at least 16 hours after Vulcanising as significant post vulcanisation changes in structure of the material may occur during this period.

Tensile Tests

These tests are the most widely used test in the rubber industry.

They are used to determine rate of cure and optimum cure, quality check on the compound, effect of immersion in liquids etc.

Two shapes of test specimen are most popular-dumb bells and rings. The dumb bell so called because of its shape has tabbed ends for gripping in the test machine tapers to a central constricted section of uniform width. Bench mark 1" apart is stamped on the constricted section to facilitate observation of the elongation during test. The dumb bell specimen is clicked out with the help of a die.

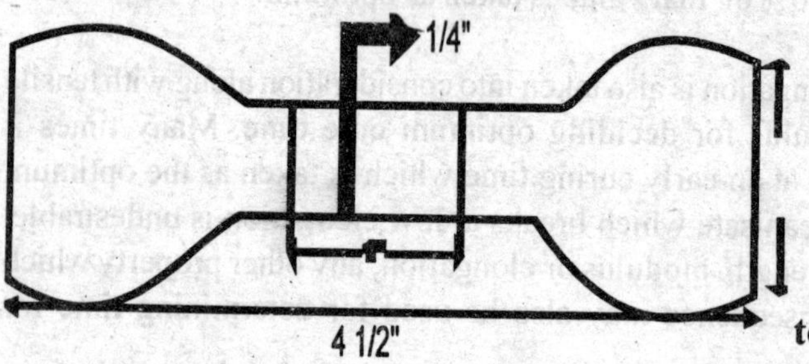

Width narrow of constricted part = 1/4"

Thickness of rubber 0.1" tolerance 0.001"

Advantages of using dumb bell specimen are ease of preparation and breakage in the area meant for following the elongation :

The ring specimen may have the following size :

Inner dia	-	44 mm
Outside dia	-	52.6 mm
Radial width	-	4 mm
Thickness of specimen	-	6 mm

The ring is held by lubricated rollers in the machine so that the stress is equalised. Advantages of using ring specimen is possibility of using clamp separation as good measure of elongation and distribution of stress over a greater length.

The speed maintained for testing is machine jaw or spindle separation rate of 20 ± 2 inch per minute. Dumb bell specimen gives result higher than ring specimen.

Tensile strength is the maximum tensile stress reaches in stretching a test piece to its breaking point. The force required is expressed as force per unit area of the original cross-section of the test length.

Elongation is the extension between bench marks produced by a tensile force applied to the test piece and is expressed as a percentage of the original distance between the marks. Elongation at break or ultimate elongation is the elongation at the moment of rupture.

Modulus is the stress required to produce a certain elongation. The standard temp. for conditioning and testing the samples is 23 ± 2°C. The tests should be made along the grain in the rubber *i.e.* parallel to direction of passage through the mill.

Hardness

Hardness, as applied to the rubber, may be defined as the resistance to indentation under conditions that the rubber is not punctured.

Hardness is one of the most useful and often quoted properties of rubber. However the values mentioned can be misleading due to mechanical limitations of the instrument and personal error.

The spring-loaded pocket durameter is the most popular instrument for measuring hardness of rubbers. The scale is from zero hardness for a liquid to 100 for a hard surface such as of glass. It has a different indenter and stiffness spring. The instrument is portable and can be used for even irregular surfaces. However, differences of 5 units in reading are common.

Dead-load hardness testers are less convenient than durameters but the measurements are more reproducible. Here a dead load is applied to the indentor for a specified time and the hardness is obtained from the depth of the identation.

Rebound Tests

Resilience is the ability of a rubber vulcanisate to return the energy used to deform it during its recovery from deformation. It is expressed in percent. The simplest test for resilience is the falling ball rebound. If the drop height of the steel ball is divided into 100 equal parts, the rebound height is equal to the resilience.

In a pendulum rebound test, the specimen is held at the rest position of the pendulum (zero degree) and is impacted by the centre of percussion of the arm. The angle of rebound is noted on a scale and resilience calculated by the formula :

$$R = \frac{1 - \cos \text{ angle of rebound}}{1 - \cos \text{ angle of fall}} \times 100$$

Lupke pendulum is popular in Europe. The rubber is subjected to only one half cycle of deformation. In a rebound test, the specimen should be preconditioned with six impacts before a reading is taken as the rebound height is then stabilised. The method is applicable to elastomers with hardness ranging from 30-85 IRHD only.

Tear Test

Tear test results depend on type of specimen used, the rate of tearing and the temp. The method is therefore useful for only laboratory comparison and cannot be applied for service evaluation.

Different types of Dies can be used to prepare specimen as shown below :

ASTM DIEA
(Gescent)

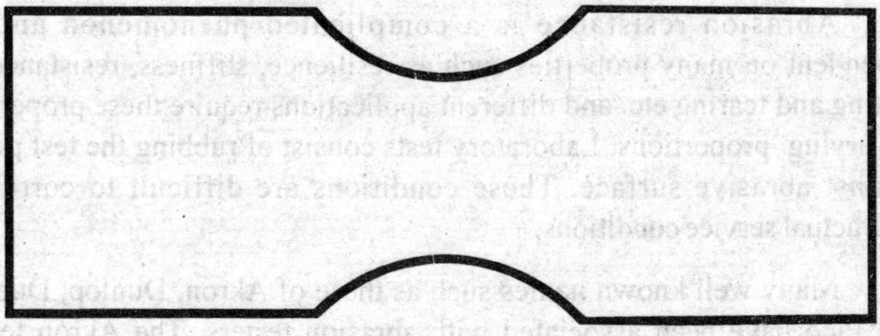

ASTM DIEB

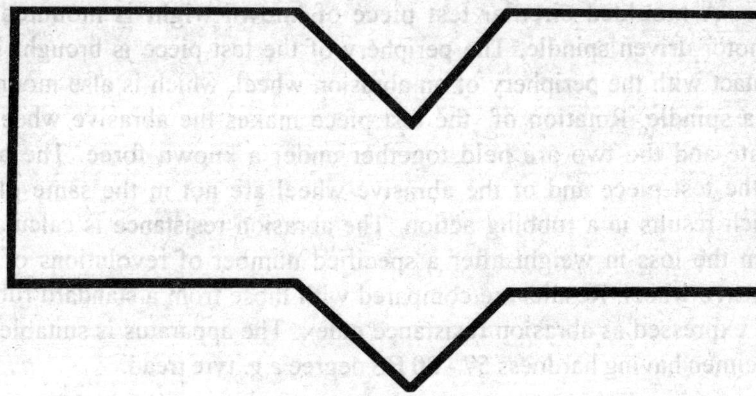

ASTM DIEC

No Nick has to be cut in ASTM Die C specimen, while nicks of prescribed lengths are cut into the region of desired stress concentration.

The rate of stretching is kept at 20 inches per minute. The results are expressed as the force required to tear a specimen of given thickness while in ASTM type, it is dependent on width as well as thickness.

Abrasion Tests

Abrasion is the progressive wearing away of a rubber article in service. In many applications, resistance to wear is one of the most important properties of a rubber article although it is one of the most difficult to measure. The type of wear undergone by an automobile tyre on a road is very different from the wear on a hose used for sand-blasting.

Abrasion resistance is a complicated phenomenon and is dependent on many properties such as resilience, stiffness, resistance to cutting and tearing etc. and different applications require these properties in varying proportions. Laboratory tests consist of rubbing the test piece against abrasive surface. These conditions are difficult to correlate with actual service conditions.

Many well known names such as these of Akron, Dunlop, Dupont and Pico have been associated with abrasion testers. The Akron tester is described below :

Akron

A moulded circular test piece of known wight is mounted on a motor driven spindle. The periphery of the test piece is brought into contact with the periphery of an abrasion wheel, which is also mounted on a spindle. Rotation of the test piece makes the abrasive wheel to rotate and the two are held together under a known force. The axes of the test piece and of the abrasive wheel are not in the same plane which results in a rubbing action. The abrasion resistance is calculated from the loss in weight after a specified number of revolutions of the abrasive wheel. Results are compared with those from a standard rubber and expressed as abrasion resistance index. The apparatus is suitable for specimen having hardness 57 - 80 BS degree *e.g.* tyre tread.

Ageing Tests

Heat Ageing

Tests for heat ageing are carried out for two purposes. Firstly to establishe changes in physical properties at elevated service temperatures. Secondly they serve as accelerated ageing tests at high temperatures which try to predict the long-term life at low temperatures. ISO 188 lays down methods using an air oven or an oxygen pressure chamber.

The test consists of ageing test pieces are for a given period at a specified temperature and then measuring the physical properties such as tensile strength, modulus, elongation at break and hardness. Comparison is thereafter made with non-aged test pieces.

In the oven method, the test pieces are exposed to air at atmospheric pressure. The total volume of the test pieces should not exceed 10%

of the free air space in the oven. The air flow must be steady and between 3-10 complete changes of air per hour. No copper or its alloys should be used in the construction of the oven because they may have an accelerating effect in ageing. The temperature may be as required. However 70°C or 100°C are most commonly used. The duration of the test is recommended as 1,3,7,10 or a multiple of 7 days. In the oxygen chamber method, the temperature is maintained at 70°C and a pressure of 2.1 MPa (300 psi).

The ageing period should not be too long to prevent determination of ultimate physical property. After vulcanisation of specimen, a minimum period of 24 hours and a maximum of 14 days prior to commencement of ageing should be allowed.

Resistance to liquids

Elastomer when in contact with a liquid may absorb the liquid or the liquid may extract some soluble constituents from the elastomer or there may be chemical reaction between the two. Absorption is normally greater than extraction resulting in increase in volume which is called swelling.

The international standard for resistance to liquids in ISO 1817 which specific choice of liquid, conditioning, temperature and duration of the test.

The size of the test pieces when measuring change in volume should be 1-3 cm with a uniform thickness of 2 mm and should not be longer or broader than 50 mm. The test consists of completely immersing the test piece in the liquid in a stoppered glass bottle at the required temperature. The volume of the liquid must be at least 15 times the volume of the test piece.

Compression Set

Rubbers deform under load and the difference between the original and final dimensions is known as permanent set and can be measured in compression.

Small cylindrical disks of size 13 mm. diameter by 6.3 mm. thickness or 29 mm. by 12.5 mm. are compressed to a fixed height in a jig which of two or more flat parallel rigid metal plates of proper size to hold the test pieces. The plates are clamped together with nuts and bolts. Steel spacers of appropriate thickness in the form of rings around each belt are placed between the plates to control the thickness of the test pieces while compressed.

Three test pieces should be used for each determination and the average value should be taken. The bolts are tightened so that the plates are drawn together uniformly until they are in contact with the appropriate spacers sized to give a compression of 25%.

The duration of the test is 72 hours at 23°C or 24 hours at elevated temperature of test which can be one of the nine temperatures between 70°C - 250°C and for which the compressed test pieces have to be kept in the central part of an oven maintained at the test temperature. After the specific time, the test pieces are removed and allowed to recover at 23°C for 30 minutes before the thickness is measured.

The compression set is the difference between the original thickness of the test piece and the one after the recovery expressed as a percentage of the initally applied compression as shown in figure.

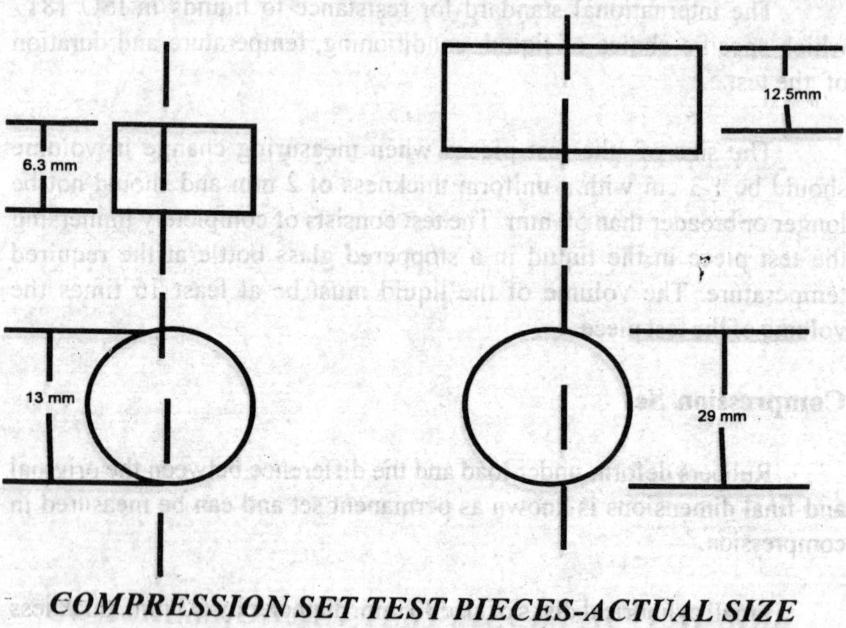

COMPRESSION SET TEST PIECES-ACTUAL SIZE

The compression set at constant strain =

$$\frac{t_a - t_b}{t_a - t_c} \times 100$$

Where t_a = original thickness of the test piece

t_b = thickness of the test piece after recovery

t_c = thickness of the spacer

Compression set value provides an indication of the degree of vulcanisation and unsuitable compounds can be identified if the value comes in high range.

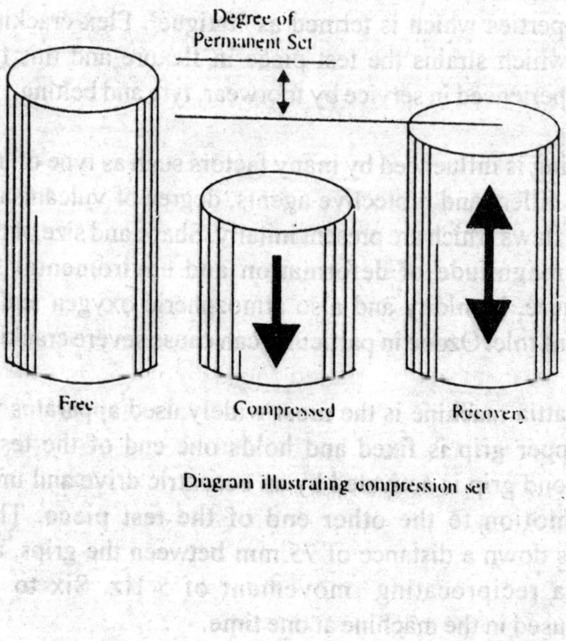

Diagram illustrating compression set

Typical values for a few elastomers are given in the following table :

Compression Set Values of Some Elastomers

	Temperature °C				
	20	70	100	150	200
Natural rubber	5	20	45	—	—
Neoprene	5	15	25	—	—
Nitrile	10	20	40	—	—
Silicone	10	10	10	15	40
Fluoro silicone	10	10	10	20	70
Fluoro carbon	10	10	15	20	25

Fatigue - Flex Cracking

After prolonged action of stress or strain on rubber, there is a change in its properties which is termed as 'fatigue'. Flex cracking test is a fatigue test which strains the test piece in flexure and this type of deformation is experienced in service by footwear, tyre and belting.

Flex cracking is influenced by many factors such as type of rubber, additives such as fillers and protective agents, degree of vulcanisation or cross-linking and flaws which are present initally. Shape and size of the article, nature and magnitude of deformation and enviromental factors such as temperature, humidity and also atmospheric oxygen and ozone also play important role. Ozone in particular can cause severe cracking.

The De Mattia machine is the most widely used apparatus for this test. In it, the upper grip is fixed and holds one end of the test piece stationary. A second grip is activated by an eccentric drive and imparts a reciprocating motion to the other end of the test piece. The ISO specification lays down a distance of 75 mm between the grips, a travel of 57 mm and a reciprocating movement of 5 Hz. Six to 12 test pieces should be used in the machine at one time.

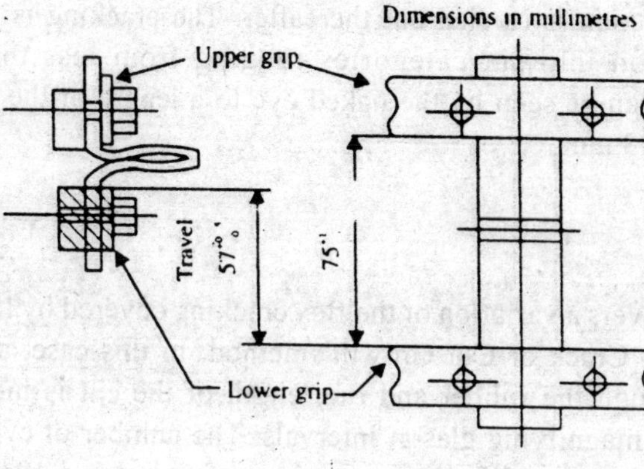

Principle of the De Mattia machine

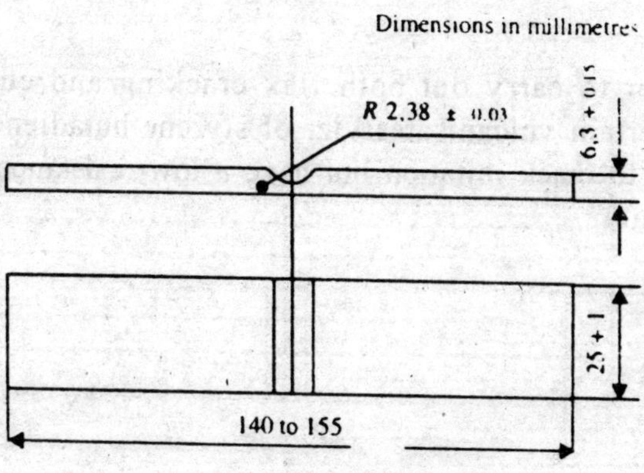

De Mattia test piece

The test piece is a strip of rubber with a moulded groove. The results depend on the thickness of the test pieces. The test pieces are flexed until the appearance of first minute sign of cracking and the number of flexing cycles is noted. The machine is restarted and the number of flexing cycles is increased in geometric progression of 1.5 each time. Inspection is carried out thereafter. The cracking is graded at each inspection into six categories ranging from less than ten pinpricks which can be seen by the naked eye to a length of the largest crack greater than 3 mm.

Cut Growth

ISO 133 covers a variation of the flex cracking covered by ISO 132 and is known as 'Crack or Cut Growth' method. In this case, a 2 mm cut is made through the rubber and the length of the cut is measured with the aid of a magnifying glas at intervals. The number of cycles for cut to extend by 2 mm and further extensions of 6 mm and 10 mm are recorded.

It is better to carry out both flex cracking and cut growth tests because certain vulcanisates viz. of styrene-butadiene rubbers show resistance to crack initation but have a low resistance to crack or cut propagation.

28
Trade Names and Chemical Compositions

Elastomers

Trade Name	Designation ASTM D 1418	Chemical Composition	Manufacturer
Ameripol	IR	Polyisoprene Synthetic	Goodrich
Cariflex	IR	Polyisoprene Synthetic	
Breon	NBR	Nitrile (Butadiene-acrylonitrile)	B.P.Chemicals U.K.
Chemigum	NBR	Nitrile (Butadiene-acrylonitrile)	Goodyear Tyres

Trade Name	Designation ASTM D 1418	Chemical Composition	Manufacturer
Hycar	NBR	Nitrile (Butadiene-acrylonitrile)	Goodrich
Krynac	NBR	Nitrile (Butadiene-acrylonitrile)	Polysar, Canada
Perbunan	NBR	Nitrile (Butadiene-acryonitrile)	Mobay,Germany
Cisrub	BR	Polybutadiene	
Hypalon	CSM	Chlorosulphonated Polyethylene	Du Pont
Cynoprene		Thermoplastic elastomer	American Cyanamide
Hytrel		Thermoplastic elastomer	Du Pont
Fluorel	FPM	Fluororubber	3M Company, USA
Viton Kalrez		Fluororubber	
Hycar	ACM	Acrylic Elastomer	Goodrich, USA
Vamac	ACM	Acrylic Elastomer	Du Pont, USA
Nipol	ACM	Acrylic Elastomer	Nippon Zeon, Japan
NR	NR	Natural Rubber	

Trade Name	Designation ASTM D 1418	Chemical Composition	Manufacturer
Neoprene	CR	Polychloroprene	Denka, USA, DuPont, USA Bayer, Germany Showa, Japan.
Krylene	SBR	Styrene Butadiene (SBR)	
Synaprene	SBR	Styrene Butadiene (SBR)	Synthetics and Chemicals Ltd., Bairelly
Nordel	EPDM	Ethylene Propylene Diene	Du Pont, U.S.A.
Vistalon	EPDM	Ethylene Propylene Diene	Exxon Chemical Co.
Silastomer	PVMQ	Silicone Rubber Phenyl Methyl Vinyl Silaxone	G.E.C.
Siliplus		Silicone Rubber	Dow
Thiokol	T	Polysulphide	Thiokol
Vikollin	AO	Polyurethane	Bayer, Germany
Vibrathene	AO	Polyurethane	Uniroyal
Chemigum	AO	Polyurethane	Good Year
Polysar	IIR	Butyl	Polysar
Opanol	IIR	Butyl	Bedischer Co.
Vistanex	IIR	Butyl	Exxon Chemical Co.

Thermoplastic Elastomers

Kraton	Styrene Block Copolymer
Elexar	Styrene Block Copolymer

Plastics/Resins

Trade Name	Chemical Composition	Manufacturer
Araldite	Epoxy	Ciba
Epon	Epoxy	Shell
Bakelite	Phenol-formaldehyde	Union Carbide
Durez	Phenol-formaldehyde	Hooker
Cellobond	Phenolic resin	
Alkathene	Polyethylene	
Indothane	Polyethylene	
Marlex	Polyethylene	Philips Chemicals
Hostalane	Polyethylene	American Hoechest
Breon	Polyvinyl chloride & copolymers	
Geon	Polyvinyl chloride & copolymers	Goodrich
Vinylite	Polyvinyl chloride & copolymers	Union Carbide
Caprolan	6-Nylon	Allied

Trade Name	Chemical Composition	Manufacturer
Dartek	66-Nylon	Du Pont, Canada
Krylene	Polypropylene	
Profax	Polypropylene	Hercules
Styron	Polystyrene	Dow chemicals
Siliastic	Silicone	Dow
Teflon	Polytetrafluoroethylene	Du Pont
Halon	Polytetrafluoroethylene	Allied
Implex	Polymethyl methacrylate	Rohm and Hass
Plexiglas	Polymethyl methacrylate	Rohm and Hass
Cordura	Viscose rayon	Du Pont
Kodapak	Cellulose acetate	Eastman
Arnel	Cellulose triacetate	Celanese
Beetle	Urea-Formaldehyde	American Cynamide

Fillers

Trade Name	Chemical Composition	Manufacturer
Aerosil	Fumed silica	Deggusso Corporation
Hisil	Precipitated silica	PPG Industries
Catalpo Clay	Precipitated Aluminium Silicate	Feeport Kaolin Co.
Mansit	Precipitated Aluminium Silicate	
Fortimax 423	Modified Precipitated calcium carbonate	ICI
Nytal 200	Talc slurry	
Rutiox	Titanium dioxide	
Titanox	Titanium dioxide	NL Industries
Silane	Coupling Agent	Union Carbide
Winofil	Activated calcium Carbonate	ICI
Witcarb	Precipitated Calcium Carbonate	
Albacar	Precipitated Calcium Carbonate	
York White	Natural Calcium Carbonate	Whitee New York

Softners

Trade Name	Chemical Composition	Manufacturer
Circosol 4240	Naphthenic oil	
Dutrex R	Mineral oil	
Okerin	Microcrystalline wax	
MRX	Mineral Rubber	
Sunpar 2280	Paraffin oil	

Accelerators

Trade Name	Chemical Composition	Manufacturer
Altax	Slow curing accelerators	
Banton	ZMBT	
Delac S	CBS	Uniroyal Inc.
Vulcafor DAU	CBS	
Butyl zimate	Ultra accelerator	
Ethyl zimate	Ultra accelerator	
Sitsit 9	Ultra accelerator	
Tiex	TMTD	
Zetax	Thiazole	

Antioxidants

Agerite stalite S		
Agerite Superlit		
DPPD	Diphenylpara diamene	
Nonox WSP	Phenol aldehyde	
PBN	Phenyl-B-napthalamine	

Aniozonates

Antoziie		

Blowing Agents

Vulcacel BN	Dinitrosopenta methylenetramine	

Emulsifiers

Tamon N	Sodium salt of naphthalene sulphanic acid formaldohyde Condensate	(W.R.Grace)

Peroxides

Di Cup HOKE	Dicumyl peroxide 40%	Hercules Ine.
Cadex	Benzoyl peroxide	Noury Chemical New York
Luperco AST	Benzoyl peroxide	Penwatt corp. New York

Stablisers

Vulcastab LW	Non-ionic stabliser	

29

Suppliers of Plant & Machineries for Rubber & Allied Products

Alfa Thermal Engg. Co.
B-119, Mayapuri Industrial Area,
Phase-I, New Delhi - 110 064
Tel : 5132648
Product : Mfr. of Heater Boiler

Aloona Industries
T-89, Vishnu Garden,
New Delhi - 110 018
Tel : 5421342
Product : Butyl Tube Flap Mould/Automatic Hydraulic Press

Anand Sintex Equipments Pvt. Ltd.
A-68/1, G.T. Karnal Road,
Industrial Area,
Delhi - 110 033
Tel/Fax : 7225888
Product : Special purpose machines Used in Rubber Processing Plant

Anant Corporation
Bassi Road,
Sirhind - 140 406
Tel : (Off) 40187
(Res.) 40474
Product : Manufacturers of Rubber Goods Processing machinery

Anant Corporation
B-83, First Stage, PIE,
Bangalore - 58
Tel : 8394808
Fax : 080 - 8391434
Product : Hand & Hydraulic Presses, Mixing Mills, Calenders, Extruders For Manufacturing Auto Tyres & Tubes, Rubber Footwear, Rubber Beltings, Moulded Parts etc.

Anant Engg. Works
Bassi Road,
Sirhind-140 406
Tel: 40037
Product : Mfrs. of Mixing Mill, Extruder Worm, Calendering Machine & Hydraulic Belt Press

Anant Enterprises
P.B.No.5, Bassi Road,
Sirhind - 140 406 (Punjab)
Tel : (Off) 40452, (Res) 40852
Product : Mfrs. of Rubber Procesing Machinery i.e. Rubber Mixing Mills, Calender Machines

Chadha Engg. Works
52, Aman Nagar, Indl. Area,
Jalandhar - 144 004 (Punjab)
Product : Mfrs. & Rubber Machinery & Rubber Chappals Dies

Crupp Metals
C-36, Inder puri,
New Delhi-110 012
Tel : 5183085, 5745154
Fax : 91-11-5726682
Product : Mfrs. of IBR & Non-IBR Boilers, Incinerators, Oil Burners & Dust Collectors

Deep Mechanical Works
8 Anju Bldg.,
Malbar Hill Road,
Mulund,
Mumbai - 82
Tel : 5650147

Dhiman Metal Fabrics
B-XXII/501, Dashmesh Nagar,
Ludhiana-141 003 Punjab
Tel :(Off) 530760 (Res.) 535576
Product : Mfrs. of Dies

Equipment Agencies (Bangalore)
3&4, 109, J.C Road, Bangalore - 2
Tel : 2223751, 2223750
Product : Rubber Mixing Mill, Extruders, Calendering Machines

G.S.S. Engg. Works
Chowk Moni,
Amritsar - 143 001 (Punjab)
Tel : (Res.) 234210
Product : Mfrs. of Rubber and Plastic Dies

Gagan Hydraulic Industries
14432, Street No.3, Kalsi Nagar,
G.T.Road, Ludhiana - 141 003
Tel : 672630
Product : Mfrs of Cycle Tube, Tyre Hydraulic Press, Kneader Machine & Mono band Machines

Hind Hydraulics & Engineers
Plot No. 13, Sector-24,
Faridabad - 121 005
Tel : 0129 - 233308, 234295
Fax : 0129 - 234294
Product : Rubberised Coir Foam Plant, Tyre & Tube Machine, V-Belts, Fan Belts, Conveyor Belts, Machinery for Shoe & Automobile Industry (Automatic Bias Cutting Slitting, Clickers for Shoe Uppers), Rubber Bale Cutters, Compression, Transfer & Injection Moulding Presses

Indimech
A-7, Bonanza Industrial Est.
Kandivli E, Mumbai - 101
Tel : 8874716

Industrial Machinery Company
205, Kanchan Hse,
Karampura Complex,
New Delhi - 110 015
Tel : 5116159
Fax : 91-11-5431706
Product : Mfrs. of Rubber processing Machinery

Indus Engineering Pvt. Ltd.
1A, Peenya Industrial Area,
II Phase, Bangalore - 560 058
Tel : (080) 8394983
Fax : 080-8394893, 5543402

International Fluid Valves
170, Sidco East, Amb,
Chennai - 98
Tel : 654011

J.P.Engg. Works
G.T.Road Bye Pass,
Nr. New Tpt. Nagar,
Jalandhar - 144 009.
Product : Mfrs. of Rubber Strap Moulds & Sole & Sheet Die Cutters

Jainsons (India)
5140/2, Ist Floor,
Krishan Nagar, Dev Nagar,
New Delhi - 110 005
Tel : 5769550
Telefax : 5725060
Product : Rubberised Coir Plant, Hydraulic Presses & Other Machinery.

JRD Rubber & Plastic Techonology
K-49, Model Town,
Delhi - 110 009
Tel : 7234947, 7128281
Product : Mfrs of Rubber Comp./ Transfer/Injection Moulding Machines & Moulds

Jogindra Engineering Works
70, Rama Road.,
New Delhi - 110 015
Tel/Fax : 5442112, 5412323, 5117614/011-5453836
Product : Plastic Processing Machinery

Kamal Rubber & Agri Engg. Works
B-XVII-2817,
Street No. 1, Jammu Colony
Nr. Preet Palace,
Ludhiana - 141 003 (Punjab)
Tel : 35149
Product : Mfrs. of Hydraulic Press, Monobend, Moulded Tube Press, Hydraulic Pump etc.

Kuka Sales Corpn.
B-62/1, Wazirpur Indl. Area,
Delhi - 110 052
Tel/Fax : 7118141
Product : Rubber Mixing Machine

Kuldip Engineering Works
Gali No. 4D, Plot No.4B,
Anand Parbat Indl. Area,
New Delhi - 110 005
Product : Hydraulic Presses for bakelite Moulding, Rubber Moulding, Broaching Machine, Hydraulic Pumps & Hydraulic Jacks.

L & T Mc Neil Ltd.
Mt Poonamalle Road,
Chennai - 98 (T.N)
Tel : 2341932

Ludhiana Hydraulic Inds.
577/10, Tagore Col,
Nr. New Cycle Mkt.,
Miller Ganj,
Ludhiana - 141 003 (Punjab)
Tel : (Off) 536632,
(Res.) 490229.
Product : Mfrs. of Hydraulic Presses for Plywood & Rubber Goods, Cycle Seats etc.

M.B.Engg. Works (Regd.)
A-57/1, G.T.Karnal Road,
Indl. Area,
Delhi - 110 033
Tel/Fax : 7118618
Product : Injection Moulding Machine for PVC Footwears

Manjit Industries
A-57, Mayapuri Indl.Area,
Phase-II, New Delhi - 110 064
Tel/Fax : 5401784, 5400782
Product : Rubber Machine

Manoj Engg. & Scientific Industries
Plot No. 3, Gali No. 1,
Anand Parbat Indl. Area,
New Delhi - 110 005
Tel/Fax : 5714314
Product : Hydraulic double action press, Metal Embossing Machines, Powder Compacting Hydraulic Press, Bakelite, Rubber Moulding Machines, Plywood Making Machines.

Modern Machine Works
Khasra No.5,
Kamrudin Nagar, Nangloi,
New Delhi - 110 041
Tel/Fax : 5476620
Product : Full Circle Tyre Retreading Machines & Allied equipments

Modern Metal Works
9/95, Kirti Nagar Indl. Area,
New Delhi - 110 015
Tel/Fax : 525041,
533199/011-539128
Product : Tyre Retreading Machines

Modern Hydraulics
5 Italian Building, Ground Floor,
381 Sane Guruji Marg,
Agripada, Mumbai - 3082365
Tel : 3082365

Micro Machine Tools
92, Sect.-24,
Faridabad - 121005 (Haryana)
Tel/Fax : 232379
Product : Rubber Mixture & Extruder

Om Dutta Steel Fabricators
G.T.Road,
Sherpur,Opp. Hero Cycles,
Ludhiana - 141 003 (Punjab)
Tel : (Off) 674846, 673615
(Res) 673615
Product : Mfrs. of Vulcanizers

Orleon machinery Corporation
122/2, Thambu Chty Street,
Chennai - 1
Tel : 513238

P.L.Engg. Works
397, Indl. Area - A,
Ludhiana - 141 003 (Punjab)
Tel : 661309
Product : Mfrs. of Rubber Processing Machinery

Premier Engineers
Post Box No. 11,
Opp. Railway Microwave Tower,
Sirhind - 140 406 (Punjab)
Tel : 40260
Product : Manufacturers of Dispersion Kneader, Extruder, Mixing Mill, Hydraulic Press & Three Bowl Calender

Product Engineering Industry
93-A N P Indl. Est., Chennai - 98 (T.N)
Tel : 652032

Psycho Enginering Corporation
PP-41, Gali No.10,
Anand Parbat Indl. Area,
New Delhi - 110 005
Tel/Fax : 5749619, 5757659, 5757634
Product : Rubber Thread Covering Machines, Surface Grinder Machine

R.S.Matharoo Dic Centre
11539, Partap Nagar, St.No.4,
Ludhiana - 141 003 (Punjab)
Product : Mfrs. of All Kinds of Rubber Aluminimum Oil Seals Moulding Dies

Rajhans Products
48, Defence Colony, Main Market,
New Delhi - 110 024
Tel : 4636374
Product : Hydraulic presses

Rana Hydraulic Industries
WZ-34/1, Khyala Village,
New Delhi - 110 018
Product : Auto Tube Plant, Tyre & Tube Mould, Hydraulic Press & Flap Mould Etc.

Ravi Engg. Works
29/19, St.No.6, New Rohtak Road,
Anand Parbat Indl. Area,
New Delhi - 110 005
Tel : 5725517

Ravi Engg. Works
18/34, Street No. 5,
Anand Parbat Indl. Area
New Delhi - 110 005
Tel : 5755332, 5755351, 5726630, 5725517
Fax : 91-11-5764369
Product : Mfrs & Exp. of Dispersion Kneader, Rubber Mixing Mills, All Types of Hydraulic Presses, Extruders, Two/Three/Four Roil Calenders, Rubber Sheeting Line, etc.

Realway Mechanical Works
WH-3, Mayapuri Indl. Area,
Phase - I,
New Delhi - 110 064
Tel/Fax : 5132523
Product : Rubber Converting Machines

Rub-Plast Mech. India Pvt. Ltd.
11-12, Swan Park, Mundka,
New Delhi - 110 041
Tel/Fax : 5473384,
5471638/011-5471638
Product : Rubber & Plastic Processing Machinery

Rubbermac (P) Ltd.
Outer Bye Pass Road,
Sirhind - 141 406 (Punjab)
Tel : 416
Product : Manufacturers of Rubber Processing Machinery, Mixing Mill, Calendering Machine

Sant Enginerring Co.
G.T.Road,
Model Town,
Ambala City - 134 003
Tel : 440442, 440823
Product : Rubber Processing Machines

Shree Dashmesh Castings
A - 4, Industrial Estate,
Malerkotla - 148 023 (Punjab)
Tel : (Off) 53496, 50433
(Res.) 53369
Fax : 91-54086
Product : Mfrs. of Chilli Roil Barrels for Rubber Mills & Hydraulic Ram

Sidhu Engg. Works
67, Sodal Road,
Jalandhar - 144 004 (Punjab)
Tel : 290637
Product : Manufacturers and Suppliers of Rubber, Plastic Moulds for Straps, Soles & Sheets etc.

Sifter International
Plot-83, Sector 6,
Faridabad - 6
(Haryana)
Tel : 240150

Slach Hydrates Equipt. (P) Ltd.
15 Najafgarh Road,
New Delhi - 110 015
Tel : 5441917, 538230
Fax : 91-11-5441916
Product : Mfrs. of Rubber Injection Moulding Machines & Injection Systems & Entire Range of Rubber Processing Machines

Slach Hydrates Equipt. Pvt. Ltd.
BE-294,295, Gali No.5,
Hari Nagar, New Delhi - 110 064
Tel/Fax : 5401991/011-5441916
Product : Rubber Polymer & Processing Machine

Spall Mech. Works
Bassi Road,
Sirhind - 140 406 (Punjab)
Tel : 40723
Product : Mfrs. of Rubber Processing Machinery & Spare Parts

Saroj Rubber Industries
WZ-119/1, Khyala, New Delhi.
Tel : 5112244
Product : Hydraulic Presses

Standard Cycle Industries
511, Industrial Area - B,
Ludhiana - 141 003 (Punjab)
Tel : 532392
Product : Specialist in Rubber Mixing Mill, Rubber Moulding Hydraulic Press, Hydraulic Pump, Extruder, Cycle & Auto Tyre Machinery, Monoband, Tube Jointing machine.

T.K. Rubber Inds. Pvt. Ltd.
24, Focal Point,
Mehta Road,
Amritsar (Punjab)
Tel : 231949, 230433
Product : Mfrs. of Rubber Rolls for Paper Textile Jannery & various other Inds.

Tarsem Singh & Co
WZ-490, Asri Nagar,
New Delhi - 110 034
Tel : 7182997
Product : Cycle Tyre and Tube

Technocrat Mouldings Pvt. Ltd.
4/7, Kirti Nagar Indl. Area,
New Delhi - 110 015
Tel/Fax : 5433578,
5431483/011-5457619
Product : Plastic & Rubber Head, Double Station Shoe Soles Making Machines, Extruder Driven-Model Technica & Ten Station with Rotating Table, PVC & Foam Footwear machine

Tri-Star Engineers
Plot No. 1, Sect.-24,
Faridabad - 121005 (Haryana)
Tel/fax : 232753
Product : Hydraulic Presses & Equipments

Unimech
J-117, MIDC,
Tarapur Boisar,
Thane - 401501
Tel : 02525 70540

Uttam Singh & Sons
B-61, Mayapuri Indl. Area,
Phase-II,
New Delhi - 110 064
Tel/Fax : 5400757,
5404716/011- 5457099,
5432729
Product : Dispersion Kneader Machine, Rubber Mixing Mill, Hydraulic Press, Calender machine, Extruder Etc.

Vishnu Machines
Plot No. 11,
SIDCO Industrial Estate,
Ambattur,
Chennai - 600 098 (T.N)
Tel : 653625

Walia & Sons
2801, Chunna Mandi,
Pahar Ganj,
New Delhi - 110 055
Tel : 7538624
Product : Motor Bus Fittg

White Machines
59, Najafgarh Road,
Tel : 5417077
Delhi - 110 015.

30

Suppliers of Rubber Raw Materials and Chemicals

Aar Tee Rubber Chemicals
300-A, Indl. Area-A,
Ludhiana - 141 003
Punjab
Tel : 661661
Product : Deals in Zinc oxide, Sulphur Powder & other Rubber Chemical

Action Chemicals
16-17, Indl. Area-A,
Chowk bagh Sufflan,
Ludhiana - 141 003.
Punjab
Tel : 660376
Product : Dealers in Raw Rubber & Rubber, Paint, P.V.C. Chemicals

Advance Chemical Co.
42, Strand Road,
Calcutta - 700 001
Tel : 242-7796/6475
Product : Calcium carbonate, Fillers, Activators, Reinforcing Agents, Mould Release Agents, Rubber Substitutes, Blowing Agents, Abrasive, Solvents, Protective Agents & Rubber Crumb etc.

Ahuja Rubber Chemicals
1443/4, Iqbal Market,
Pan Mandi, Sadar Bazar,
New Delhi - 110 006
Tel : 7774590
Product : Dealer of Raw Rubber Chemicals

Albert International
B-10/7557,
Vasant Kunj,
New Delhi - 110 070
Tel : 6897883
Product : Rubber-Malayasia

Allied Rubber & Chemicals
1H/260,
Opp. Dayanand School,
Faridabad - 1 (Harayana)
Tel : 8213603

Alka Minerals & Chemicals
25 DSIDC Sheds,
Jhilmil Industrial Area,
Delhi - 110 095
Tel : 228 5830
Product : Aluminium Silicate, Chinaclay, Soapstone

Alpha Trading Co.
9/14, Old Rly. Road-1,
Gurgaon (Haryana)
Tel : 320603

Arichem Sales (India)
B-44,
Industrial Estate,
Ludhiana (Punjab)
Tel : 534899, 534968
Product : Dealers in Rubber Chemicals, Minerals, Raw Rubber)

Arora Chemicals
Kesar Ganj Road,
Ludhiana - 141 003 (Punjab)
Tel : (Off) 400925,
(Works) 400925

Ashoka Sales Corpn.
18/21-A, New Rohtak Road,
Industrial Area,
Delhi - 110 005
Tel : 5719837
Product : Dealer of Raw Rubber

Ashutosh Rubber Chemicals
33/34, west Patel Nagar,
New Delhi - 110 008
Tel : 5743360
Product : D lr. of Rubber Chemical

A.I.G. Rubbers (P) Ltd.
Jhingran Road, Chanalon,
Kurali - 140 103 (Punjab)
Product : Mfrs. of Raw Rubber

Bhagat Rubber & Chemicals Co.
Kotwali Bazar,
Jalandhar - 144 001 (Punjab)
Tel : 2737
Product : Deals in Raw Rubber & chemical & Colours

Bajaj Rubber Company
15, Khurshid Market,
Sadar Bazar, Delhi - 110006
Tel : 7773460, 7526037

Batra Rubber Company
48/38, Gali No.1,
Nai Basti, Anand Parbat.
Delhi - 110 005
Tel : 5710934

Bhagat Ji Chemicals
4/5, GI-4, New Rohtak Road,
Anand Parbat,
New Delhi - 110 005.
Tel : 5727015

Bharat Sales Corpn.
133-134, Indl. Area-A,
Ludhiana - 141 003 (Punjab)
Tel : 661945, 661908
Fax : 91-161-609908
Product : Dealer of Raw Rubber Latex & Chemicals

Bharat Industrial Corporation
Plot No. 8/2,
WoodinnLoc Shopping Centre,
Kirti Nagar,
New Delhi - 110 015
Tel : 5116754
Product : Manufacturer of Rubber Raw Material

Bhimrajka Impex Ltd.
708, Maker Chambers V,
Nariman Point,
Mumbai - 400 021
Tel : 002-2875715/2044476
Fax : 022-204 8289
Branch : 1523, Ansal Tower,
38, Nehru Place,
New Delhi - 110 019
Tel : 011-6461361/6465619
Fax : 011-6224054
Product : For Speciality Elastomers from Dupont Dow Elastomes L.L.C & Rubber Chemicals

Cal - Chem
305, Shri Niwas, 382/84,
Narshi Natha Street,
Mumbai - 400 009
Tel : 344 5088
Product : Calcium Carbonate Minerals

Chawla Sales Agencies
133-134,
Indl. Area-A,
Ludhiana - 141 003 (Punjab)
Tel : 661945, 661908
Fax : 91-161-609908
Product : Carbon & OCL Stearic Acid, Dealer of Rubber & Paint Chemicals

Chemical Traders
B-V/546,
Fateh Ganj,
Ludhiana - 141 008 (Punjab)
Tel : 21437, 21943
Product : Deals in Reclaimed Rubber & Rubber Chemicals

Chowdhury Rubber & Chemical Co.
1403, Pan Mandi,
Sadar Bazar,
Delhi - 110 006.
Tel : 7773373, 751698
Fax : 753 4153
Products: Deal In All Types of Synthetic/Natural/ Silicon/ Reclaim Rubber/ Rubber Chemical/ Silicon Emulsion/ Swagat Zinc Oxide/ Pigment Powder/ Stearates/ Silicate/ Blowing Agent/ Stearic Carbon Gram Rub Chem/ Oil

Colour Chem Ltd.
Khetan Bhawan, 198,
Jamshed ji Tata Road,
Church Gate,
Mumbai - 400 020
Tel : 2830882/4
fax : 22-2876095
Product : Popular Pigments For Rubber : Permanent Yellow DHG-ID, Novaperm yellow HR-ID, Permanent Orange G-ID, Permanent Lake Red LC-ID, Permanent Rubine CA-E, Vulcan Fast Blue BBR, Hostaperm Blue CBR, Hostaperm Green GN, Hostaperm Green GNX, Hostaperm Voilet RL Spec-ID

C P M Trading Corp.
N-14, Kirti Nagar,
New Delhi - 110 015
Tel : 5116739
Product : Dealer Of Kerala Raw Rubber

Dharnendra Trading Co.
6926/A
Chandrawal Road.
Clock Tower,
Delhi - 110 007
Tel : 2913639

Crompton Industrial & Chemical Company
36, M.G Road,
Calcutta - 700 009
Tel : 350-8604, 350-5762
Product : All Grades of Furnace Type Carbon Black, Also Deals in Zinc Oxide & Stearic Acid.

Elite Rubber Chemicals
7/24, GI-7 A,
Anand Parbat Industrial Area,
Delhi - 110 005.
Tel : 57515726

Elastochemie Impex Pvt. Ltd.
57, 2nd Rd, R A Prm,
Chennai - 28
Tel : 4935450

Flexo Chemical Co.
327/1, Mansarovar Park,
G.T.Road,
Shahdra,
Delhi - 110 032
Tel : 2293193

Friends Trading Company
A-4/69,
New Kondli,
Delhi - 110 096
Tel : 2474156
Product : Dealers in Rubber

G.R.Rubber Chemicals
3/14,
Kirti Nagar Industrial Area,
New Delhi - 110 015
Tel : 532259

General Trading Corporation
E-2/10, Shastri Nagar,
Sarai Rohila,
New Delhi - 110 052
Tel : 5761600
Product : Rubber Raw Material

Gogia Chemicals
1452, Pan Mandi, Sadar Bazar,
New Delhi - 110 006
Tel : 735337
Product : Dealers of Chemical Goods

Goradha Industries
2nd floor,
8 Mirza Street,
Mumbai - 400 003
Tel : 340 125

Gyanesh Aggarwal
5934/4, Street-1,
Dev Nagar,
Karol Bagh,
New Delhi - 110 005
Tel : 5759671
Product : Dealers of Chemical Goods

Happy Rubber Inds.
New Colony, Tanda Road
Jalandhar - 144 004
Tel : 291889, 291238
Product : Mfrs. & Supl. of Chemicals & Rubber Goods

Hilla Industries
141/4-B, P H Road,
Chennai - 107
Tel : 4871844

Hindustan Petroplast
117, Allied House,
Inderlok,
Delhi - 110 035
Tel : 5469077
Fax : 5119555
Product : Nitrile & Syn. Rubber, Dnpt & Tmtd, Rosin, Zno Stearic Acid, Glycerine Etc.

ICI India Limited
34, Chowringhee Road,
Calcutta - 700 071
Tel : 91-33-290406, 91-33-298694, 91-33-298420
Fax : 91-33-2496330
Product : Rubber Chemicals

Jain Enterprises
C-57/3, Wazirpur Indl. Area,
Delhi - 110 059
Tel : 7220419
Product : Rubber Raw material

Jain Plastics
Bazar Nauhrian,
Jalandhar - 144 001
Product : Dealers in Rubber Chemicals pigments Colours Etc.

Jet Colour Chemicals
38, Harris Road,
Chennai - 2
Tel : 8520596
Product : Rubber Process Oil Naphthenic, Aromatic, Paraffanic, Spindle Oil, Pinetar

J.R. Inds.
11-A, Textile Colony,
Indl. Area-A,
Ludhiana - 141 003 (Punjab)
Tel : 21437, 21943
Product : Mfrs. & Suppliers of Rubber Reclaimed

Jyoti Rubber Chemicals
42, DLF Shop No. 52,
Kirti Nagar,
Delhi - 110 015
Tel : 5435399

Kapoor Rubber Reclaimer
Street No. 4,
Sameypur,
Delhi - 110 042
Tel : 7293944
Product : Mfrs. of Super fine Quality Tyre Reclaims

Karamsar Trade Links
Indra Colony, Indl. Area - A,
Ludhiana - 141 003 (Punjab)
Tel : 660808
Product : Mfrs. of All Kinds of Raw Material for Rubber, Paint & P.V.C. Industries

Kaypan Vanijya Pvt. Ltd.
2 Vardhman Complex,
L B S Marg, Vikhroli W,
Mumbai - 79
Tel : 5785880

Kerala Rubber House
Kotwali Bazar,
Jalandhar - 144 001 (Punjab)
Product : Dealers in Raw Rubber Grade Rubber & Latex

Kishore Rubber Products Pvt. Ltd.
681/1, Gavhane Estate,
Landewadi, Bhosari,
Pune - 411 039
Tel : 792391/2/792672
Fax : 0212-792390
Product : Rubber Raw Materials including Synthetic & Natural Rubber, Rubber Chemicals, Processing Aids, Extenders, Fillers & Reinforcing Materials, Auxiliary & Surface Materials & Colours.

Lakshmi Steels
105, New Cycle Market,
Gill Road,
Ludhiana - 144 003 (Punjab)
Tel : (Off) 538177, 660398
(Works) 660396,
(Pager) 122243
Product : Dealers of Raw Rubber & Latex

Luthra Rubber Inds.
Hoshiarpur Road,
Jalandhar - 144 004
Tel : 292500, 292600
Fax : 91-181-292005
Product : Dealers in Raw Rubber & Latex

Mahavir Enterprises
274/3,
Adarsh Nagar Market,
Jalandhar - 144 008
Tel : 251809
Product : Dealers of Raw Rubber Chemicals & P.V.C. Chemicals

Mahalaxmi Polychem
3856, G.B.Road,
Delhi - 110 006
Tel : 7531838
Product : Whole Sale Supp.

Manchanda Rubbers
C-12, Vishal Encalve,
New Delhi - 110 027
Tel : 5410292
Product : Making Tyre Tube

Mangal Chemical Industries (P) Ltd
D-193, Lajpat Nagar-Ist,
New Delhi - 110 024
Tel : 6844867
Product : Mfrg. of Sp Oil, Ch Oil)

Mercury Rubbers
Kapurthala Road, Basti Bawa Khel,
Ludhiana - 144 021 (Punjab)
Product : Dtb. of Ralson Carbon. Dlr.of Carbon Black, Rubber Chemicals & Dyes

Mohan Chemicals
2187/5, Beri Market,
Hingabeg,
Delhi - 110 006
Tel : 2510409
Product : Rubber Paint Chemicals

Moni Metal Inds.
F-113, Allied Hse, Inderlok,
Delhi - 110 035
Tel : 531452

National Rubber
2173, Tilak Bazar, Khari Baoli,
Delhi - 110 006
Tel : 2510216

Omsons Chemicals
N.B.175-B, Laxmipura,
Jalandhar - 144 044 (Punjab)
Product : Dlr.of Rubber, Chemicals

Oriental Agencies
4 Block, H.No. 593, Dev Nagar,
Delhi - 110 006
Tel : 5745591
Product : Trading of Raw Rubber

Pawan Rubber Inds.
Sherpur Chowk,
Nr. Military Camp,
Ludhiana - 141 003 (Punjab)
Tel : 672010 (PP)
Product : Mfrs. of Rubber Reclaimed & Rubber Crumb

Pioneer Rubber Works
82 & 106, N M Road,
Chennai - 29
Tel : 4835086

Pooja Intnl
2317/23, Floor-2,
Nanak Market, Gali Hinga Beg,
Tilak Bazar,
Delhi - 110 006
Tel : 2930999

Pukhraj Engg. & Chemicals Pvt. Ltd.
122, Govt. Industrial East Kandivli W, Mumbai - 67
Tel : 6054927

Petro Chemicals (I)
302, Himland, H S Karampura Comp
New Delhi - 110 015
Tel : 5411231

Plastic Point
215/22, Floor 3rd,
Gali Loharan, Ajmeri Gate,
Delhi - 110 006
Tel : 7512827

Plastic Chemicals C
204 C-In-C Rd,
Chennai - 105
Tel : 8272047

Premier Engineers
Post Box No. 11,
Opp. Railway Microwave Tower,
Sirhind - 140 406 (Punjab)
Tel : 40260
Fax : 01763-40560
Product : Mfrs. of Mixing Mill, Dispersion Kneader, Extruder, Hydraulic Press, Three Bowl Calender.

Pritam Rubber Industries
210-A, Hind Saurashtra East,
Andheri Kurla Road,
Mumbai - 59
Tel : 5772610

Pumm Chem. India (Regd.)
83, Aman Ngr.,
Near Pathankot Bye Pass,
Jalandhar - 144 004 (Punjab)
Tel : 291351

Rohit Sales Corpn.
Nr. Preet Ngr. Chowk,
Jalandhar - 144 004 (Punjab)
Tel : 290269
Product : Deals in Chinaclay Calcite Powder, Other Minerals DPG, Glue Powder & Chem.

Rubber Chemical Coroporation
9 Rehman Market, Sadar Bazar,
Delhi - 110 006
Tel : 251557
Product : Dlr of Raw Rubber

Rubber Linkers
46-A, Neelam Bata Road,
Faridabad - 121 001
Tel : 216796
Product : Rubber & Chemicals

Rubber Mineral Products
Shop No. 1418,
Iqbal Market Lane,
Near Narain Market,
Sadar Bazar,
Delhi - 110 006
Products : Natural Rubber, Rubber Chemicals, Silicon Rubber, Synthetic Rubber, Zinc Oxide, Carbon Black, Titanium Di-Oxide etc.

Rubber Products
203, Linghi Chty Street,
Chennai - 1
Tel : 5341503

Rubo - Chem Industries Pvt. Ltd.
403, Laxmi Commercial Complex,
Senapati Bapat Marg, Dadar(W),
Mumbai - 400 028
Tel : 4223578, 4227538
Fax : 5567626
Branch : 20/29, Dutt Saw Mill Road,
Kallai, Calicut.
Tel : 0495-304634
Product : Rubber Raw Materials ***Suppliers***- Stearic Acid, Powerene Aparene, Blowing Agent, Pigment Colours, Bonding Agents, Calcium Carbonate.

R. S. Chemicals
Narayani Building, 27,
Biplabi Trailokya Maharaj Sarani,
Calcutta - 700 001
Tel : 242-2408, 242-4683
fax : 220 0527
Product : All Types of Rubber Chemicals & Raw Materials including Zinc Oxide, Carbon Black

Sachdeva Rubber Chemicals
F-31, New Rohtak Road,
Anand Parbat Industrial Area,
Delhi - 110 005
Ph : 571 7683

Sachin Chemical Udyog
1414/2, Gali Chulhewali,
Sadar Bazar,
Delhi - 110 006
Tel : 7520316
fax : 3558887
Product : Sulphur Powder Mineral

Sharma Enterprises
623, Pocket A,
Sector-6, Rohini,
Delhi - 110 085
Tel : 7164408
Product : Mfr. of Tyre Raw Material

Shama Rub - Chem Co. Pvt. Ltd.
3&4 - A, Sai Niketan,
345, Mount Road, Mazagoan,
Mumbai - 400 010.
Tel : 3765193/3716380
Fax : 91-22-3738707
Product : White Reclaim Rubber for Canvas Shoes, Micro Sheet, Rubber Hose, Hawai Chappal, Rubber Ball, Hospital Rubber Sheeting, Rice Rubber Roller, Rubber Matting, Different Grades of Whole Tyre Reclaim Rubber.

Shree Ram Silicates (P) Ltd.
Hoshiarpur Road,
Jalandhar - 144 004 (Punjab)
Tel : 291838, 292403
Product : Mfrs. of Precipitated Silica

Shivalak Inds.
E-433, Phase-VI,
Focal Point,
Ludhiana - 141 001 (Punjab)
Tel : 661828
Product : Mfrs. of Rubber Reclaimed & Rubber Crumb

Silica House
406, Suneja Tower - I,
Distt. Centre, Janak Puri,
New Delhi - 110 058
Tel : 5617557, 5601318
Tele Faxv : 5613384
Product : Imp. of Synth. Rubber, SBR, NBR, PBR, Butyl, Also Deals in Zinc Oxide, Zincolet, Cal Carbonate, Latex Chem.

Silicons India
55, Halls Road,
Chennai - 10
Tel : 6440891

Singh Plasticisers & Resins P Ltd
1178,
Arjun Nagar,
Safdarjang Enclave,
New Delhi - 110 029
Tel : 6169709
Product : Mfg. of Rubber Antioxidants, Wet/Dry Bonding Agents for Oil Seals, Auto parts, Tyre, Hoses, Belts

Soni Rubber Chemicals
L-116, Sadar Bazar,
Delhi - 110 006
Tel : 3557396
Product : Heat, Corrode Proof

Sneh Industries
167-169, Ajmeri Gate,
Delhi - 110 006,
Tel : 7518061

Sucheda Agencies
15, Gee Gee Aptts.,
8 Kasturi Est.,
Chennai - 86
Tel : 499 0274

Super India Rubber Works
B-54, Sector - 5,
Noida - 201301 (U.P)
Tel : 91 - 527739 / 541619
Product : Mfr. of All Kinds Of Reclaim Rubber

Super Pine Tar Mfrs. Co.
E-39,
West Jyoti Nagar Extn.
Shadhra - 110 032
Tel : 2277790

Synthetics & Chemicals Ltd.
7 Jamshedji Tata Road,
Oriental House,
Church Gate,
Mumbai - 20.
15, Community Centre,
New friends Colony,
New Delhi - 110 065.
Tel : 2820161,
683 0897/683 1330 (Delhi)
Fax : 2870299,
011-6843514 (Delhi)
Product : Mfr. of Styrene Butadiene Rubber and latex, also manufacture Industrial Alcohol, Styrenated Phenol.

Synthetics & Chemicals
15-C, Centre New Friends Colony,
New Delhi - 110 065
Tel : 6831330
Product : Mfrs. Tyre

Teknos (India) & Co. Pvt. Ltd.
1/18-B, Asaf Ali Road,
New Delhi - 110 002
Tel : 3235993, 3230050
Product : Silicone Emulsion, Oil & Rubber

The C. B. Royal Chemicals
643, Vishwakarmapuri,
St.No.2, Gill Road,
Ludhiana - 141 003 (Punjab)
Tel : 24819, 456399
Product : Dealers Paints & Rubber Chemicals

United Enterprises
44-45,
Central Market, Gill Road,
Ludhiana - 141 003
Tel :(Off) 537894
Product : Dealers of Raw Rubbers Latex & Chemicals

V. R . Rubbers Chemicals
1307-C, Pan Mandi, Sadar Bazar,
Delhi - 110 006
Tel : 524877

Vardhman Trading Corpn.
4-14, Parijat 95 Marine Drive,
Mumbai - 2,
Tel : 3437812

Vardhman Chemicals
G-4, WZ-14B, Rohtak Road,
Manohar Park,
Delhi - 110 026
Tel : 5411266, 5475373
Product : Authorised Distributor of Dewan Reclaim Rubber

Vikas Chemical Agencies
5335, Gandhi Market,
Sadar Bazar,
Delhi - 110 006.
Tel : 7776833

Vikas Elastochem Agencies (P) Ltd.
57, 2nd Mn Rd., R A Prm,
Chennai - 28
Tel : 4937417

31

Project Profiles

- Asbestos Gasket Sheet
- Auto Tyre, Tube & Flaps
- Cycle Tyres & Tubes
- Crumb Rubber
- Disposable Surgical Examination Gloves
- Hard Rubber Battery Container
- Hawai Chappals
- Industrial Gloves
- Latex Rubber Condoms
- Oil Seals

- Rubber Balls
- Rubber Auto Parts
- Rubber Beading For Automobiles
- Rubber Sheet For Automobiles
- Rubber Hose Pipe
- Rubber Hoses For Automobiles
- Rubber Powder
- Rubberised Cloth
- Rubber Band
- Rubberised Coir
- Rubber Process Oil
- Rubber Transmission Belt & V-Belt
- Tyres, Tubes & Flap (Moped To Truck)
- Tyre Retreading By Cold Process

PLANT ECONOMICS OF ASBESTOS GASKET SHEET

Rated Plant capacity = 500.00 KGS/day

LAND & BUILDING (Land 600 Sq.mts.) Rs. 8,80,000.00

PLANT & MACHINERY

Rubber mixing mill size 16" x 42" complete with chilled cast iron rolls,reduction gearbox, 60HP motor & starter Rubber mixing mill 12" x 30" complete with reduction gear 30 HP Baby boiler Cap: 100 kgs./hr, 5 Roll calendering unit 8"x10" with M.S. roll & reduction gearbox with 10 HP motor starter etc. Vulcanisation unit steam heated 9'x 5' with trollies, Weighing maching plate type to weigh 300 kgs, Cooling water tank, pumps and piping & washing arrangement, Transformer 20 KVA Misc Tools & accessories etc. Testing equipment: Thickness gauge, Hardness Tester, Tensile Testing machinery, Compression Testing apparatus, Impact Tester, Abrader, Ross Flex machine, Ageing Block, Asbestos fibre making machine, Mixing tanks M.S. Cap: 3 CUM Blender Mixer Cap: 100 kg/hr for controlled feeding of rubber strip from mill & complete with 10 HP motor & Treaddie head etc, Cutting & Sizing equipment.

TOTAL **Rs. 9,82,500.00**

OTHER FIXED ASSETS Rs. 2,40,000.00

WORKING CAPITAL REQUIREMENT/MONTH

RAW MATERIALS

1. Asbestos fibre
2. Natural Rubber Latex 30%

3. Carbon Black Qty. 255 Kgs.
4. Napthenic oil Qty. 128 kgs.
5. Coumarone resin Qty.128 kgs.
6. Stearic acid Qty. 128 kgs.
7. Paraffin wax Qty. 64 Kg.
8. Sulphur (Vulcaniser) Qty. 128 kgs.
9. Graphite Powder Qty. 128 kgs.
10. TMTD (Accelerator) Qty. 128 kg.

TOTAL	**Rs. 1,20,360.00**

TOTAL WORKING CAPITAL/MONTH

1.	RAW MATERIAL	Rs. 1,20,360.00
2.	SALARY & WAGES	Rs. 52,500.00
3.	UTILITIES & OVERHEADS	Rs. 53,400.00
	TOTAL	**Rs. 2,26,260.00**

TOTAL CAPITAL INVESTMENT

TOTAL FIXED CAPITAL	Rs. 21,02,500.00
TOTAL WORKING CAPITAL	Rs. 6,78,780.00
TOTAL	**Rs. 27,81,280.00**

TURN OVER/ANNUM

Recipts from sale of Asbestos Gasket Sheet **Rs. 48,75,000.00**

PROFIT SALES RATIO = Profit / Sales x 100 = 26.31 %

RATE OF RETURN = Operating profit / T.C.I x 100 = 46.11 %

BREAK EVEN POINT (B.E.P) = 52.16 %

PLANT ECONOMICS OF AUTO TYRE, TUBE & FLAPS

Rated Plant capacity = 65.00 NOS./day

LAND & BUILDING
(Land required 750 sq.mt.) Rs. 19,50,000.00

PLANT & MACHINERY Rs. 3,50,000.00

OTHER FIXED ASSETS Rs. 85,000.00

WORKING CAPITAL REQUIREMENT/MONTH

RAW MATERIALS

1. Tread rubber sheet 2500 kg
2. Synthetic rubber 800 kgs
3. Smoked sheet (not rubber) 1300 kg
4. Reclaimed rubber 864 kgs
5. Stearic acid 48 kg
6. Zinc Oxide 100 kg
7. Carbon black 320 kg
8. Chin clay 2880 kg
9. Antioxident 53 kg
10. Accelerator (PBN, HAM, DIG) 48 kg
11. Pinc oil
12. Paraffin 5 kg
13. Process oil 15 kg
14. Sulphur 7.2 kg
15. Fabric with tyre cord cotton
16. Printing ink
17. Copper plated steel wire 360 kg
18. Valve fillings 9120 kg
19. Solvent oil 430 kg

TOTAL **Rs. 1,64,284.40**

TOTAL WORKING CAPITAL/MONTH

1.	RAW MATERIAL	Rs. 1,64,284.40
2.	SALARY & WAGES	Rs. 73,000.00
3.	UTILITIES & OVERHEADS	Rs. 64,000.00
	TOTAL	**Rs. 3,01,284.40**

TOTAL CAPITAL INVESTMENT

TOTAL FIXED CAPITAL	Rs. 23,85,000.00
TOTAL WORKING CAPITAL	Rs. 9,03,853.20
TOTAL	**Rs. 32,88,853.20**

TURN OVER/ANNUM

1. By sale of 6,000 Jeep tyres
2. By sale of 6,000 Jeep Tubes
3. By sale of 7500 nos of flaps

TOTAL **Rs. 60,75,000.00**

PROFIT = RECEIPTS - COST OF PRODUCTION = 15,43,103.50

PROFIT SALES RATIO = Profit / Sales x 100 = 25.15 %

RATE OF RETURN = Operating profit / T.C.I x 100 = 46.42 %

BREAK EVEN POINT (B.E.P) = 40.20 %

PLANT ECONOMICS OF CYCLE TYRES & TUBES

Rated Plant capacity = 1467.00 NOS/day

LAND & BUILDING

(Land required 1200 sq.mt) Rs. 29,20,000.00

PLANT & MACHINERY

Rubber mixing mill size 14" x 36" Complete with driving arrangements, reduction gears, etc 40 HP motor, 2 Bowl vertical tread calender of size 6" x 14", 5 HP motor, Cycle tyre vulcanization press with 4 set of moulds, pumps and all accessories, Air bag vulcanizing press complete with moulds, Rubber spreading machine 60"x18" brid type with electrical and Mechanical drives, steam chest, etc., Rubber solution mixer, Monobond tyre building machine, Hand operated case form,

Tube Section : Rubber mixed mill Size 20"x30" with all accessories 40 HP, Vulcanizer with troley arrangement 5'x10' Valve nut tightening machine, Valve nut punching machine (double action), Air removing machinery complete with all accessories, Handrel made out of aluminium.,

Common for both Section : Air compressor 2050 lb Cap. 15 HP, Rubber extruder, Boiler 150 psi 1500 lg/hr, Printing machine (small) Laboratory equipments.

TOTAL **Rs. 27,60,000.00**

OTHER FIXED ASSETS Rs. 2,75,000.00

WORKING CAPITAL REQUIREMENT/MONTH

RAW MATERIALS

Synthetic Rubber (SBR), Smoked Sheet (not rubber) ,Reclaimed Rubber, Stearic acid, Zinc Oxide, Carbon black China Clay, Antioxidant, Accelerator (PBN, HAN, DIG), Pine oil, Paraffin, Process oil, Sulfer, Fabric 62" wite tyre cord Cotton, Printing ink, Copper plates lead wire, Valve fillings, Solvent oil, Packing material

TOTAL	**Rs. 4,36,852.50**

TOTAL WORKING CAPITAL/MONTH

1. RAW MATERIAL	Rs. 4,36,852.50
2. SALARY & WAGES	Rs. 1,17,875.00
3. UTILITIES & OVERHEADS	Rs. 1,23,000.00
TOTAL	**Rs. 6,77,727.50**

TOTAL CAPITAL INVESTMENT

TOTAL FIXED CAPITAL	Rs. 59,55,000.00
TOTAL WORKING CAPITAL	Rs. 20,33,182.50
TOTAL	**Rs. 79,88,182.50**

TURN OVER/ANNUM

Receipt by sale of 2,20,000 tyres & tubes	Rs.1,36,40,000.00

PROFIT SALES RATIO = Profit / Sales x 100 = 21.15 %

RATE OF RETURN = Operating profit / T.C.I x 100 = 36.05 %

BREAK EVEN POINT (B.E.P) = 56.19 %

PLANT ECONOMICS OF CRUMB RUBBER

Rated Plant capacity = 2.00 TON/day

LAND & BUILDING

(land area required 600 sq.mt.) Rs. 9,00,000.00

PLANT & MACHINERY

1. Washing tanks for preliminary washing of scrap rubber filted with water spray nozzles.
2. Drier (Tray) for drying of washed rubber scrap.
3. Rotary precutter size 11 x 22" complete with IV carbide tipped blades and extra heavy duty
4. Chambers and rator but without 35 H.P. motor 144 RPM and electricals.
5. Chapper complete with heavy duty angle iron frame and gears but without 5 HP motor 96 RPM & electrical
6. Compulsary spares:
   (a) Disc
   (b) Blade
7. (c) Water box
   (d) Tep
8. Magnetic separator for removal of iron pieces.
9. Rubber grinder size 24" complete with water cooling system both the discs & vibration hopper
10. But without 60 HP motor 1440 RPM and electricals.
11. Ruching sieve size 8'x2' (single) complete with extra heavy duty angle iron frame
12. System but without 3 HP motor 1440 RPM and electricals.
13. Motor 60 HP.
14. Motor 35 HP.
15. Motors of 3 HP & 2 HP
16. Starters & Switches
17. Storage containers cap 5 m3
18. Miscellaneous equipments viz, jigs, fixtures etc.

TOTAL **Rs. 7,17,703.00**

OTHER FIXED ASSETS Rs. 1,80,000.00

WORKING CAPITAL REQUIREMENT/MONTH

RAW MATERIALS

Rubber scrap (*i.e.* used tyre)	Rs. 2,10,000.00

TOTAL WORKING CAPITAL/MONTH

1.	RAW MATERIAL	Rs. 2,10,000.00
2.	SALARY & WAGES	Rs. 61,875.00
3.	UTILITIES & OVERHEADS	Rs. 37,000.00
	TOTAL	**Rs. 3,08,875.00**

TOTAL CAPITAL INVESTMENT

TOTAL FIXED CAPITAL	Rs. 17,97,703.00
TOTAL WORKING CAPITAL	Rs. 9,26,625.00
TOTAL	**Rs. 27,24,328.00**

TURN OVER/ANNUM

By sale of 600 M.T. rubber powder	**Rs. 57,00,000.00**

PROFIT SALES RATIO = Profit / Sales x 100 = 22.80 %

RATE OF RETURN = Operating profit / T.C.I x 100 = 47.71 %

BREAK EVEN POINT (B.E.P) = 47.72 %

PLANT ECONOMICS OF
DISPOSABLE SURGICAL EXAMINATION GLOVES

Rated Plant capacity = 900000.00 DOZ/day

LAND & BUILDING **(Land required 1000 sq. mt)**	Rs. 8,50,000.00
PLANT & MACHINERY	Rs. 52,44,800.00
OTHER FIXED ASSETS	Rs. 2,75,000.00

WORKING CAPITAL REQUIREMENT/MONTH

RAW MATERIALS

1. Natural Rubber Latex
2. Zinc Oxide
3. Couanidines
4. Sulphur
5. Other miscellaneous chemicals

TOTAL	**Rs. 5,21,900.00**

TOTAL WORKING CAPITAL/MONTH

1. RAW MATERIAL	Rs. 5,21,900.00
2. SALARY & WAGES	Rs. 36,625.00
3. UTILITIES & OVERHEADS	Rs. 1,72,000.00
TOTAL	**Rs. 7,30,525.00**

TOTAL CAPITAL INVESTMENT

TOTAL FIXED CAPITAL	Rs. 63,69,800.00
TOTAL WORKING CAPITAL	Rs. 21,91,575.00
TOTAL	**Rs. 85,61,375.00**

TURN OVER/ANNUM

By selling of Surgical Examination gloves Rs.1,62,00,000.00

PROFIT SALES RATIO = Profit / Sales x 100 = 26.20 %

RATE OF RETURN = Operating profit / T.C.I x 100 = 49.57 %

BREAK EVEN POINT (B.E.P) = 50.06 %

PLANT ECONOMICS OF HARD RUBBER BATTERY CONTAINER

Rated Plant capacity = 400.00 NOS/day

LAND & BUILDING
(Land required 500 sq.mts) Rs. 55,000.00

PLANT & MACHINERY

1. Rubber Mixing Mill with chilled rolls 16"x 42 30 H.P. motor drive.
2. Hydraulic press 50 tonnes power driven 24"x24" electronically heated
3. Weighing balance platform type,
4. Weighing balance pan type
5. Moulds for container
6. Lab testing equipments
7. Installation and Erection
8. Electric fitting and commissioning
9. Miscellaneous

TOTAL **Rs. 4,77,000.00**

OTHER FIXED ASSETS Rs. 30,000.00

WORKING CAPITAL REQUIREMENT/MONTH

RAW MATERIALS

1. Reclaimed Rubber
2. Natural Rubber
3. Synthetic Rubber
4. Sulphuric Acid
5. Ebonite
6. Carbon black
7. China Clay
8. Spindle oil

9. Hydraulic Lime
10. Vovager 3A

TOTAL	**Rs. 5,13,600.00**

TOTAL WORKING CAPITAL/MONTH

1.	RAW MATERIAL	Rs. 5,13,600.00
2.	SALARY & WAGES	Rs. 26,640.00
3.	UTILITIES & OVERHEADS	Rs. 28,200.00
	TOTAL	**Rs. 5,68,440.00**

TOTAL CAPITAL INVESTMENT

TOTAL FIXED CAPITAL	Rs. 8,62,000.00
TOTAL WORKING CAPITAL	Rs. 17,05,320.00
TOTAL	**Rs. 25,67,320.00**

TURN OVER/ANNUM

Return by sale of Battery Container	Rs. 96,00,000.00

PROFIT SALES RATIO = Profit / Sales x 100 = 22.55 %

RATE OF RETURN = Operating profit / T.C.I x 100 = 84.30 %

BREAK EVEN POINT (B.E.P) = 28.18 %

PLANT ECONOMICS OF HAWAI CHAPPALS

Rated Plant capacity = 80.00 DOZ/day

LAND & BUILDING

(Land Required 2 KANALS) Rs. 7,50,000.00

PLANT & MACHINERY

1. Dispersian Kneader 50 Ltr, capacity with 50 H.P. motor & gear box.
2. Mixing Mill 14" X 36" with 50 H.P. motor are chilled rolls and Redicon gear box.
3. Hydraulic Press 36" x 36",5 daylight 20 " Ram, with 20 H.P. motor
4. Hydraulic press 14 X 20 with 10 H.P motor 6 day light for straps
5. Boiler Oil type with oil fired and 5 H.P. motor
6. Volcariser/Chamber 100 pair Capacity with compressor of 10 H.P. motor
7. Cutting press (power press) 10 Ton with 10 H.P. motor
8. Dies and Moulds
9. Hard tools etc.
10. Testing equipment
11. Cutter and grinder for Waste Grinding with 20 H.P. and 20 H.P. motor.

TOTAL **Rs. 28,20,000.00**

OTHER FIXED ASSETS Rs. 25,000.00

WORKING CAPITAL REQUIREMENT/MONTH

RAW MATERIALS

1. Rubber compound comprising of RMA, SBR other ingredinets, chemicals & colours
2. China Clay & other filler

3. Cloth
4. Solution, Stamps and other items

TOTAL	**Rs. 8,40,000.00**

TOTAL WORKING CAPITAL/MONTH

1.	RAW MATERIAL	Rs. 8,40,000.00
2.	SALARY & WAGES	Rs. 25,185.00
3.	UTILITIES & OVERHEADS	Rs. 80,000.00
	TOTAL	**Rs. 9,45,185.00**

TOTAL CAPITAL INVESTMENT

TOTAL FIXED CAPITAL	Rs. 35,95,000.00
TOTAL WORKING CAPITAL	Rs. 28,35,555.00
TOTAL	**Rs. 64,30,555.00**

TURN OVER/ANNUM

1. By sale of 24000 dozens of Hawai chapples
2. By sale of rubber sheets
3. By sale of 24000 Nos. Rubber sheets

TOTAL	**Rs.1,47,60,000.00**

PROFIT = RECEIPTS - COST OF PRODUCTION = 15,10,884.10

PROFIT SALES RATIO = Profit / Sales x 100 = 10.11 %

RATE OF RETURN = Operating profit / T.C.I x 100 = 23.50 %

BREAK EVEN POINT (B.E.P) = 61.44 %

PLANT ECONOMICS OF INDUSTRIAL GLOVES

Rated Plant capacity = 250.00 PAIRS/day

LAND & BUILDING

(Land required 500 Sq.Mt.) Rs. 7,50,000.00

PLANT & MACHINERY

1. Ball mill with accessories.
2. De-ammoniation tank.
3. Compounding tank with stirrer.
4. Dipping tank(Aluminium)
5. Leaching tank.
6. Air ovens for drying or vulcanisation.
7. Weighing balance.
8. Table balance.
9. Moulds for industrial gloves.
10. Miscellaneous laboratory equipment pipe fitting & other accessories.

TOTAL **Rs. 4,90,500.00**

OTHER FIXED ASSETS Rs. 2,35,000.00

WORKING CAPITAL REQUIREMENT/MONTH

RAW MATERIALS

1. NR Latex
2. Potassium hydroxide
3. Potassium laurate
4. Sulphur
5. Zinc diethyl dithio carbamate
6. Antioxidant (2-2' methylene-bis (4-ethyl-6-t-butyl-phenol)
7. Zinc Oxide

8. Miscellaneous chemicals, *viz,* french chalk, calcium nitrate, colour pigments etc.
9. Packaging materials.

TOTAL	**Rs. 74,248.75**

TOTAL WORKING CAPITAL/MONTH

1.	RAW MATERIAL	Rs. 74,248.75
2.	SALARY & WAGES	Rs. 45,186.00
3.	UTILITIES & OVERHEADS	Rs. 54,600.00
	TOTAL	**Rs. 1,74,034.75**

TOTAL CAPITAL INVESTMENT

TOTAL FIXED CAPITAL	Rs. 14,75,500.00
TOTAL WORKING CAPITAL	Rs. 5,22,104.25
TOTAL	**Rs. 19,97,604.25**

TURN OVER/ANNUM

By sale of 75,000 pairs of Industrial Gloves

TOTAL	**Rs. 45,00,000.00**

PROFIT SALES RATIO = Profit / Sales x 100 = 42.20 %

RATE OF RETURN = Operating profit / T.C.I x 100 = 94.64 %

BREAK EVEN POINT (B.E.P) = 34.19 %

PLANT ECONOMICS OF
LATEX RUBBER CONDOMS

Rated Plant capacity = 48000.00 PCS/day

LAND & BUILDING **(Land area required 500 sq.)**	Rs. 16,25,000.00
PLANT & MACHINERY	Rs. 10,00,000.00
OTHER FIXED ASSETS	Rs. 2,25,000.00

WORKING CAPITAL REQUIREMENT/MONTH

RAW MATERIALS

1. 60% NR Latex
2. KOH
3. Potassium laurate
4. Sulphur
5. Zinc oxide
6. Antioxidant
7. ZDBC
8. ZMBT
9. Packaging charges

TOTAL	**Rs. 1,34,767.00**

TOTAL WORKING CAPITAL/MONTH

1.	RAW MATERIAL	Rs. 1,34,767.00
2.	SALARY & WAGES	Rs. 67,372.00
3.	UTILITIES & OVERHEADS	Rs. 37,200.00
	TOTAL	**Rs. 2,39,339.00**

TOTAL CAPITAL INVESTMENT

TOTAL FIXED CAPITAL	Rs. 28,50,000.00
TOTAL WORKING CAPITAL	Rs. 7,18,017.00
TOTAL	**Rs. 35,68,017.00**

TURN OVER/ANNUM

By selling 1,44,00,000 No. Condoms **Rs. 63,36,000.00**

PROFIT SALES RATIO = Profit / Sales x 100 = 37.14 %

RATE OF RETURN = Operating profit / T.C.I x 100 = 66.39 %

BREAK EVEN POINT (B.E.P) = 40.20 %

PLANT ECONOMICS OF
OIL SEALS

Rated Plant capacity = 53333.34 NOS/day

LAND & BUILDING
(land area required 500 sq.mt) Rs. 3,50,000.00

PLANT & MACHINERY

1. Rubber mixing mill
2. Hydraulic press with steam heating
3. Baby boiler (coal filled)
4. Power press
5. Centreless grinder/lathe
6. Extruder/Calender Mechanical
7. Steam heated press
8. Weighing machine (platform type)
9. Testing equipments
10. Moulds/Assorted
11. Miscellaneous Tools

TOTAL **Rs. 2,74,200.00**

WORKING CAPITAL REQUIREMENT/ANNUM

RAW MATERIALS

1. Nitric Rubber
2. Sulphur
3. Stearic acid
4. Non-ox-B-3
5. GPE black
6. Mexplas
7. Tractoly phosphate
8. Zinc oxide
9. Vulca for PMT

TOTAL **Rs. 94,39,500.00**

TOTAL WORKING CAPITAL/ANNUM

1.	RAW MATERIAL	Rs. 94,39,500.00
2.	SALARY & WAGES	Rs. 3,11,488.00
3.	UTILITIES & OVERHEADS	Rs. 2,02,000.00
	TOTAL	**Rs. 99,52,988.00**

TOTAL CAPITAL INVESTMENT

TOTAL FIXED CAPITAL	Rs. 7,01,620.00
TOTAL WORKING CAPITAL	Rs. 24,71,863.00
TOTAL	**Rs. 31,73,483.00**

TURN OVER/ANNUM

By Selling of 1,60,00,000 oil seals Rs.1,60,00,000.00

PROFIT SALES RATIO = Profit / Sales x 100 = 34.09 %

RATE OF RETURN = Operating profit / T.C.I. x 100 = 169.88 %

BREAK EVEN POINT (B.E.P) = 13.52 %

PLANT ECONOMICS OF RUBBER BALLS

Rated Plant capacity = 1500.00 TOY/day

LAND & BUILDING (Land 150 sq.mts) Rs. 1,50,000.00

PLANT & MACHINERY

1. Ball Mill (Small)
2. Rubber mixing mill with complete accessories
3. Vulcaniser with complete accessories
4. Moulding machine revolving type
5. Oven and drying chamber with hot air blower
6. Baby boiler
7. Laboratory testing equipments
8. Stainless steel tank
9. Miscellaneous

TOTAL **Rs. 2,45,000.00**

OTHER FIXED ASSETS Rs. 1,00,000.00

WORKING CAPITAL REQUIREMENT/MONTH

RAW MATERIALS

1. Latex 60%
2. Casein 10% Solution
3. Whiting
4. Sulfur
5. Zinc Oxide
6. ZDC
7. Dispersing agent
8. Wetting agent solution

9. Processing oils, accelerations
10. Packing films, carboard cartons labels, etc.

TOTAL	**Rs. 1,61,930.00**

TOTAL WORKING CAPITAL/MONTH

1.	RAW MATERIAL	Rs. 1,61,930.00
2.	SALARY & WAGES	Rs. 23,520.00
3.	UTILITIES & OVERHEADS	Rs. 22,350.00
	TOTAL	**Rs. 2,07,800.00**

TOTAL CAPITAL INVESTMENT

TOTAL FIXED CAPITAL	Rs. 4,95,000.00
TOTAL WORKING CAPITAL	Rs. 6,23,400.00
TOTAL	**Rs. 11,18,400.00**

TURN OVER/ANNUM

By sale of 4,50,000 Nos of Rubber balls	Rs. 36,00,000.00

PROFIT SALES RATIO = Profit / Sales x 100 = 23.65 %

RATE OF RETURN = Operating profit / T.C.I x 100 = 76.13 %

BREAK EVEN POINT (B.E.P) = 35.57 %

PLANT ECONOMICS OF RUBBER AUTO PARTS

Rated Plant capacity = 333.33 KGS./day

LAND & BUILDING

(Land area 1000 sq.mts.) Rs. 18,00,000.00

PLANT & MACHINERY

1. Rubber mixing mill
2. Banbury mixer
3. Compression moulding machine
4. Hydraulic press
5. Steam heated presses
6. Vulcaniser
7. Boiler
8. Moulds/Assorted
9. Weighing machine platform
10. Weighing machine brenger type
11. Miscellaneous tools
12. Testing equipments; thickness gauge
13. Hardness tester
14. Tensile testing machine
15. Impact tester
16. Compression testing Apparatus
17. Ross flex Machine
18. Abrasor
19. Ageing block

TOTAL **Rs. 7,17,000.00**

OTHER FIXED ASSETS Rs. 5,80,000.00

WORKING CAPITAL REQUIREMENT/ANNUM

RAW MATERIALS

1. Natural Rubber 15 M.T.
2. Synthetic Rubber SBR 25 M.T.
3. Nitrile Rubber (imported) 4 M.T.
4. China Clay 30 M.T.
5. Whiting 30 M.T.
6. Zinc Oxide 2 M.T.
7. Stearic Acid 1 M.T.
8. Carbon Black 1 M.T.
9. Accelerators 0.5 M.T.
10. Antioxidants 0.5 M.T.
11. Antiozonats 0.2 M.T.
12. Paraffin Wax 0.3 M.T.
13. Wood Rosin 0.3 M.T.
14. Spindle Oil 800 litre.
15. Plasticizers DBP 1500 kgs.
16. Sulphur 800 kgs.
17. Aluminium Silicate 800 kg.
18. Aluminium Chloride 400 kgs.
19. Sodium Nitrite 400 kgs.
20. Silicones & Other Misc. Chemicals
21. Packing Materials
22. Colours.

TOTAL **Rs. 28,17,400.00**

TOTAL WORKING CAPITAL/ANNUM

1.	RAW MATERIAL	Rs. 28,17,400.00
2.	SALARY & WAGES	Rs. 8,40,000.00
3.	UTILITIES & OVERHEADS	Rs. 7,17,000.00
	TOTAL	**Rs. 43,74,400.00**

TOTAL CAPITAL INVESTMENT

TOTAL FIXED CAPITAL	Rs. 30,97,000.00
TOTAL WORKING CAPITAL	Rs. 10,85,408.00
TOTAL	**Rs. 41,82,408.00**

TURN OVER/ANNUM

Suspension Parts & Engine Mountings Sales of 100 M.T.(Auto Rubber Parts)	Rs. 70,00,000.00

PROFIT SALES RATIO = Profit / Sales x 100 = 23.01 %

RATE OF RETURN = Operating profit / T.C.I x 100 = 38.01 %

BREAK EVEN POINT(B.E.P) = 50.42 %

PLANT ECONOMICS OF RUBBER BEADING FOR AUTOMOBILES

Rated Plant capacity = 67.5 MT/ANNUM

LAND & BUILDING
(Land reqd. 600 sq.mtrs.) Rs. 11,00,000.00

PLANT & MACHINERY

1. Mixing mill 14" x 36" with 40 H.P. motor
2. Extruder 63mm (21/2") 7.5" with other accessories
3. Horizontal steam vulcanizer 3'x14"
4. Steam boiler 150 kgs/hr.
5. G.I. trays (Circular & rectangular)
6. Hand fly press 12"x12"
7. Testing equipments, moulds & dies etc.
8. Weighing balance
9. Miscellaneous tools pipe and pipe fittings etc.

TOTAL **Rs. 8,00,000.00**

OTHER FIXED ASSETS Rs. 1,60,000.00

WORKING CAPITAL REQUIREMENT/ANNUM

RAW MATERIALS

1. Natural Rubber 20,000 kgs
2. Zinc oxide 1500 kgs
3. P B N 300 kgs.
4. Clay 25,000 kgs.
5. Whiting 6000 kgs.
6. FEF black 6000 kgs.
7. Naphthenic oil 1500 kgs.
8. Paraffin Wax 300 kgs.
9. CBS 300 kgs.

10. Sulphur 750 kgs.
11. Stearic acid 600 kgs.
12. Other consumables like talc, separating agents, adhesive etc.

TOTAL	**Rs. 19,01,800.00**

TOTAL WORKING CAPITAL/ANNUM

1.	RAW MATERIAL	Rs. 19,01,800.00
2.	SALARY & WAGES	Rs. 7,35,476.00
3.	UTILITIES & OVERHEADS	Rs. 12,46,000.00
	TOTAL	**Rs. 38,83,276.00**

TOTAL CAPITAL INVESTMENT

TOTAL FIXED CAPITAL	Rs. 20,60,000.00
TOTAL WORKING CAPITAL	Rs. 9,70,819.00
TOTAL	**Rs. 30,30,819.00**

TURN OVER/ANNUM

Receipt By sale of 67.5 tons of Rubber beading for automobiles

TOTAL	**Rs. 54,00,000.00**

PROFIT SALES RATIO = Profit / Sales x 100 = 12.57 %

RATE OF RETURN = Operating profit / T.C.I x 100 = 22.62 %

BREAK EVEN POINT (B.E.P) = 70.24 %

PLANT ECONOMICS OF RUBBER SHEET FOR AUTOMOBILES

Rated Plant capacity = 2.00 TON/day

LAND & BUILDING

(Total Land required 4840 Sq Yds.) Rs. 21,35,200.00

PLANT & MACHINERY

1. Rubber mixing mill 12"x30" with chilled castrols,40 HP motor, reduction gear&other accessories
2. Extruder 2.5" with 10 HP motor with accessories
3. Hydraulic Press of plate size
4. Steam heated presses (heat operated 16"x16")
5. Steam heated press (heat operated 24"x24")
6. Vulcanizer with trolly arrangement
7. Boiler (oil fired)
8. Moulds assorted,
9. Weighing machine
10. Miscellaneous tools, jigs, fixtures etc..

TOTAL **Rs. 36,15,000.00**

OTHER FIXED ASSETS Rs. 8,60,000.00

WORKING CAPITAL REQUIREMENT/MONTH

RAW MATERIALS

1. Synthetic scrap rubber
2. Synthetic -rubber SBR
3. China Clay
4. Whiting (Precipitated calcium carbonate)
5. Zinc Oxide
6. Stearic acid

7. Accelerators
8. Antioxidants
9. Plasticizers DBP
10. Sulphur

TOTAL	**Rs. 11,77,600.00**

TOTAL WORKING CAPITAL/MONTH

1.	RAW MATERIAL	Rs. 11,77,600.00
2.	SALARY & WAGES	Rs. 1,13,125.00
3.	UTILITIES & OVERHEADS	Rs. 1,66,000.00
	TOTAL	**Rs. 14,56,725.00**

TOTAL CAPITAL INVESTMENT

TOTAL FIXED CAPITAL	Rs. 66,10,200.00
TOTAL WORKING CAPITAL	Rs. 43,70,175.00
TOTAL	**Rs.1,09,80,375.00**

TURN OVER/ANNUM

By Sale of 600 tonnes of Rubber sheets	Rs.2,70,00,000.00

PROFIT SALES RATIO = Profit / Sales x 100 = 24.57 %

RATE OF RETURN = Operating profit / T.C.I x 100 = 60.41 %

BREAK EVEN POINT (B.E.P) = 39.60 %

PLANT ECONOMICS OF RUBBER HOSE PIPE

Rated Plant capacity = 120.00 PCS./day

LAND & BUILDING

(Land Required 1000 Sq.Mts.) Rs. 16,15,000.00

PLANT & MACHINERY

1. Mixing mill 16" x 42" with chilled cast iron rolls and 50 H.P. electric motor.
2. Mixing mill 14" x 36" with 40 H.P. motor.
3. Extruder size 4" with 10 H.P. motor
4. Braiding machine, size 6" x 18" with 5 H.P. motor.
5. Cross head extruder.
6. Lead press or lead extruder.
7. Churning mill (225 litre) with 5 H.P. motor.
8. Vulcanising pan with trolley 24"dia 60" long.
9. Oil fired boiler 250 Kg/hr. evaporation capacity with chimney, water softener and all other accessories.
10. Air compressor 100 psi.
11. Drum winding machine.
12. Clamping press machine.
13. Stripping machine.
14. Moulds of different sizes
15. D.G. set of 100 KVA.

TOTAL **Rs. 20,70,000.00**

OTHER FIXED ASSETS Rs. 4,20,000.00

WORKING CAPITAL REQUIREMENT/MONTH

RAW MATERIALS

1. Natural Rubber 4000 Kgs.
2. SBR 2000 Rubber 2000 Kgs.
3. Reclaimed Rubber 2000 Kgs.

TOTAL	**Rs. 3,68,000.00**

TOTAL WORKING CAPITAL/MONTH

1.	RAW MATERIAL	Rs. 3,68,000.00
2.	SALARY & WAGES	Rs. 41,875.00
3.	UTILITIES & OVERHEADS	Rs. 42,750.00
	TOTAL	**Rs. 4,52,625.00**

TOTAL CAPITAL INVESTMENT

TOTAL FIXED CAPITAL	Rs. 41,05,000.00
TOTAL WORKING CAPITAL	Rs. 13,57,875.00
TOTAL	**Rs. 54,62,875.00**

TURN OVER/ANNUM

1. By Sale of 6000 M.T. of Precision
2. By sale of 36000 pieces of Rubber Hose Pipes
3. Recovery from Sale of Steel Scraps

TOTAL	**Rs.14,46,00,000.00**

PROFIT SALES RATIO = Profit / Sales x 100 = 95.01 %

RATE OF RETURN = Operating profit / T.C.I. x 100 = 2,498.99 %

BREAK EVEN POINT (B.E.P) = 1.58 %

PLANT ECONOMICS OF RUBBER HOSES FOR AUTOMOBILES

Rated Plant capacity = 333.33 NOS./day

LAND & BUILDING

(Land Required 600 Sq.Mts.) Rs. 9,00,000.00

PLANT & MACHINERY

1. Mixing mill (14" x 36") 40 H.P
2. Extruder (5") 8 H.P.
3. Spreading Machine. (60" x 18")
4. Auto Clave 4' x 10' with trolleys & accessories.
5. Solvent Mixer 150 litre 5 H.P. (Crushing Mill).
6. Boiler, 250 Kgs. Capacity.
7. Air Compressor, 100 psi.
8. Wrapping Machine.
9. Mandrels.
10. Hose Braiding Machine complete with accessories.
11. Miscellaneous, Pumps, Weighing Machine, Building roller, Building tables, hand tools etc.

TOTAL **Rs. 14,00,000.00**

OTHER FIXED ASSETS Rs. 3,20,000.00

WORKING CAPITAL REQUIREMENT/MONTH

RAW MATERIALS

1. Natural Rubber
2. Zinc Oxide
3. Stearic Acid
4. S R F Black

5. Hard Clay
6. Precipitated Calcium Carbonate
7. Naphthenic Oil
8. Antioxide PBN
9. CBS
10. TMTD
11. Sulphur
12. Pure Tar
13. Fabric
14. Solvent Oil
15. Packaging Materials (Hessian Bags).

TOTAL	**Rs. 2,01,918.37**

TOTAL WORKING CAPITAL/MONTH

1.	RAW MATERIAL	Rs. 2,01,918.37
2.	SALARY & WAGES	Rs. 61,247.00
3.	UTILITIES & OVERHEADS	Rs. 39,600.00
	TOTAL	**Rs. 3,02,765.37**

TOTAL CAPITAL INVESTMENT

TOTAL FIXED CAPITAL	Rs. 26,20,000.00
TOTAL WORKING CAPITAL	Rs. 9,08,296.11
TOTAL	**Rs. 35,28,296.11**

TURN OVER/ANNUM

By Sale of Rubber Hoses for Automobiles (Radiator)	Rs. 60,00,000.00

PROFIT SALES RATIO = Profit / Sales x 100 = 19.52 %

RATE OF RETURN = Operating profit / T.C.I x 100 = 33.15 %

BREAK EVEN POINT (B.E.P) = 58.13 %

PLANT ECONOMICS OF RUBBER POWDER

Rated Plant capacity = 2.00 M.T/day

LAND & BUILDING

(Land required 600 sq. mt) Rs. 11,91,000.00

PLANT & MACHINERY

1. Pre-cutter machine size 11* 22" without 30 H.P motor & switches starter
2. Chopper machine without 3 H.P motor & switches starter
3. Masson Grinder without 60 H. P motors & switch starters
4. Rocking sieve without 2 H.P motor & switches starter
5. Motors 60 H.P
6. Motors 30 H.P
7. Motors of 3 H.P & 2 H.P
8. Starters & switches
9. Storage containers cap:- 5 M3 (Made of mild steel)

TOTAL **Rs. 5,10,000.00**

OTHER FIXED ASSETS Rs. 1,31,000.00

WORKING CAPITAL REQUIREMENT/MONTH

RAW MATERIALS

Rubber scrap (*i.e.* used tyre)

TOTAL **Rs. 3,00,000.00**

TOTAL WORKING CAPITAL/MONTH

1.	RAW MATERIAL	Rs. 3,00,000.00
2.	SALARY & WAGES	Rs. 41,936.00
3.	UTILITIES & OVERHEADS	Rs. 53,500.00
	TOTAL	**Rs. 3,95,436.00**

TOTAL CAPITAL INVESTMENT

TOTAL FIXED CAPITAL	Rs. 18,32,000.00
TOTAL WORKING CAPITAL	Rs. 11,86,308.00
TOTAL	**Rs. 30,18,308.00**

TURN OVER/ANNUM

Receipt through sale of
600 M.T. Rubber powder

TOTAL **Rs. 72,00,000.00**

PROFIT SALES RATIO = Profit / Sales x 100 = 22.22 %

RATE OF RETURN = Operating profit / T.C.I x 100 = 53.00 %

BREAK EVEN POINT (B.E.P) = 45.04 %

PLANT ECONOMICS OF RUBBERISED CLOTH

Rated Plant capacity = 100.00 KGS./day

LAND & BUILDING

(Land required 500 sq.mts.) Rs. 9,27,000.00

PLANT & MACHINERY

1. Ball Mill or Pot Mill S.S. made,
2. Hobart Type Mixer with all accessories.
3. Baby Boiler
4. Storage Tanks
5. Spreading Machine (automatic) complete.
6. Miscellaneous (Tools & other equipment.)

TOTAL Rs. 19,60,000.00

OTHER FIXED ASSETS Rs. 5,40,000.00

WORKING CAPITAL REQUIREMENT/MONTH

RAW MATERIALS

1. Latex (NR) .
2. Zinc oxide
3. Whiting Powder
4. Potassium Hydroxide
5. Zinc Dibutyl dithiocarbonate -
6. Sulphur
7. Nonax S.P.
8. Oleic Acid
9. CMC
10. T.D.

TOTAL Rs. 1,21,287.50

TOTAL WORKING CAPITAL/MONTH

1.	RAW MATERIAL	Rs.	1,21,287.50
2.	SALARY & WAGES	Rs.	45,625.00
3.	UTILITIES & OVERHEADS	Rs.	66,600.00
	TOTAL	**Rs.**	**2,33,512.50**

TOTAL CAPITAL INVESTMENT

TOTAL FIXED CAPITAL	Rs. 34,27,000.00
TOTAL WORKING CAPITAL	Rs. 7,00,537.50
TOTAL	**Rs. 41,27,537.50**

TURN OVER/ANNUM

By sale of 30,000 kgs.of Rubberized Cloth,

TOTAL **Rs. 66,00,000.00**

PROFIT SALES RATIO = Profit / Sales x 100 = 38.08 %

RATE OF RETURN = Operating profit / T.C.I x 100 = 61.29 %

BREAK EVEN POINT (B.E.P) = 42.10 %

PLANT ECONOMICS OF
RUBBER BAND

Rated Plant capacity = 120.00 KG/day

LAND & BUILDING

(Total area required 200 sq.m.) **Rs. 1,42,000.00**

PLANT & MACHINERY

1. Storage vessels (Fixed with agitator)
2. Kheader 2 rool type equipped with ratar etc.
3. Automatic cutting machine with 12 No of blades
4. Baby baiter
5. Motor & other miscellaneous accessories
6. Transportation and operation charges
7. Powder canling & piping etc.

TOTAL **Rs. 1,57,000.00**

OTHER FIXED ASSETS Rs. 29,000.00

WORKING CAPITAL REQUIREMENT/MONTH

RAW MATERIALS

1. National Rubber Latex
2. Potassium Hydroxide (10%)
3. Sulphur
4. 2 MBT
5. 2 D.D.
6. N Odioxide D
7. TiO^2
8. ZnO

TOTAL **Rs. 50,687.50**

TOTAL WORKING CAPITAL/MONTH

1.	RAW MATERIAL	Rs.	50,687.50
2.	SALARY & WAGES	Rs.	15,125.00
3.	UTILITIES & OVERHEADS	Rs.	42,700.00
	TOTAL	**Rs.**	**1,08,512.50**

TOTAL CAPITAL INVESTMENT

TOTAL FIXED CAPITAL	Rs.	3,28,000.00
TOTAL WORKING CAPITAL	Rs.	3,25,537.50
TOTAL	**Rs.**	**6,53,537.50**

TURN OVER/ANNUM

Sales receipt by selling of Rubber band **Rs. 18,00,000.00**

PROFIT SALES RATIO = Profit / Sales x 100 = 17.26 %

RATE OF RETURN = Operating profit / T.C.I x 100 = 47.63 %

BREAK EVEN POINT (B.E.P) = 60.04 %

PLANT ECONOMICS OF RUBBERIZED COIR

Rated Plant capacity = 125.00 PIECES/day

LAND & BUILDING (Land 4000 sq.mt) Rs. 45,50,000.00

PLANT & MACHINERY

1. Willow for coir fibres, Cards, Fibre cutter, wooden frames of assorted sizes.
2. Boiler (Oil fired)
3. Hot air chambers electrically heated
4. Storage tanks
5. Miscellaneous machines

TOTAL **Rs. 36,00,000.00**

OTHER FIXED ASSETS Rs. 4,00,000.00

WORKING CAPITAL REQUIREMENT/MONTH

RAW MATERIALS

1. Rubber Sheet 4" thick 12500 sqm.
2. Properly extracted and washed fine quality coir 12500 kg or 9000/-per MT
3. Various ingredients for making Bonding Compound 19000 kgs/-
4. Dyes for coir fibres

TOTAL WORKING CAPITAL/MONTH

1.	RAW MATERIAL	Rs.	19,94,750.00
2.	SALARY & WAGES	Rs.	1,79,375.00
3.	UTILITIES & OVERHEADS	Rs.	1,20,000.00
	TOTAL	**Rs.**	**22,94,125.00**

TOTAL CAPITAL INVESTMENT

TOTAL FIXED CAPITAL	Rs. 85,50,000.00
TOTAL WORKING CAPITAL	Rs. 68,82,375.00
TOTAL	**Rs. 1,54,32,375.00**

TURN OVER/ANNUM

By selling mattress 37500 pieces of mattress	**Rs. 4,12,50,000.00**

PROFIT SALES RATIO = Profit / Sales x 100 = 23.06 %

RATE OF RETURN = Operating profit / T.C.I x 100 = 61.15

BREAK EVEN POINT (B.E.P) = 38.26 %

PLANT ECONOMICS OF RUBBER PROCESS OIL

Rated Plant capacity = 6.00 TON/day

LAND & BUILDING

(Land required 2000 sq.mts.) Rs. 22,65,000.00

PLANT & MACHINERY

1. Distillation plant 1000 litre lube oil charge per hr Bubble Cap type
2. Condenser (Shell and Tube type)
3. Chilling plant of Capacity 5 tons
4. Frame and Plate type filter press
5. Water Cooler
6. Storage tank for lube oil capacity
7. Lead lined Reactor vessel
8. Boiler steam Producing 1000 kg/hr Vertical Types oil fired steam pressure
9. Acid storage tank
10. Miscellaneous (Pipe lines, valves) Compressed air etc.
11. Instrumentation & Process Control Equipment

TOTAL **Rs. 61,00,000.00**

OTHER FIXED ASSETS Rs. 10,40,000.00

WORKING CAPITAL REQUIREMENT/MONTH

RAW MATERIALS

1. Crude lubricating oil
2. Acid Sulfuric
3. Alkali Sodium hydroxide
4. Filter Cloth
5. Miscellaneous chemicals &

Packaging Materials.
viz. Barrels etc.

TOTAL	**Rs. 20,22,000.00**

TOTAL WORKING CAPITAL/MONTH

1.	RAW MATERIAL	Rs. 20,22,000.00
2.	SALARY & WAGES	Rs. 1,77,125.00
3.	UTILITIES & OVERHEADS	Rs. 1,58,000.00
	TOTAL	**Rs. 23,57,125.00**

TOTAL CAPITAL INVESTMENT

TOTAL FIXED CAPITAL	Rs. 94,05,000.00
TOTAL WORKING CAPITAL	Rs. 70,71,375.00
TOTAL	**Rs. 1,64,76,375.00**

TURN OVER/ANNUM

1. By selling 1500 Tons of Rubber Process Oil.
2. By Selling Slack wax

TOTAL	**Rs. 4,05,00,000.00**

PROFIT SALES RATIO = Profit / Sales x 100 = 17.78 %

RATE OF RETURN = Operating profit / T.C.I x 100 = 43.21 %

BREAK EVEN POINT (B.E.P) = 48.34 %

PLANT ECONOMICS OF RUBBER TRANSMISSION BELT & V-BELT

Rated Plant capacity = 1.00 MT/day

LAND & BUILDING (Land 1000 sq.mts) Rs. 25,50,000.00

PLANT & MACHINERY

1. M.S. Mixing Mill for Rubber compoun with two chiled cast iron roll size 14" x 36" 25 H.P.
2. Calendering machine, 3 rolls (Bowl rolls type) similar to mill rolls
3. Complete hydaraulic belt vulcanizin press size 500x100 mm. corssisting of side per pressig device etc.1 No
4. Belt press 12 No x 2 size 36"x7" `indouble moulding arrangement
5. Moulds M.S. made of various size
6. Boiler 250/kgs/m steam generator
7. Triming and outting machine
8. Other ancilliary equipments
9. Miscellaneous, pipe, fitting and other equipments

TOTAL **Rs. 17,50,000.00**

OTHER FIXED ASSETS Rs. 4,50,000.00

WORKING CAPITAL REQUIREMENT/MONTH

RAW MATERIALS

1. Cotton ducks (canvas, soft types)
2. Nitrite Rubber
3. FEF Black
4. D.O.P

5. Coumarine Indone Resin
6. Zinc oxide
7. Stearic acid
8. A.O.P BNA
9. ETDO Type A.O.
10. TMTD
11. Sulphur
12. Hard clay

TOTAL	**Rs. 24,94,000.00**

TOTAL WORKING CAPITAL/MONTH

1.	RAW MATERIAL	Rs. 24,94,000.00
2.	SALARY & WAGES	Rs. 1,77,500.00
3.	UTILITIES & OVERHEADS	Rs. 1,69,750.00
	TOTAL	**Rs. 28,41,250.00**

TOTAL CAPITAL INVESTMENT

TOTAL FIXED CAPITAL	Rs. 47,50,000.00
TOTAL WORKING CAPITAL	Rs. 85,23,750.00
TOTAL	**Rs. 1,32,73,750.00**

TURN OVER/ANNUM

By sale of 300 tons of Rubber Transmission & V-belts

TOTAL	**Rs. 4,50,00,000.00**

PROFIT SALES RATIO = Profit / Sales x 100 = 17.25 %

RATE OF RETURN = Operating profit / T.C.I x 100 = 58.40 %

BREAK EVEN POINT (B.E.P) = 37.52 %

PLANT ECONOMICS OF TYRES, TUBES & FLAP (MOPED TO TRUCK)

Rated Plant capacity = *Moped : 180000 tubes/annum*
Bus Truck : 432000 tubes/annum
Flap : 360000 per day.

(AMOUNT - IN THOUSAND RUPEES)

LAND & BUILDING

(Land 30 acres) Rs. 1,46,450.00

PLANT & MACHINERY

1. Rubber mixing mill size 16" X 42" complete with chilled cast iron reduction gear 12" centre with
2. 60 H.P. 960 RPM, TEFC slip ring motor with starter, dectromagnetic brake, etc.
3. Rubber mixing mill 32" X 86" with 120 H.P., 1000 RPM motor complete with all accessories.
4. Vertical tread calender of size 6'X 14' complete with drive arrangement and 5 HP motor and all accessories.
5. Vertical tread calender 12' X 28' size with 20 H.P. motor and accessories.
6. Tyre vulcanizing press complete with sets of moulds, hydraulic pump and accessories.
7. Air bag vulcanizing press complete with mould.
8. Rubber spreading 60" X 18" braided type complete with electrical and mechanical drives, steam chest
9. Rubberised rolls of 8" dia and all other accessories.
10. Rubber spreading machine 120" X 36" long braided type complete with -

11. electrical and mechanical drives, steam chest, rubberised rolls and other accessories.
12. Rubber solution mixer size, 2'X 3' (double drum) connected with 5 HP motor.
13. Tyre building machine complete with electrical accessories.
14. Fabric slitting machine
15. Spool wrapping machine
16. Value nut punching machine
17. Chilling plant 10 tons capacity
18. Rubber compounding machine size 14" X 16" made of mild steel 30 RPM motor of 5 HP.
19. Rubber extruder with 5 HP motor and double jacketed steel body with cooling arrangement.
20. Tube vulcanizing system.
21. Mandrel made of aluminium
22. Automatic edge cutter
23. Tyre vulcanizer complete with trolly arrangements, hinged doors and all other accessories.
24. Extruder complete with electrical/ mechanical drives and all accessories.
25. Tyre vulcanizing press, complete with sets of moulds, hydraulic pump and all accessories.
26. Hoist, compressor, motor, agitator etc.
27. Tanks
28. Boiler (oil fired) : 10 MT/hr. evaporation capacity with all accessories.
29. Stand by electric power generation arrangements
30. Transformer
31. Valve nut tighting machine

TOTAL **Rs. 4,45,550.03**

OTHER FIXED ASSETS Rs. 1,09,500.00

WORKING CAPITAL REQUIREMENT/MONTH

RAW MATERIALS

1. **FOR TUBE** : Butyl Rubber
2. G.R.F.Black (M-660)
3. Paraffin oil
4. Zinc oxide
5. Stearic acid
6. T M.T.
7. MBT
8. Sulphur
9. **FOR TYRE :-**
   SBR (1712)
10. FEF Black
11. SRF Black
12. Paraffin oil
13. Coumarie resin
14. Zinc oxide
15. Stearic acid
16. Vulkanox 4020
17. Vulkacite MOZ
18. Paraffin wax
19. M.B.T.
20. M B T S
21. Sulphur
22. Fabric
23. Wire ring

TOTAL **Rs. 1,99,572.75**

TOTAL WORKING CAPITAL/MONTH

1.	RAW MATERIAL	Rs.	1,99,572.75
2.	SALARY & WAGES	Rs.	10,990.25
3.	UTILITIES & OVERHEADS	Rs.	31,000.00
	TOTAL	**Rs.**	**2,41,563.00**

TOTAL CAPITAL INVESTMENT

TOTAL FIXED CAPITAL	Rs. 7,01,500.03
TOTAL WORKING CAPITAL	Rs. 7,24,689.00
TOTAL	**Rs. 14,26,189.03**

TURN OVER/ANNUM

1. By sale of Moped tyre
2. Moped tube
3. Truck tyre
4. Truck tubes
5. Flaps

TOTAL **Rs. 38,04,300.00**

PROFIT SALES RATIO = Profit / Sales x 100 = 13.86 %

RATE OF RETURN = Operating profit / T.C.I x 100 = 37.05 %

BREAK EVEN POINT (B.E.P) = 51.63 %

FLAP PRESS

PLANT ECONOMICS OF TYRE RETREADING BY COLD PROCESS

Rated Plant capacity = 60.00 NOS/day

LAND & BUILDING

(Total area required 2000 Sq.Mt.) Rs. 24,30,000.00

PLANT & MACHINERY

1. One full circle tyre-retreading plant, suitable for retreading truck,& bus tyres, pneumatically operated
2. One full circle tyre-retreading plant, suitable for retreading jeep & car tyres, pneumatically operated
3. One full circle tyre-retreading plant, suitable for retreading scooter tyres, with 3 set of matrices.
4. Boiler complete with safety valves etc.
5. One Buffer *i.e.* Buffing Machine with 5 H.P. Motor
6. Air compressor
7. Hand Buffer
8. Cut repairing machine
9. Tyre-spreader
10. Miscellaneous tools like hammer,

TOTAL Rs. 3,14,000.00

OTHER FIXED ASSETS Rs. 85,000.00

WORKING CAPITAL REQUIREMENT/MONTH

RAW MATERIALS

1. Used Tyres
2. 500 Car/Tractor
3. 250 Scooter Tyres

4. Rubber Retread Compounds
5. Other miscellaenous chemicals like solvent oil, Gum based adhesives etc.
6. Rubber adhesives

TOTAL	**Rs.**	**5,71,667.00**

TOTAL WORKING CAPITAL/MONTH

1. RAW MATERIAL	Rs.	5,71,667.00
2. SALARY & WAGES	Rs.	39,687.50
3. UTILITIES & OVERHEADS	Rs.	67,500.00
TOTAL	**Rs.**	**6,78,854.50**

TOTAL CAPITAL INVESTMENT

TOTAL FIXED CAPITAL	Rs.	28,29,000.00
TOTAL WORKING CAPITAL	Rs.	20,36,563.50
TOTAL	**Rs.**	**48,65,563.50**

TURN OVER/ANNUM

1. Receipt through sale of 9000 truck tyres
2. Receipt through sale of 6000 car tyre
3. Receipt throught sale of 3000 Scooter tyres

TOTAL	**Rs. 1,08,00,000.00**

PROFIT SALES RATIO = Profit / Sales x 100 = 14.01 %

RATE OF RETURN = Operating profit / T.C.I x 100 = 31.09 %

BREAK EVEN POINT (B.E.P) = 52.22 %

32
Details of Rubber Processing Equipments and Machineries

RUBBER MIXING MILLS

Rubber Mixing Mills are designed for a rapid and homogenous mastication and Mixing of natural and Synthetic Rubber, Beckolite, Melomine, P.V.C and Industrial chemicals with other compounding ingredients as per desired specification. The Mixing Mills are supplied with chilled Cast Iron Rolls with efficient cooling and heating system. Reduction gear unit. Electric motor, starter and electro magnetic brake for emergency stoppage on request.

Model Nos.		RMM 1	RMM 2	RMM 3	RMM 4	RMM 5	RMM6	RMM 7
Roll dia	Inc. mm	6" 150	8" 200	10" 250	12" 300	14" 350	16" 400	22" 550
Face Width	Inc. mm	16" 400	18" 450	24" 600	30" 750	36" 900	42" 1050	60" 1500
Batch cap	kg	2	4	8	20	30	40	100
Motor	H.P. R.M.P.	7.5 960	10 960	20 960	30 960	40 960	60 960	125 960
Worm Type gear box	Ratio	10:1	10:1	10:1	10:1	10:1	10:1	10:1
Helical gear box (V-Beltdriven)	Ratio	4:1	4:1	4:1	4:1	4:1	4:1	4:1

RUBBER MIXING MILL

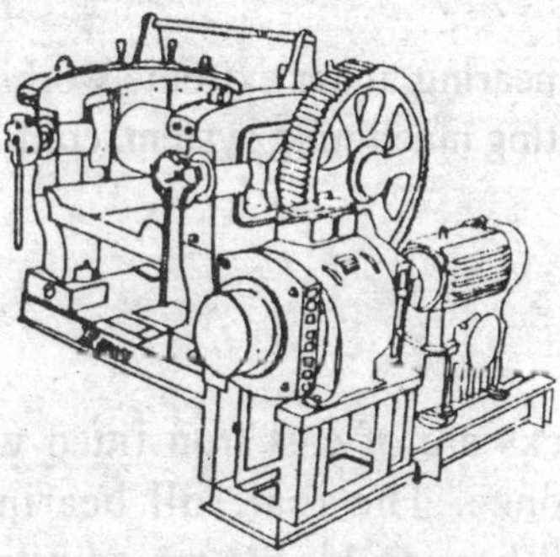

RUBBER MIXING
MILL WITH REDICON
GEAR BOX

SALIENT FEATURES

BASIC RMM SERIES

RMM series cover Rubber Mixing Mill from laboratory to production sizes. These are extra heavy duty models with comparable sizes and are of sturdy design and construction. Although many, of the machine characteristics are identical in various Rubber Mixing Mills manufactured all over India. It will be interesting to note that ours is a more or less self contained unit, relating to design machining and testing facilities. Design efficiency relating to rigidity were checked by preliminary study of scale models and finally by inspection of finished in our factory.

BASE PLATE

The main base plate will be of chanel steel fabrication and has perfectly machined top & bottom surface it required no foundation. Can be installed & operated on upper floors of the building or in basement. Economic and easy to remove or re-install.

STAND AND CAPS

Well designed for load bearing under extreme working conditions, Graded casting with single setting machining system, confirms consistent accuracy and alignments.

BEARING BLOCK

The rolls bearings blocks are of cast iron fitted with full circle gun metal/Phosphorous bronze. The rear roll bearing blocks are stationary while the front roll bearing blocks are adjustable by means of screw with square threads.

ROLLS

The machine is provided with chilled alloy cast iron rolls/carbon steel rolls hollowed for efficient cooling/heating are provided. Depth of the chill is taken care of normal wear, journals of rolls are machine ground.

WORM GEAR BOXES

RADICON/ELECON worm reduction gear box of appropriate specifications ratio 10:1 with torque absorping coupling on motor and machine ends are provided for climbinating power losses.

HELICAL GEAR BOX

Self designed and manufactured, V-Belt driven type helical gear box ratio 4:1 is perfectly alignment having balance class IV steel shafts and helical machine-cut gears. Driven in roller and Ball Bearings. Driven shaft of the Gear box has the pinion for power transmission to big super gear, having hob cut helical teeth and machined all round and balanced.

MATERIAL SPECIFICATION

Roller	Chilled cast iron
Hardness & depth	500 BHN. 12 to 35 mm
Friction gears	EN.9 forged steel hob cut
Bull gear	Graded casting/Railway wheel/steel fabricated
Driving pinion	EN. forged steel hob cut
Frame	Graded cast iron
Caps	Graded cast iron
Bearing	Gun metal/Phosphorous bronze
Bearing hausing	Cast iron
Bed plate	Channel steel fabricated
Lubrication System	Dip lubrication & forced lubrication pump also be supplied on request in suitable ratio.

ACCESSORIES

Gear covers, receiving tray, lubrication glass, water cups for cooling of rolls.

EXTRA ACCESSORIES

Electro Magnetic brake, Safety trip switch, Manual-cutter, Rotory joints, Forced lubrication-pump, Motorised nip roll adjustment.

HYDRAULIC PRESS

The application of Hydraulics in Rubber Processing through Hydraulic Presses is most convenient and effective method. Upstroking, Hot Platen Hydraulic Presses serve the purpose more sufficiently and conveniently.

ZERO DEFLECTION

The rugged design of press frames reduces the deflection of platens to practically zero at full load moulding, resulting in uniform moulding force over the entire platen surface.

ONE-PIECE CYLINDER

Cylinders are one-piece. No welding or fabricated cylinders- No failures.

GLAND RING WITH ZERO LOADING

Specially designed cylinder assembly assures nearly zero load on gland and studs for accurate and safe working of chevron packers. "No gland stud breaking at all".

CHEVRON PACKINGS

Well designed, endless Chevron Packings are made out of oil resistant nitrile rubber with accurate lips for positive sealing. This gives practice "Zero-leak" at all pressures.

RAM

Solid ram, machined, ground and hard chrome plated to give long life to chevron packings. It does not rust in idle periods.

PLATENS

Accurately machined with precisely pitched steam or electrical heating channels for absolutely even temperature distribution over the entire surface.

POWER PACK

Single discharged piston pumps. Double discharge "Standard Hydraulic" power packs for fast closing of press with slow pressing action.

HYDRAULIC PRESSES SINGLE UNITS FRAME TYPE

Single units in platen size 12" x 12" to 60" x 60" or more in single and multi daylight models in steam or electrically heated versions, with manual semi automatic and automatic operation. Capacity : 30 to 500 tons.

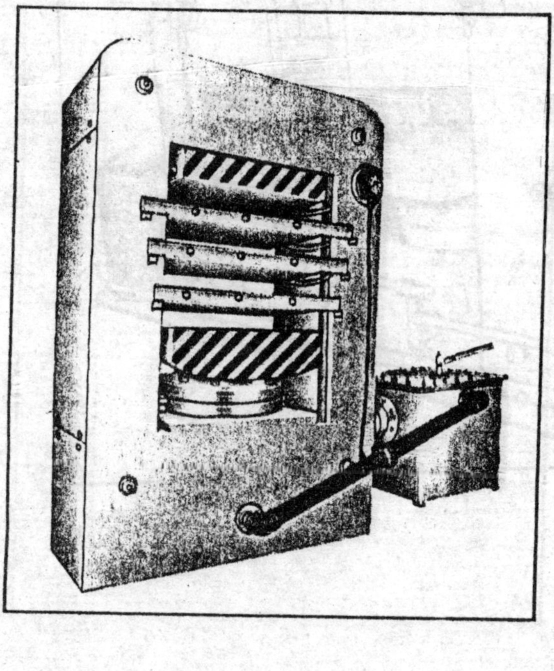

BATTERY OF PRESSES

Battery of 2,3 or 4 presses driven by common power pack to save floor space to maximise utilisation of labour and for mass production of similar components.

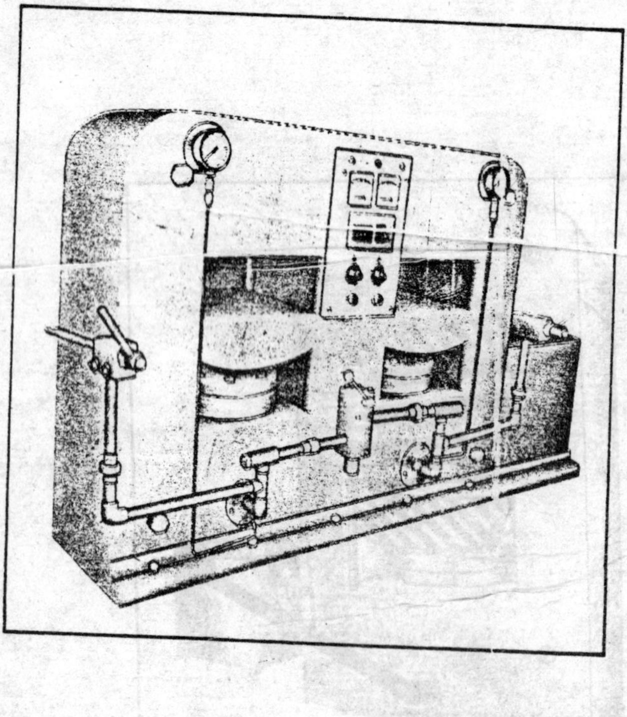

PRE QURED TREAD RUBBER PRESS

Pre-qured Tread Rubber Press is a sophisticated, heavy duty machine. It's construction is very sturdy and completely concealed. It is unique as it can be fitted with variable lengths of press and variable platen widths. This precision built machine ensures consistant non- porous High density tread rubber production. Two, three, Four numbers of standards daylights are provided and can be varied. The six hydraulic cylinders of the press ensures equal & constant pressure. It has an easier and safer loading and unloading system.

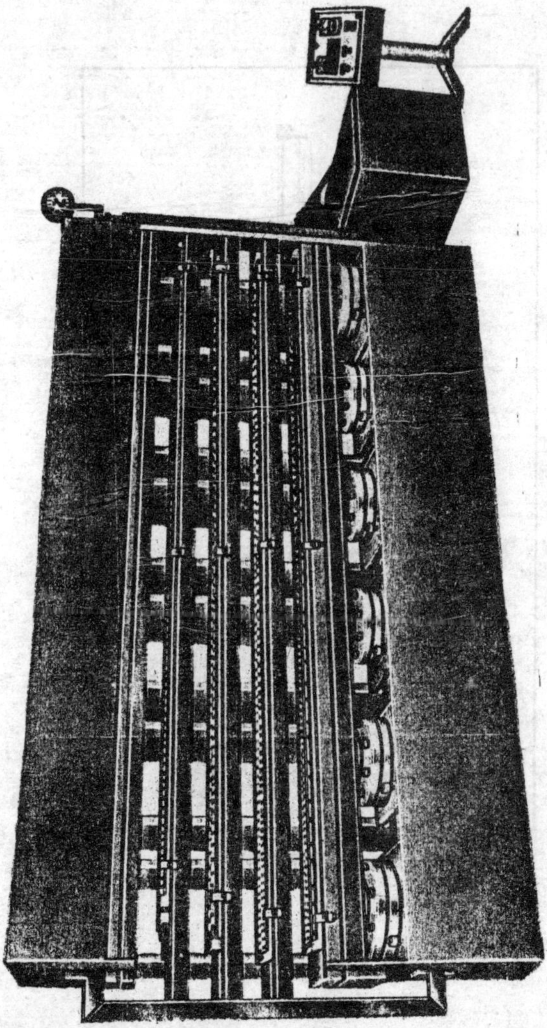

RUBBER BALE CUTTER

Primary need in rubber Industry is to cut natural/synthetic rubber bales to desired sizes/pieces.

Bale cutting Machine, serving this need, is hydraulically operated down-stroking cutting machine with sharp alloy-steel blade. The table to rest bulky bales, consists of idler rollers on which the bale could be moved easily. The appropriate cutting pressure optimum speed is the essence of Rubber Bale Cutter design.

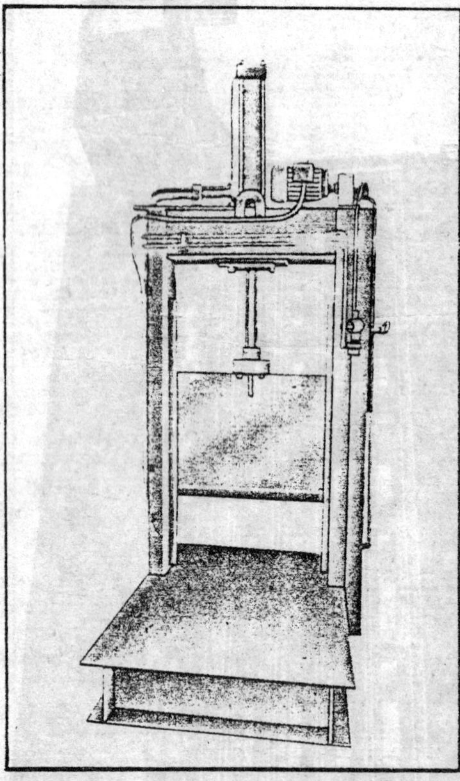

RUBBER BALE CUTTER

FLAP PRESS

High Quality-Sturdy-Reliable Versatile & Simple in operation for tyre, tubes & flap. With gear pump, semi automatic, fully automatic power pack.

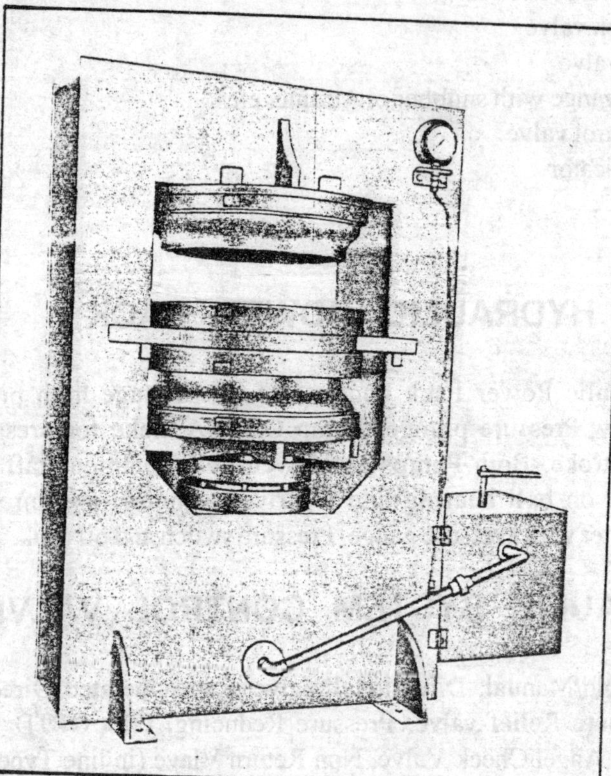

FLAP PRESS

SEMI/AUTOMATIC POWER PACK

The high pressure pump is coupled to the electric motor and is mounted either on tank or on separate base plates.

The other components include :-

1. Solenoid/pilot operated DC valve
2. Safety relief valve
3. Low pressure relief valve
4. Non return valve
5. Exhaust valve
6. Pressure gauge with snubber oil strainer etc.
7. Flow control valve.
8. Level indicator
9. Breather
10. Strainer

HYDRAULIC POWER PACK

Hydraulic Power Pack consists of a two stage high pressure pump for low Pressure .plunger Pump OSAKA make for pressing at the end of stroke. Both Pumps are driven by a common staff which is supported on ball bearing and is driven - motor, pressure relief valve, Oil Filter with Pressure gauge, Pressure switch and oil tank.

HYDRAULIC SYSTEM CONTROL VALVES

Solenoid/Manual, Directional Valve, Cam Operated Directional Valve, Pressure Relief valve, Pressure Reducing, Pilot OPTD. Check Valve, Right Angel Check Valve, Non Return Vlave (in line Type) Flow Control Valve, Pressure Compensated, Flow regulator Valve, Power Saving Valve, Yuken, Polyhydron, Dounty, Standard Make Hydraulic Equipments.

DISPERSION KNEADER

Dispersion Kneader is a rugged and versatile machine for fast mixing of material. The machine is designed to suit for vaired nature of dispersion kneading jobs. It is available in four different models ranging from a capacity of 25 litres to 75 litres. Tilting arrangement provide for taking out the mixed products.

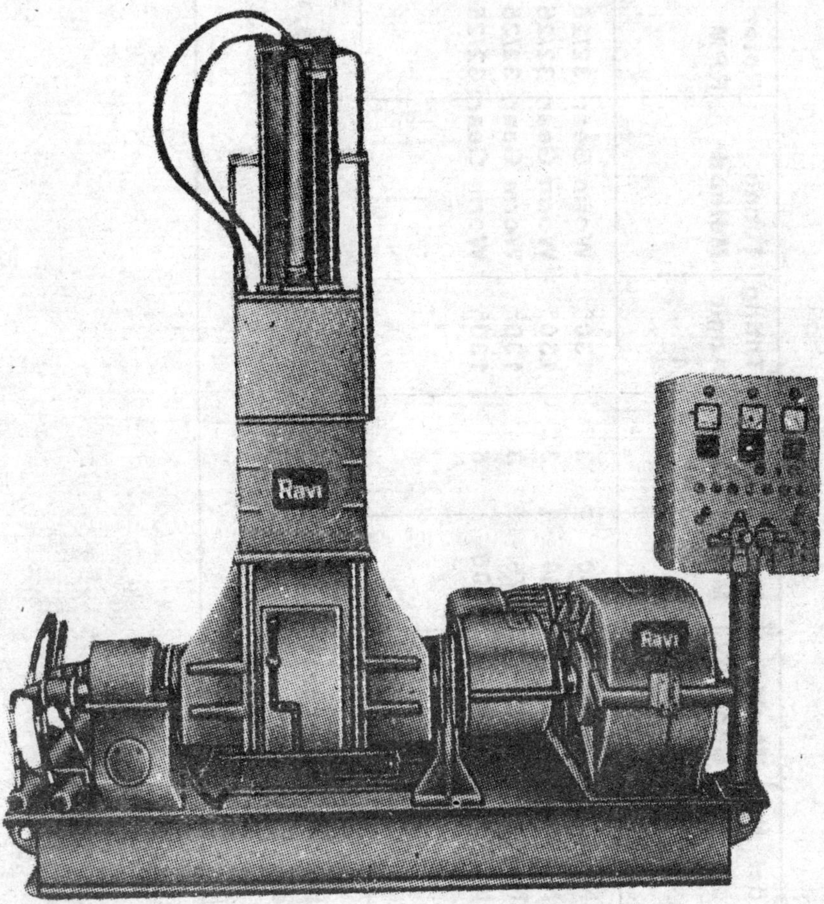

Model No.	Working Capacity (in liters)	Main Motor	Tilting Motor (H.P.)	Tilting Angle	Tilting Method	Rotor RPM	Required Compresser (H.P.)	Dust Collector Motor
R.N.25	25	40	2	130°	Worm Gear	32/25	5	2 H.P.
R.N.35	35	60	3	130°	Worm Gear	32/25	5	2 H.P.
R.N.55	55	75	3	130°	Worm Gear	32/25	5	2 H.P.
R.N.75	75	100	5	130°	Worm Gear	32/25	5	2 H.P.

Technological improvements may result in change specifications, which customer will have to accept.

FEATURES

MAXIMUM DISPERSION

Double blades, proper clearance and high cooling effect jacket construction enable maximum dispersion.

MORE THREE TIMES OUT PUT

Kneader out put four times than mixing mill with lower labour & electricity.

ROTORS

The integral part of the whole machine the Rotor is manufactured out of high alloy steel. The edges of the rotors are "Stelite" and finally grounded on a profile grinding machine. These Rotor are also tested to check for any possible leakages before mounting. The temperature in the Rotors can be varied through the water path provided in them.

THERMOCOUPLE

The thermocouple is projected into mixing chamber, temperature measurement can be done more accurately.

MECHANICAL PACKING

Special alloy for Rotor contact surface and new materials for packing. Replacement and cleaning of packing are done with a simplified manner.

COMMON BED

The machine has common bed on to which mixer, reducer and motors are compactly arranged. Common bed for easy installation. No need for designing of foundation.

APPLICATION

Rubber compound for Hawai Chappal, Micro Sheet, Tyre & Tube, Gasket, Hoses, V-Belt, Rubber Sheet, Battery container and other type of Rubber compound.

PLASTICS

Plastics Moulded Products, Compounds, Engineering Plastics.

ELECTRICALS

Magnetic Tapes.

CALENDER MACHINE

Description and Techenical Specification of Calender Machines

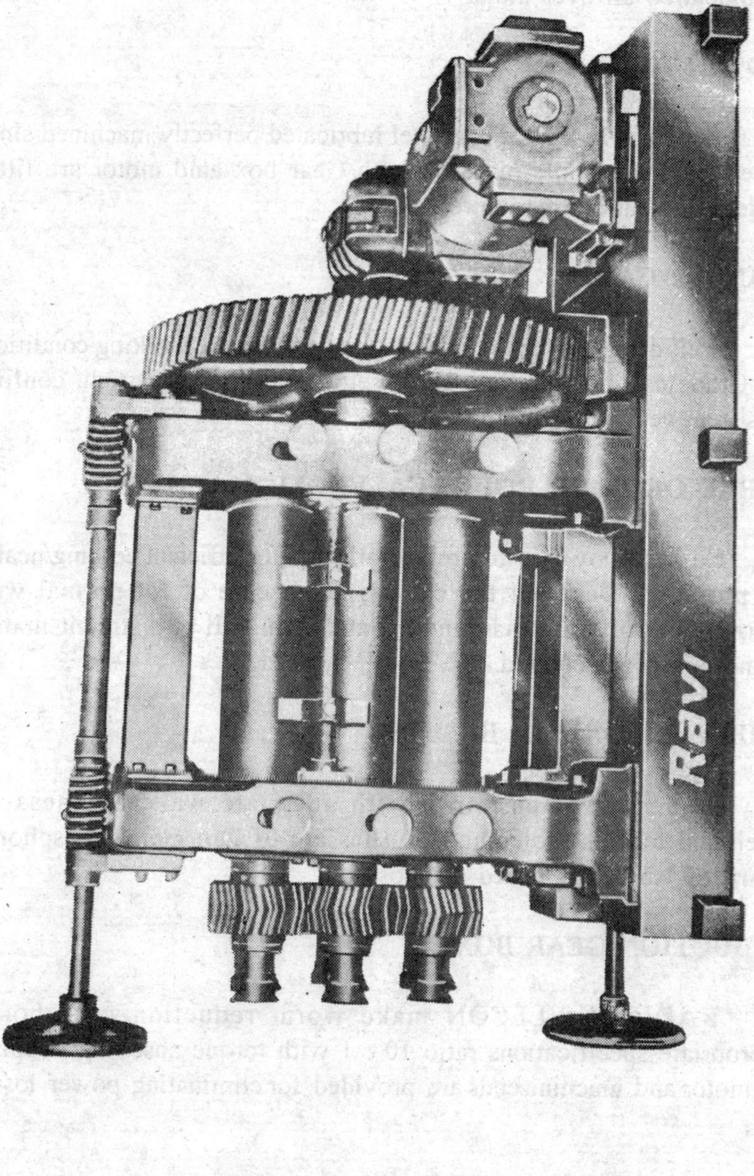

BASIC C.M. SERIES

These are extra heavy duty models with comparable sizes and are sturdy design and construction. Although many of the machine characterstics are identical in various Calender Machines manufactured all over india.

BED PLATE

The basic bed-plate is a steel fabricated perfectly machined single piece on which whole machine with Gear box amd motor are fitted. No deep foundation are required.

STAND & CAPS

Well designed for load bearing under extreme working conditions, A - Grade casting steel fabricated setting machining system, confirms consistent accuracy and alignments.

THREE OR FOUR ROLLS CALENDER MACHINE

Chilled alloy cast iron rolls, hollowed for efficient cooling/heating are provided. Depth of the chill is taken care of for normal wear. Journals of rolls are machine ground. Nip roll adjustment manual or motorised as required.

JOURNAL BOXES & BUSHES

Made out of cast iron with adequate wall thickness and machined to close tolerance. Bushes are of gun metal/phosphorous bronze of laboratory tested composition.

REDUCTION GEAR BOXES

RADICON/ELECON make worm reduction gear box of appropriate specifications ratio 10 : 1 with torque absobing couplings on motor and machine ends are provided for climinating power losses.

CAPACITIES OF CALENDER MACHINES

Type	Calender Machines				Required Electric Motor	
	Roll Size		Size in mm		H.P.	RPM
Model Nos.	Dia	Length	Did	Length		
C.M.1	6"	18"	150	450	5	960
C.M.2	8"	24"	200	600	10	960
C.M.3	10"	30"	250	750	15	960
C.M.4	12"	36"	300	900	25	990
C.M.5	14"	42"	350	1050	30	960
C.M.6	16"	48"	400	1250	40	960

EXTRUDER MACHINE

Discription & Technical Specification of

RUBBER EXTRUDER MACHINE

FEATURES OF RUBBER EXTRUDER MACHINE

BASIC E.M. SERIES

E.M. series cover Rubber Extruder Machines from laboratory to products sizes. These are extra heavy duty models with comparable sizes and are of sturdy design and construction. Alongwith many of the machines characterstics are identical in various Rubber Extruder Machines manufactured all over India.

BED PLATE

The basic bed plate is heavily steel fabricated/cast iron perfectly machined single place on which whole machine with gear box & motor can be fitted which not required foundation.

WORM

The Mill cut & polished worm of steel is used in single double and tripple feed type and can be brought out from the machine by removing a single nut and provision for water cooling to maintain the temperature of machine.

BEARINGS

Jacketed with heavy duty single, double taper roller as per extruder loads.

DRIVE

Worm directly connected with cast iron/steel casting helical gear or connected with antivibration flexible coupling with worm reduction gear box of RADICON/ELECON Make.

HEATING & COOLING

Cast iron/steel fabricated body jacketed for water coolant and steam heating system.

CAPACITIES OF RUBBER EXTRUDER MACHINES

Model No.	Dia of Worm	Required H.P.	R.P.M Worm	Capacity in Kgs. per Hour
E.M. 1	1"	2	50	25
E.M. 2	2"	3	45	50
E.M. 3	3"	5	35	75
E.M. 4	4"	15	28	100
E.M. 5	4-1/2"	20	25	125
E.M. 6	6"	25	22	150
E.M. 7	8"	40	18	200

Note : All the above machineries details and pictures have been provided by **M/s. Ravi Engineering Works, New Delhi.**

124. ACRYLIC FIBRES
125. AUTO PISTON & PISTON RING (Piston Assembly - Al. Alloy)
126. ASPIRIN
127. AUTOMATIC PLANT for toffee/ Candy Manufacture
128. ATRAZIN PESTICIDE
129. AMMONIA LIQUOR
130. ACRYLIC YARN
131. ADHESIVE FOR CORRUGATION DRY POWDER & PASTE
132. AUTOMATIC CANDLE UNIT
133. ALUMINIUM KNOBS (for Domestic Electric Appliances)
134. ACETYLENE BLACK (CARBON BLACK)
135. ADHESIVE POWDER for Electric Lamps
136. ALUMINIUM CIRCLE
137 ALUMINIUM HYDROXIDE
138. AMMONIUM DI-CHROMATE
139. AUTO SPOKES
140. ANGORA RABBIT WOOL
141. AAC & ACSR ALUMINIUM CONDUCTORS
142. ALUMINIUM CANS FOR CAPACITORS
143. AMMONIUM SULPHATE
144. AUTOMATIC VENDING MACHINE FOR HOT & COLD BEVERAGES
145. ASBESTOS FIBRE
146. ACRYLIC SHEET & MOULDED PRODUCTS
147. AUTOMOBILE POLISH
148. ASPHALTIC ROOFING SHEET
149. ASH TRAYS for Maruti Cars
150. ADHESIVE TAPES (Pressure Sensitive)
151. ALUMINIUM/STAINLESS STEEL PRESSURE COOKER & WATER FILTER
152. ADHESIVE (For Photo Album)
153. ACTIVATED CARBON from Rice Husk
154. AUTOMOBILE BLINKERS
155. ASAFOETIDA (HING)
156. AUTOMOBILE GASKET
157. ACETYLENE GAS
158. ANTISTATIC POLYTHENE BAGS
159. ALUMINIUM SILICATE
160. ARTIFICIAL FISH MEAL for Poultry Feed
161. AMMONIUM CHLORIDE TABLETS
162. AUTOMOBILE PARTS FOR MARUTI VEHICLE
163. AUTOMOBILE PART
164. AUTOMOBILE RUBBER PARTS
165. AZO-DYE STUFFS
166. AUDIO CASSETTES SCREW
167. AUTO TELEPHONE RECORDING & ANSWERING M/C.
168. AUTO GEARS
169. ABRASIVE PAPER
170. ALUMINIUM UTENSIL
171. ACRYLIC & COTTON YARN SPINDLES
172. AUTO PART (Rubber)
173. ABRASIVE (Carborandam Cloth)
174. AGRICULTURAL & GARDENING HOSE PIPE
175. ABRASIVE EMERY
176. BULK DRUGS
177. BUTTON FROM HOOVE HORN
178. BALL BEARING
179. B.O.P.P ADHESIVE TAPES
180. BESAN PLANT
181. BORAX

182. BLANKETS
183. BIO COAL From Agro Waste
184. BLEACHING DYEING, PRINTING/ FINISHING OF CLOTH
185. BRAKE LININGS
186. BALL POINT PEN REFILLS & INKS
187. BED SHEET, BED COVERS, FURNISHING, ETC.
188. BRAKE OIL, COOLANT & PACKING OF LUBE OIL & GREASE
189. BRAKE OIL
190. BRASS/COPPER SHEET CIRCLES & UTENSILS
191. BLACK/WHITE TV PICTURE TUBE
192. BOILER DE-SCALING COMPOUNDS
193. BLISTER FILM PVC
194. BI-METAL BUSHES
195. BLACK PEPPER
196. BAMBOO STICKS FOR AGARBATTIES
197. BOOT/SHOE POLISH
198. BORIC ACID
191. BARIUM COMPOUND
192. BEER PLANTS
193. BLEACHING LIQUOR (Calcium Hypo Chlorite Liquor)
194. BRA & PANTY (HOSIERY)
195. BANANA PUREE
196. BREAD PLANT
197. BLACK & GALVANIZED STEEL CONDUIT PIPES
198. BINDIA & SINDUR
199. BUILDING HARDWARE OF ALUMINIUM
200. BASMATI RICE TRADING
201. BATTERY PLATE
202. BETA NAPHTHOLS
203. BLOWING AGENT
204. BENZYL BENZOATE
205. BUTT HINGES OF BRASS SHEET
206. BONE MILL
207. BARBED WIRE
208. BLOWMOULDED PLASTIC CONTAINER
209. BRICK from Fly Ash
210. BLOOD BAGS
211. B.P HARD COKE
212. BAKELITE MOULDED PRODUCTS
213. BITUMINOUS ROAD EMULSION
214. BADMINTON RACKETS
215. BOARD MILL BASED ON RICE STRAW
216. BLUE DETERGENT POWDER
217. BAKERS YEAST
218. BENZENE
219. BAND SAW BLADES
220. BRASS HOLDERS
221. BUFFING & POLISHING COMPOUNDS
222. BONE CRUSHING
223. BUS TRANSPORT COMPANY
224. BENZENE HEXA CHLORIDE
225. BANANA & ITS BYE PRODUCTS
226. BALLOONS (All Type)
227. BATTERY CONTAINER
228. BAKERY UNIT (Buns, Bread, Pastry, Cakes & Toffees)
229. BARIUM CARBONATE
230. BUBBLE GUM & CHEWING GUM
231. BABY DIAPERS
232. BRASS & COPPER TUBES
233. BI-CHROMATES OF SODIUM POTASSIUM & AMMONIUM
234. BITUMINIZED COMPOUND FOR WATER PROOFING
235. BOLTS (MILD STEEL)
236. BRANDY
237. BICYCLE PARTS
238. BAYGON SPRAY
239. BRIQUETTED FUEL FROM AGRO WASTE
240. BRASS UTENSILS
241. BANANA POWDER
242. BLOCK BOARD
243. BEES WAX
244. BLEACHING POWDER
245 .BUFFALO MEAT PROCESSING
246. BEES WAX REFINING & BLEACHING
247. BAKELITE SHEETS (PHENOLIC SHEETS) ELECTRICAL GRADE
248. BALL POINT PEN REFILLS

Price Rs.3000/- for each "Detailed Project Report" Payable in advance through Draft/Cash/M.O. in favour of "ENGINEERS INDIA RESEARCH INSTITUTE". Immediate Delivery or Ask by V.P.P. PH.: 2918117/ 2916431 Fax : 291 6431.

(100% EOU)
249. BUTTONS (PLASTIC) From Polyester Sheets & Rods
250. BAKING POWDER
251. BACTERICIDA FOR CANE JUICE
252. BOTTLING PLANT
253. BRASS SHEET ROLLING
254. BROILER CHICKEN
255. BARIYAN & PAPPAD
256. BITUMEN
257. BLOCK MAKING
258. BAKELITE ELECTRICAL ACCESSORIES (Switch, Socket, Plug)
259. BUSINESS CENTRE (JOB WORK)
260. BANQUET HALL
261. BENZYL PEROXIDE
262. BRASS PIPES
263. BRASS WARES
264. BUS AND TRUCK BODY BUILDING
265. BLEACHING & MORDANT DYEING OF YARN
266. BADMINTON SHUTTLE COCKS
267. BRASS STAIRCASE & WROUGHT IRON, RODS, RAILING, GATE & GRILL
268. BLEACHING & REFINING OF BEES WAX
269. CASSETTE RECORDER/ PLAYER (STEREO)-COST OF REPORT - Rs.2500/-
270. COLD PROCESSED TYRE RETREADING
271. CAMPHOR
272. CHINA CLAY
273. CRAYON WAX
274. CATTLE & POULTRY FEED
275. COPPER WIRE DRAWING & ENAMELING
276. COLD DRINKS
277. CORD LESS PHONE
278. CARBON DIOXIDE
279. CONCENTRATION OF MANGANESE ORE
280. COPPER & BRASS TUBES
281. CORRUGATED SHEET BOARD & BOXES
282. COPPER BOTTOM STAINLESS STEEL UTENSILS
283. CAR BURGLAR ALARM
284. COOLING COILS FOR AIR CONDITIONERS
285. CHOKES, TRANSFORMERS & ELIMINATORS
286. COLOUR LAB (QSS-PHOTO)
287. CANNED FRUITS & VEGETABLES
288. COMPUTER CONTI-NUOUS STATIONERY
289. COMPUTER ASSEMBLY
290. COMPUTER MONITOR
291. COOLANT ENGINE
292. CALCIUM CARBONATES
293. CIGARETTES
294. CALCIUM CARBIDE
295. CUTTING OIL
296. COLD STORAGE
297. COLD STORAGE & ICE
298. COTTON ADHESIVE TAPES & PLASTER OF PARIS BANDAGES For Hospital

EIRI
We Create Industrialists
Recipient of
Udyog Rattan Award

299. COLOUR & B/W TV
300. CAUSTIC SODA
301. CHOLORINATED PARAFFIN WAX
302. COSTUME JEWELRY
303. CEMENT PLANT
304. CHEESE (Processed)
305. COTTON SEED OIL
306. CARBON BLACK
307. CARBON ELECTRODE (for Battery Cell)
308. CEMENT ROOFING TILES
309. COTTON YARN
310. CONDUIT IRON PIPES (C.I.PIPES)
311. CARBONATED BEVERAGES
312. CHICKEN/MUTTON (SHEEP MEAT) PROCESSING
313. COIR FOAM (RUBBERIZED COIR) as Cushion & Mat etc.
314. CARBON BRUSHES
315. CONCRETE HOLLOW BRICK/ BLOCKS
316. CONDENSED MILK
317. COLD ROLLING MILL
318. CEMENT FROM RICE HUSK
319. COCONUT OIL
320. COPPER NITRATE
321. CONCENTRATE OF TOMATO (TOMATO PASTE)
322. CERAMIC TILES (GLAZED)
323. CONFERENCE BAG, FOLDERS ETC. (PLASTIC)
324. CHROME PLATED (C.P.) BATH ROOM FITTINGS
325. C.I. CASTINGS (FOUNDRY) BY INDUCTION FURNACE
326. CORN FLAKES
327. CERAMIC INSULATOR
328. CAPACITORS
329. CALCIUM SILICATE BLOCKS
330. COMPUTER RIBBON
331. CITRONELLA OIL
332. CINEMA HALL
333. CARD BOARD SLATE
334. COATING ON PLASTICS
335. CALCIUM CARBONATE BASED ON STEAM COAL
336. COPPER OXY-CHLORIDES
337. CARBON MONO-OXIDE for Water Gas
338. CELLULOSE ACETATE
339. CHAIN LINK FENCING OUT OF PVC COATED WIRE
340. CHEWING TOBACCO
341. CASING UNIT OF SAUSAGE FOOD (100% EOU)
342. CHROMIC ACID
343. COPPER PHTHALOCYNINE BLUE & GREEN
344. CHOCOLATE
345. COATED PAPER & BOARD (ART & CHROME)
346. CARPET WOOL YARN SPINNING
347. CITRIC ACID BY MOLASSES
348. CONVERTER
349. CHOKES & PATTIES
350. COPPER CLAD LAMINATES FOR PCB'S (PAPER & FABRIC BASED)
351. COPPER RODS from Scraps
352. COLLECTION OF MILK & PACKAGING IN POLYTHENE POUCHES (MILK CHILLING)
353. CANNING OF MANGO PULP & MANGO SLICES
354. CEMENT WATER PROOF COMPOUND
355. CYCLE TYRE & TUBES
356. CAFFEINE BY TEA WASTE
357. COURIER SERVICES
358. CHINESE SOYA SAUCE
359. CALCINED / PETROLEUM COKE
360. CONFECTIONERY
361. CUBICAL ELECTRICAL PANEL BOARD (SWITCH BOARD)
362. CALCIUM CARBONATE, MAGNESIUM CARBONATE & METAL FROM DOLOMITE
363. CALCIUM CASEINATE & SODIUM CASEINATE
364. CUSHION COMPOUND, THREAD & VULCANIZING SOLUTION, FORMULATION AND MANUFACTURE
365. CAR AIR FRESHNER
366. CASTOR OIL
367. CATTLE FEED
368. CARBON POTENTIO METERS
369. CAST STEEL PANS for Melting Furnace
370. CALCINING OF MANGANESE & DEAD BURNT MANGA-NESE
371. COAL BRIQUETTING FROM COAL
372. CYCLE & RIKSHAW FRAMES
373. COAL BRIQUETTES FROM AGRO WASTE

Price Rs.3000/- for each "Detailed Project Report" Payable in advance through Draft/Cash/M.O. in favour of "ENGINEERS INDIA RESEARCH INSTITUTE". Immediate Delivery or Ask by V.P.P. PH.: 2918117/ 2916431 Fax : 291 6431

374. COMPUTER RIBBON REFILLING & REINKING
375. COUNTRY LIQUOR
376. COPPER STRIPS COILS
377. CEILING FAN
388. CONCAST STEEL BAR
389. CRICKET BAT/BALL
390. COLD ROLLING OF STEEL STRIPS
391. CARTONS FOR DISTILLERY
392. COATING & PRINTING OF LAMINATED PAPER POUCH
393. CLAY PLATES FOR ELECTRIC HEATERS
394. CASHEWNUT SHELL LIQUID & KERNELS (CNSL)
395. CYANIDE ZINC BRIGHTENER
396. COUNTRY LIQUOR FROM MOLASSES
397. CARPET WOOLLEN YARN DYEING
398. COSMETIC UNIT
399. COMPOSITE CONTAINER
400. CASTOR OIL REFINING
401. CASTOR OIL HYDROGENATION
402. COPPER BERYLLIUM ALLOY SPRINGS
403. COLOUR MASTER BATCH FOR VARIOUS PLASTICS
404. CANDLE (Semi Automatic)
405. CAST IRON POWDER
406. COMPACT DISC PLAYER
407. COMPACT DISC (CD)
408. COTTON FINISHING
409. CONSTANT VOLTAGE TRANSFORMER (C.V.T.)
410. CASEIN BASED PIGMENTS USED IN SPORT INDUSTRY
411. CEMENT FROM RICE HUSK
412. CHROMIC ACID
413. CORROSION CONTROLLING CHEMICAL (Pipe Line)
414. CHICKEN/MEAT PROCESSING AND PACKAGING
415. COPPER FOIL
416. COMPUTER MONITOR TUBE & T.V. PICTURE TUBE (b/w)
417. CURRY POWDER
418. COPPER & BRASS INGOTS
419. CASHEWNUT (Dried & Fried)
420. CARD/GREY BOARD
421. COMPRESSOR (HERMETIC) FOR AIR CONDITIONER
422. CHLORAM PHENICOL
423. COATING ON PLASTICS & GLASS
424. CANDLE (NON DRIP)
425. CATTLE FEED BY TAPIOCA
426. CRYSTAL TABLEWARE
427. CHELATED ZINC (Zn-EDTA)
428. CRUCIBLE BY FIRE CLAY
429. CLUTCH WIRE FROM DRAWN WIRE
430. COCONUT PLANTATION
431. CHILLI POWDER
432. COMPUTER SOFTWARE
433. CHOCOLATE
434. CHEWING GINGER & AMLOKI
435. CHROME PLATING
436. CAUSTIC SODA/CHLORINE PLANT MEMBRANE CELL
437. CRACKING OF KERNELS (DESHELLING/DECORTICATING)
438. CARBON BRUSHES
439. CEMENT PAINT
440. CEMENT PLANT
441. CINNAMON BARK OIL
442. CLOVE OIL
443. CHOKE & STARTER
444. CINE-ARC- CARBON
445. CYLINDER LINERS FOR AUTOMOBILES
446. CANNING & PRESERVATION OF FRUIT & VEGETABLE
447. CANNING & PRESERVATION OF FRUITS & VEGETABLE WITH COLD STORAGE & RAISIN (KISMISH MAKING)
448. CROCKERY WARES
449. CASSETTE TAPES (COVER)
450. CHOKE OF FLUORESCENT TUBES
451. CANVAS SHOES, JUNGLE BOOT, RUBBER KNEES AND BOOT COMBAT
452. CALCIUM SILICATE
453. CLEANING OF COOLING SYSTEM & BOILER
454. CHEWING GUM
455. COPPER SULPHATE
456. CENTRIFUGAL PUMP
457. CRITICAL AUTO BODY SHEET METAL PARTS
458. CALCIUM GLUCONATE
459. COCONUT PRODUCTS & BYE PRODUCTS PROCESSING COMPLEX (Wet Fresh) 100% EOU
460. CELLULOSE POWDER & MICRO CRYSTALLINE CELLULOSE POWDER
461. CONVEYER BELTS
462. CYCLE HANDLE BAR GRIPS
463. COMPUTER FORMS AND SECURITY PRINTING PRESS
464. COIR INDUSTRY
465. CANVAS SHOES
466. CEMENT (CLINKER)
467. CARBON POWDER
468. COMPUTER JOB WORK
469. COSMETIC (HERBAL & SYNTHETIC)
470. C.N.S.L. BASED RESIN IN LIQUID & Powder Form
471. COTTON & ACRYLIC YARN SPINDLES
472. CO-EXTRUSION MULTI-LAYER FILM
473. CLOTH (Cotton Processing & Finishing of Cloth)
474. CERAMIC NOVELTIE
475. CASTOR OIL EMULSIFIER
476. CARBON BLACK from NATURAL GAS
477. CASEIN FROM MILK
478. CARPET WEAVING
479. CERAMIC TRANSFERS (FOR PRINTING ON CERAMICS)
480. CERAMIC COATED ALUMINIUM THREAD GUIDE
481. CERAMIC THREAD GUIDE
482. CABLES FOR CABLE NETWORK
483. CANNING OF ROSGULLAS IN METAL CANS
484. COLOURED FLAME CANDLE
485. CIGARETTE & BIDI
486. CUTTING & POLISHING OF SEMI PRECIOUS STONES
487. CALCIUM NITRATE
488. COMMUTATOR FOR ELECTRIC MOTOR
489. CUT FLOWER (FLORICULTURE)
490. CIDER PLANT (APPLE WINE)
491. COTTON BUDS/SWABS
492. COMPUTER ATTENDANCE REGISTER
493. COMPUTER PRINTER
494. CERAMIC FIRING/ DECORATIVE TILES
495. CHEMICAL LABORATORY
496. CERAMIC CROCKERY WARE (Bone China - Hitkari)
497. CHEMICAL RESISTANT IRON & STEEL
498. CEMENT POLE, JALLIE & TILE
499. COATING ON METALLIZED POLYE-STER FILM/ METALLIZED PAPER/ ALUMINIUM FOILS
500. CERAMIC GLAZED TILES
501. COOLER BODY & TRUNK (FABRICATION UNIT)
502. CHEMICAL ETCHING OF STAINLESS STEEL
503. CATIONIC SOFTENER
504. COSMETIC, DETERGENT POWDER & PERFUMERY COMPOUND
505. CLUTCH PLATE FOR 4 WHEELERS
506. CHEMICAL LAMINATION OF PHOTO
507. COUNTRY LIQUOR
508. CANNING & BOTTLING of Fruits & Vegetabe Products
509. CEMENT GRINDING
510. CEMENT OXIDE
511. COBALT OCTOATE
522. CITRONELLA OIL
523. CATECHU (KATTHA) - Chemical Process
524. COMPUTER KEY-BOARD
525. CARPET DRY CLEANING
526. CONDENSER FOR MOTOR
527. CAR AIR CONDITIONERS
528. COAL GRINDING
529. CHLORINATED Rubber Based Plant
530. COCOA POWDER
531. CATTLE BREEDING
532. COTTON ROLLS
533. CLUTCH PLATE FOR 3 WHEELER

534. CARBOXY METHYL CELULOSE
535. CERAMIC MAGNET
536. COLD CREAMS
537. COSTUME/IMITATION/ ARTIFICIAL JEWELRY (CHAINS & BANGLES)
538. COMPUTER EDUCATION INSTITUTE
539. CARD BOARD MATCH BOX
540. C.I. POWDER BY GRINDING PROCESS
541. CONCENTRATE OF ROSE, JASMINE & LILLY EXTRACT
542. COPPER WINDING FOR SUBMERSIBLE PUMP & MOTOR
543. COMPACT FLUORESCENT TUBES
544. CARDINAL FROM C.N.S.L. (Cashewnut Shell Liquid)
545. CAPACITOR DISCHARGE IGNITION (CIDI Unit)
546. CLEANING POWDER (VIM)
547. CONE FOR SOFTY ICE CREAM
548. CORRUGATION OF PLAIN GALVANIZED SHEET
549. CYCLE SPOKES
550. CREPE BANDAGES
551. CASHEWNUT KERNEL EXTRACTION FROM CASHEWNUT FRUIT
552. CORN FLAKES
553. CIGARETTE (Herbal)
554. COTTON GINNING & PRESSING
555. COMPUTER PERIPHERALS
556. COMPUTER HARDWARE
557. COMPACT DISC PLAYER (AUDIO/VIDEO)
558. CARBON ZINC CELL (DRY CELL)
559. CUTTING OIL
560. CANDY HARD BOILED
561. CO_2 WELDING WIRE
562. CASHEW FENI (WINE DISTILLATION FROM FRUITS & CASHEWNUT)
563. CLUTCH FACING & BRAKE LINING
564. CARD BOARD BOXES & CARTONS (System Pack)
565. CAR PAINTS
566. CAR POLISHES
567. CEMENT TILES (LAYING OVER RCC ROOFS)
568. COPPER POWDER
569. CLEAR TRANSPARENT LACQUER FOR COATING ON BRASS BANGLES TO MAKE IT WEATHER RESISTANT
570. COPPER EXTRACTION FROM PCB WASTES
571. CASTOR OIL DERIVATIVE OLEORESIN - Cost Rs.2500/-
572. CLINICAL THERMOMETER
573. CAMEL BLACK (TREAD RUBBER)
574. COLD PROCESSED TREAD RUBBER

575. DALIA (WHEAT PORRIDGE)
576. DAIRY FARMING
577. DISPOSABLE PLASTIC SYRINGES (STERILIZED)
578. DISPOSABLE PLASTIC CUPS, GLASSES, ETC.
579. DETERGENT POWDER
580. DISTILLED WATER AMPOULES
581. DAIRY FARM & PRODUCTS
582. DETERGENT CAKE & POWDER
583. DECORATIVE LAMINATED SHEET (SUNMICA)
584. D.T.P. & OFFSET PRESS
585. DESK TOP PUBLISHING (DTP)
586. DUPLICATING STENCIL PAPER
587. DYE STUFFS
588. DAIRY PRODUCTS
589. DAIRY PRODUCTS & MILK PACKAGING IN POUCHES
590. DI-OCTYL PHTHALATE (DOP)
591. DALL/PULSE MILL
592. DISTRIBUTION TRANS-FORMER
593. DEHYDRATED ONIONS & ONION POWDER
594. DUPLEX/FILE BOARD
595. DEHYDRATION OF FRUITS & VEGETABLES
596. DEXTROSE SALINE
597. DRY ICE
598. DOOR BELL
599. DEXTROSE FROM POTATO
600. DRY DISTEMPER & LIME COLOURS
601. DI-CALCIUM PHOSPHATE FROM ANIMAL BONES
602. DI-CALCIUM PHOSPHATE FROM ROCK PHOSPHATE
603. DRY GINGER
604. DEHYDRATED GARLIC FLAKES
605. DIGITAL ELECTRONIC WATCHES
606. DISTILLATION OF ROSIN AND TURPENTINE
607. DIAMOND IMPREGNATED SEGMENTS (METAL BONDED) FOR MARBLE SAWING
608. DI-NITRO CHLORO BENZENE (D.N.C.B.)
609. DYE INTERMEDIATE
610. DI-ETHYL PHTHALATE (DEP)
611. DROSS LEAD SCRAP, LEAD POWDER
612. DODECYCLE BENZENE SULPHONATE
613. DISTILLED WATER
614. DAIRY FARM & MILK PDTS.
615. DISPOSABLE CIGARETTE GAS LIGHTER
616. DEXTRIN & STARCH BASED ADHESIVE
617. DEXTRIN
618. DEXTROSE 5%
619. DISPOSABLE NEEDLES
620. DESICCATED COCONUT POWDER
621. DIE MAKING for Sheet Metal Working
622. DHOOP BATTI STICK
623. DIAMOND TOOLS for Cutting / Drilling & Polishing
624. DIRECT BLACK DYE
625. DAIRY PLANT
626. D.G. SET
627. DISH ANTENNA
628. DEXTROSE POWDER FROM STARCH
629. DRY CELL
630. DRYING OF RED CHILLIES, HALDI, DHANIA, PEAS, AND GREEN PEAS
631. DYE FIXING AGENTS
632. DISH ANTENNA & SATELLITE EQUIPMENTS.
633. DEHYDRATION OF VEGETABLES
634. DEHYDRATED CASTOR OIL
635. DIAMOND CUTTING & EXPORT
636. DEPARTMENTAL STORE
637. DRY CELLS & STORAGE BATTERIES
638. DIAZO COATING LUMINES-CENT PIGMENT
639. DENIM JEANS & JACKETS
640. DETTOL TYPE ANTISEPTIC LOTION
641. DRY FRUIT ROASTING & PACKING
642. DEHYDRATION AND CANNING OF FRUITS & VEGETABLES
643. DIRECT COTTON DYE (No Cost Estimation)
644. DENIM CLOTH
645. DIARY EQUIPMENT
646. DUPLICATION INK
647. 4,4-DIAMINO STILBENE 2,2-DISULPHONIC ACID
648. DRUM CLOSURES
649. DI-ETHYL OXALATE
650. DEHYDRATION OF FRUITS, VEGETABLES & NON-VEGETABLE PRODUCTS (Report Cost Rs.3000/-)
651. DRIP IRRIGATION
652. DEAD BURNT DOLOMITE

Price Rs.3000/- for each "Detailed Project Report" Payable in advance through Draft/Cash/M.O. in favour of "ENGINEERS INDIA RESEARCH INSTITUTE". Immediate Delivery or Ask by V.P.P. PH.: 2918117/2916431 Fax : 291 6431

653. DETERGENT CAKE
654. DEXTROSE SALINE (I.V. FLUID) IN PLASTIC BOTTLES
655. DETERGENT WASHING POWDER (ARIEL TYPE)
656. DOOR LOCKS/PAD LOCKS
657. DISPOSABLE BABY DIAPER
658. DIAGANOSTIC CENTRE
659. DE-HULLING OF JAUN FOR BEER INDUSTRY
660. D.T.P. CUM TABLE OFFSET
661. DYEING OF HANK YARN FOR POWER LOOM
662. ETHYL ALCOHOL FROM MOLASSES
663. EUCALYPTUS OIL
664. EPABX/EPAX SYSTEM
665. EXERCISE NOTE BOOK & REGISTER
666. ELECTRONIC CHOKE
667. ELECTRICAL APPLIANCES
668. EMERGENCY LIGHT
669. ELECTRONIC FLASHER FOR AUTOMOBILES
670. ETHYL ACETATE
671. ELECTRONIC TOYS
672. E.R.W. PIPES
673. EDIBLE OIL (MUSTARD OIL)
674. ESSENCE & SOFT DRINK CONCENTRATE
675. ELECTRONIC GAS LIGHTER (MULTI SPARK)
676. ELECTRONIC TIMER
677. ELECTRONIC ENERGY METER
678. ELECTRIC IRON (SOPHISTICATED)
679. ELECTRICAL INSULATION TAPES (USING BOPP FILM)
680. ELECTRONIC BALLAST (CHOKE)
681. EXPANDED POLYSTYRENE MOULDING
682. EMBOSSING POWDER OR RESIN COMPOUND
683. ELECTRICAL LAMP (GLS)
684. EXTRACTION OF OIL (CARDAMON, JEERA ETC.)
685. ENGINE VALVE
686. ETHYL ACETATE
687. ELECTRONIC QUARTZ CLOCK/WALL CLOCK
686. ELECTRICAL STAMPING
689. EGG POWDER
690. EUCALYPTUS TREE PLANTATION
691. ELECTRONIC INDICATOR
692. ELECTRONIC TELEPHONES
693. EDIBLE & NON EDIBLE OIL
694. EMERY POWDER
695. ETHYL ACETO ACETATE FROM ALCOHOL
696. ETHYL HEXANOL from Ethyl Alcohol
697. ELECTRO MAGNETIC RELAY
698. EXTRACTION of Glue Powder
699. ENGINEERING WORKSHOP (JOB WORK TYPE)
700. ELECTROPLATING ON GOLD AND THEIR CHEMICAL TREATMENT IN GOLDEN COLOUR & SILVER THREAD
701. EPOXY RESIN
702. ELECTRICAL GLS LAMP
703. ELECTRIC FANS
704. ELECTRONIC SERVICE CENTRE
705. EXPANDED POLYSTYRENE EXTRUSION PROFILE USED FOR MATCH BOX MAKING
706. EMPTY GELATIN CAPSULES
707. E.C.G/E.E.G. PAPER
708. ELASTIC THREADS & TWINE
709. EXTRACTION OF ALKALOID from Solanium Khasianum
710. ELECTRIC GENERATORS
711. ELECTRIC MOTOR
712. EXTRACTION of Gold, Silver & Copper
713. ELECTROPLATING BRIGHTNER
714. ELECTROLYTIC CAPACITOR (MOTOR START)
715. ELECTRIC HEATER CLAY PLATES
716. EAF BASED STEEL
717. ELECTRIC LAMP ADHESIVE POWDER
718. ELECTRONIC FAN REGULATOR
719. ELECTRICAL ACCESSORIES (SWITCH, SOCKET, PLUG,)
720. ERW STEEL CONDUIT PIPE
721. EMULSION PAINTS
722. ELECTRICAL HORN FOR AUTOMOBILE
723. EARTH LEAKAGE CIRCUIT BREAKERS (ELCB)
724. EMPIRE SLEEVINGS
725. ENAMELING OF COPPER WIRE
726. EHT TRANSFORMER
727. ELECTRICAL INSULATION TAPE (USING BOPP FILM)
728. ELECTRICAL LAMP (Incandescent Lamp)
729. ELECTRICAL REPAIR
730. EXTRACTION OF ESSENTIAL OIL AND PACKING of Ground Spices (100% EOU)
731. EDTA AND ITS SALT
732. ELECTRONIC TEST & MEASURING INSTRUMENT
733. ELECTRONIC TELEPHONE
734. ETCHING OF BRASS
735. EXTRACTION OF EDIBLE OIL FROM OIL SEEDS (Expander-Extrusion Cooking Process)
736. ELECTRIC PORTABLE TOOL
737. ELECTRO POLISHING OF STEEL
738. ETCHING PROCESS
739. EXTRACTION OF ACID OIL FROM SOAP STOCK
740. ENDOSULFAN
741. ELECTRONIC T.V. TUNER
742. EXHAUST FAN
743. ELECTROPLATING CHEMICALS
744. ELECTRIC MIXER
745. EXTRACTION OF OIL FROM WAX, GENERATED AS A BYE PRODUCT FOR PETRO CHEMICALS
746. EXTRACTION OF JASMINE ESSENCE
747. ELECTRO CARDIOGRAM MACHINE (ECG MACHINE)
748. ERW TUBES
749. EXTRACTION OF ALKALOIDS FROM VINCA ROSEA
750. ELECTROPLATING SCHEME PLANT
751. ELECTROPLATING OF SILVER & SILVER
752. EXTRACTION OF CHEMICAL from d.m.o
753. ELECTRO REFINING OF ZINC
754. ELECTRONIC FLASH GUN
755. ELECTRONIC MAIL (E-MAIL)
756. ESSENTIAL OILS
757. ELECTRICAL AND ELECTRONIC PANEL METER (ANALOGUE, DIGITAL, VOLTMETER ETC.)

758. EXTRACTION OF SOYBEAN OIL FROM SOYBEAN (Expander Extrusion-Cooking Process) with Soya Grits
759. ELECTRICAL MOTOR STARTER
760. EXTRACTION AND FILTRATION OF EDIBLE OIL
761. EPOXY TRANSFORMER (CURRENT & POTENTIAL)
762. ELECTRIC SWITCHES, PLUGS, SOCKETS & OTHER ACCESSORIES
763. EXTRACTION & FILTRATION UNIT FOR EDIBLE OIL
764. ELECTRIC WATER HEATER
765. EMPTY AMPOULES
766. EMULSIFIER FOR PESTICIDE
767. ERW STEEL PIPES
768. ELECTRONIC FIRE ALARM
769. EMULSIFIER FOR CUTTING OIL
770. ELECTRIC MOTOR WINDING (FOR FAN, MIXIES ETC.)
771. ELASTIC & RIGID TAPES
772. E.R.W (Precious Type)
773. ELECTROPLATING

BRIGHTNER FOR NICKEL
774. ETHYLENE GLYCOL MONO STEARATE ETHYLENE GLYCOL DI-STEARATE
775. ELECTRICAL FIXTURES (Chokes & Starter, Patties Light-ening Fixtures etc.)
776. ELECTROPLATING UNIT (TOOL ROOM)
777. ENAMEL WARE
778. EXTRUDED ALUMINIUM SECTION
779. EASTER GUM (NOCOSTING)
780. ELECTRONIC TIMER (Processed Control)
781. EXTRACTION & REFINING OF VEGETABLE OIL
782. EMERY PAPER CLOTH
783. FOOD COLOUR
784. FLOCK PRINTING
785. FILE/DUPLEX BOARD
786. FRUIT JUICES, SQUASHES, KETCHUP ETC.
787. FURFURAL FROM RICE HUL
788. FILTERA FOR ALL VEHICLES
789. FIBRE REINFORCED PLASTIC
790. FISH FARMING
791. FISH CANNING & POUCHING
792. FLUSH DOORS
793. FISH OILS
794. FROZEN FRUITS & VEGETABLES
795. FERRO ALLOYS
796. FRUIT DRINKS IN TETRA PACKS (FROOTI TYPE)
797. FRUIT JUICE MAKING & PACKING
798. FLOPPY DISKETTES
799. FOAM AND Its Prod-ucts as Mattresses (Cushion, Pillow Sheet)
800. FLUORESCENT TUBE
801. FLY ASH BRICKS
802. FLOOR POLISH
803. FLUORESCENT TUBES & GLS LAMPS
804. FLUSH DOOR, CHIP BOARDS, INSULATING BOARDS & HARD BOARD
805. FLOAT GLASS
806. FABRICATION WORKSHOP TO MANUFACTURE TRUSSES & TANKS
807. FORMALDEHYDE
808. FERRIC ALUM
809. FERROUS SILICATE
810. FAT LIQUOR
811. FLOOR COVERING SHEET
812. F.H.P. MOTOR
813. FIRE EXTINGUISHER
814. FURNISHING FABRICS ON POWER LOOM
815. FUEL OIL
816. FLOUR MILL (Roller)
817. FLOUR MILL (Grinder/ Pulvirized)
818. FIRE BRICKS
819. FORGING (NON FERROUS)
820. FOUNDRY & MACHINING JOB WORK UNIT
821. FAST FOOD PARLOR
822. FRP PRODUCTS
823. FACSIMILE/FAX MACHINE
824. FABRICATION INDUSTRIES (WORKS) FOR S.S & M.S VESSELS WITH ELECTRO-PLATING UNIT (TOOL ROOM)
825. FIBRE GLASS
826. FERRO MANGANESE ON Alumina Thermic Process
827. FORMIC ACID
828. FERRO SILICON
829. FATTY ACID
830. FERRITE COURSE
831. FLUORESCENT TUBE & CHOKE
832. FEED MILL (CATTLE & POULTRY FEED)
833. FAST COLOUR
834. FATTY ACID FROM WASTE VEGETABLE
835. FOOD GRADE CALCIUM CHLORIDE
836. FERRIC CHLORIDE
837. FRICTION DUST (LIQUID & POWDER) FROM CNSL
838. FIRE WORKS & PYRO TECHNIQUE
839. FOOD DEHYDRATION
840. FORMAL DEHYDE RESIN
841. FILM STUDIO (video)
842. FERRO CEMENT
843. FORMULATION FOR DDT, BHC, Melethion
844. FRIED & ROASTED GROUNDNU, GRAM, PEA, etc. in pouches
845. FLUORESCENT POWDER for Flurescent Tubes
846. FRUIT PULP & JUICE CONCENTRATE (i.e. MANGO & PINEAPPLE PULP & CONCENTRATE)
847. FERRO ALLOYS (OF NIOBIUM, MOLYBDENUM, TITANIUM, TUNGSTEN & VANADIUM) - Report Rs.7500/-
848. FIBRE BASED BITUMINOUS water proof felt

849. FROZEN FOODS, FRUIT & VEGETABLE PROCESSING WITH BACKWARD LINKAGES (100% EOU) Report- Rs. 7500/-
850. FISH (PRAWN & OTHERS) & MARINE PRODUCTS - Cost of Report Rs. 7500/-
851. FRENCH POLISH
852. FUEL BRIQUETTES FROM AGRO WASTE
853. FURNACE OIL
854. FLEXO GRAPHIC & ROTO GRAVURE PRINTING INK
855. FLOURSPER BRIQUETTES
856. FERRITE MAGNETS
857. FRUIT JUICES BOTTLING
858. FISH NET
859. FLUSHING CISTERN
860. FRUITS & VEGETABLE DRYING BY FREEZE DRYING METHOD - Report Rs.7500/-
861. FLAVOURED MILK
862. FLIP TOP CANS
863. FASTENERS (H.T) (Nuts, Bolt, Rivet & Washer)
864. FISH MEAL
865. FERROUS SULPHATE
866. FORGING PLANT (Manufacture Oil/Gas Pipe Fittings)
867. FLEXO GRAPHIC & ROTO GRAVURE PRINTING
868. FRUIT JUICES, PICKLE PROCESSING & CANNING
869. FRUIT FLAVOURS (Whisky, Rum Vodka, Grape & Butter Scotch)
870. FOUNDRY/C.I. CASTINGS
871. FOAM BOOSTERS
872. FERRITE CORE TRANSFORMERS
873. FLORICULTURE (CUT FLOWER) - 100% EOU
874. FROZEN FINGER CHIP
875. GARLIC FLAKES
876. GLASS BOTTLE BY SCRAPS
877. GRINDING UNIT (CEMENT)
878. GAS PIPE (LPG)
879. GRANITE CUTTING & POLISHING UNIT
880. GINGER OIL
881. GLS LAMPS & FLUORESCENT TUBE
882. GOLD ELECTROPLATING
883. GLASS SILVERING (MIRROR)
884. G.I. WIRES
885. GOLD PLATING ON GLASS
886. GLAZED CERAMIC TILES
887. G.I. PIPE FITTINGS
888. GLACIAL ACETIC ACID
889. GARLIC POWDER
890. GLASS SHEET (AUTOMATIC PLANT)
891. GROUND NUT OIL MILL
892. GROUND NUT OIL REFINING
893. GENERATOR SET (PORTABLE)
894. GREASES MANUFACTURE
895. GRANITE & MARBLE TILES
896. GALVANIZED ERW PIPES
897. GLASS BOTTLES

Price Rs.3000/- for each "Detailed Project Report" Payable in advance through Draft/Cash/M.O. in favour of "ENGINEERS INDIA RESEARCH INSTITUTE". Immediate Delivery or Ask by V.P.P. PH.: 2918117/ 2916431 Fax : 291 6431

898. GREETING CARD BY OFFSET PRINTING PRESS
899. GLS LAMPS/BULBS
900. GEYSER & WASHING M/C.
901. GAS LIGHTER
902. GALION THREAD
903. GLASS WOOL
904. GLUE FROM LEATHER WASTE
905. GLASS SHEET FOR WINDOW PANES
906. GOLD, ROLLED GOLD & SILVER PLATING
907. GLASS MARBLES
908. GRAPHITE CARBON PLATES
909. GEMS & JEWELRY
910. GHEE, BUTTER & PANEER
911. GOLD JEWELLERY
912. GLUE EXTRACTION & GLUE WHITE POWDER
913. GINGER OIL, SANDAL WOOD OIL, NAGARMUTHA OIL
914. GREASE FROM CASTOR OIL
915. GRINDING WHEELS
916. GALVANIZING PLANT
917. GUM FROM TAMARIND SEED POWDER
918. GRINDING MEDIA BALLS
919. GRANITE CRUSHING
920. GAS FILLING OF LPG CYLINDER (LPG GAS BOTTLING PLANT)
921. GLYCERIN EXTRACTION PLANT FROM COCONUT OIL
922. GOLD ELECTROPLATING OR METALLIC JEWELLERY ARTICLE INCLUDING METALLIC WATCH STRAPS
923. GOLD & SILVER PLATING ON PVC & NYLON-6
924. GASKET SHELLAC COMPOUND
925. GEM CLIPS, PAPER PINS & STAPLE
926. GUAR GUM
927. GUAR GUM POWDER
928. GEMS Manufacture
929. G.I. PIPES
930. GLUCOSE & GLUCOSE SALINE
931. GUNNY BAGS
932. GRAM DALS & FLOUR MILLS
933. GREEN PEAS PROCESSING & CANNING
934. GRAPHITE ORE BENIFICATION UNIT
935. GOLD PLATED SILVER JEWELLERY
936. GARLIC OIL & POWDER
937. GRADED & M.I. CASTING
938. GRADES OF GUAR GUM
939. GLASS FLOORING TILES
940. GELATIN
941. GRIPE WATER
942. GOLD SALT
943. GRANULATED MIXED FERTILIZER
944. GRAVURE PRINTING CYLINDER
945. GLASS SYRINGES
946. GRANITE SLAB / TILE
947. GRAPHITE POWDER from Graphite Ore
948. GLUE POWDER FOR TECHNICAL GLUE FLAKES
949. GELATIN & OSSEIN FROM BONE

Rs. 3000/- for each Detailed Project Report or Pay Rs. 4750/- for any two Reports and Save Rs. 1250/-

950. GUM FOR PASTING LABELS/ OFFICE PASTE (GUM)
951. GRAPE DEHYDRATION
952. GRAPE WINE
953. GLASS WARE
954. GASKET
955. GLASS TUBES
956. GEMS CUTTING & POLISHING
957. GLOW SIGNS
958. GEOMETRY BOX (MATHEMATICAL INSTRUMENTS)
959. GOSSYPOL (POLYPHENOL) FROM COTTON SEED OIL
960. GRINDING OF SPICES (Turmeric, Red Chillies, Masala)
961. GLUE & GELATIN
962. GOAT FARMING
963. GOAT SLAUGHTERING & BREEDING FARM
964. GOLD EXTRACTION USING CYANIDE SOLUTION & ACID
965. GASKET SHEET (ASBESTOS FREE)
966. GOBAR GAS (BIO GAS)
967. GRANITE MONUMENT
968. GLYCERIN PURIFICATION
969. GAS MANTLES
970. GUAR GUM POWDER (FOOD GRADE)
971. GOAT & SHEEP FARMING
972. GOLF COURSE
973. GINGER POWDER
974. GREEN HOUSE, PLANT MICRO PROPAGATION
975. GATE, GRILL, WROUGHT IRON & BRASS STAIRCASE, RODS & RAILING
976. GELATIN CAPSULES (HARD)
977. GRANULES (PLASTIC) FROM WASTE
978. GRANULES (PLASTIC)
979. HYDRATED LIME
980. HDPE/LDPE MANUFACTURING FROM ETHYL-ALCOHOL
981. HAZMOLA TYPE AYURVEDIC TABLET
982. HOLIDAY RESORTS
983. HOSPITALS
984. HAWAI CHAPPAL (RUBBER)
985. HARD RUBBER BATTERY CONTAINER
986. HERBAL COSMETIC
987. HOLLOW CONCRETE BLOCK/BRICK
988. HDPE FILM / SHEET
989. HOTEL (3 STAR)
990. HOTEL (5 STAR)
991. HOTEL (NO STAR)-MOTEL
992. HOT ROLLING MILL
993. HAIR SHAMPOOS
994. HOSE PIPE (Rubber)
995. HING (ASAFOETIDA)
996. HOSPITAL (200 BEDDED)
997. HYDROGEN PEROXIDE
998. HDPE/LDPE PIPES
999. HIGH VOLTAGE WIRE
1000. HOSIERY INDUSTRY
1001. HOSIERY INDUSTRY (for Women-BRA & PANTY)
1002. HOSPITAL RUBBER GOODS & SHEETS
1003. HATCHERY FARMING (Broiler)
1004. HOMEOPATHIC MEDICINE
1005. HOSIERY & TAILORS LABEL
1006. HELMET
1007. HURRICANE LANTERN/ STOVE
1008. H.M BAGS
1009. HERBAL TOOTH PASTE & TOOTH POWDER
1010. HIGH ALUMINA CERAMICS
1011. HAND TOOLS
1012. HESSIAN BAG (LAMINATED) WITH PRINTING
1013. HARD BOARD FROM RICE HUSK
1014. HARD BOARD FROM

BAGASSE
1015. HELICAL SPRING (COIL SPRINGS)
1016. HESSIAN CLOTH
1017. HDPE/PP WOVEN SACK/BAG
1018. HEPTAL DEHYDE
1019. HERBAL*SHAMPOO/ CREAM
1020. HYDROGE NATION OF CASTOR OILS
1021. HINGES (PianoType)
1022. HINGES (M.S.)
1023. HDPE/LDPE PIPE & FITTING
1024. HYDROCHLORIC ACID (HCL)
1025. H - ACID
1026. H.T. & M.V. INDUSTRIAL CUBICAL SWITCH BOARDS
1027. HEALTH CLUB CUM BEAUTY PARLOUR WITH HAIR SALOON & SONA BATH
1028. HOSPITAL BED
1029. HONEY PROCESSING & PACKING
1030. HYDROGEN PEROXIDE BY AUTO OXIDATION PROCESS
1031. HAWAN SAMAGRI
1032. HACK SAW BLADE
1033. HARD COKE
1034. HARD CHROMIUM PLATING
1035. HDPE PIPE & FITTING
1036. HAND MADE PAPER
1037. HDPE & LDPE PIPE FITTING
1038. HYDRAULIC BRAKE CYLINDER
1039. HOT DIP GALVAINZING
1040. HAND LOOM PRODUCTS- KHES, BED SHEET, BED COVERS, FURNISHING & TAPESTRY CLOTH
1041. HOSIERY PRODUCTS LIKE CHILDREN KNITWEAR, T-SHIRTS & ACRYLIC FIBRE - Cost of Report Rs.2500/-
1042. HERBAL KUM-ROLI
1043. HYDROFLUORIC ACID
1044. HYDRAULIC DOOR CLOSER
1045. HEAT TRANSFER LABEL for Rubber
1046. HYBRID SEED
1047. HDPE TARPAULINS
1048. HEXAMINE FROM FORMALDEHYDE
1040. HEAT TRANSFER LABEL by Screen Process
1050. HEAT TREATMENT OF LEAF SPRING
1051. HYDRATED CALCIUM SILICATE BRICKS
1052. HAIR DYE IN CREAM FORM
1053. HAMMER
1054. HDPE BOX STRAPPINGS
1055. HOMOEO & BIO MEDICINES WITH MOTHER TINCTURE
1056. HUME PIPES
1057. HEAT CHAMBER PAINTING
1058. HAMMER TONE PAINTS
1059. HYPODERMIC NEEDLES FOR DISPOSABLE SYRINGES
1060. HELMET FOR COAL MINES
1061. HIGH RUPTURING CAPACITY (HRC) FUSES
1062. HAIR FIXER
1063. HOT ROLLED (HR) COILS
1064. HALOGEN LAMPS
1065. HAIR DYE POWDER
1066. HARD CHROMIUM & NICKEL CHROMIUM PLATING
1067. HYDRAULIC LIFTING DEVICES (FOR AUTOMOBILE SERVICING & REPAIR)
1068. HANDKERCHIEF
1069. HEALTH CENTRE
1070. HANDICRAFTS
1071. HERBAL MEDICATED CIGARETTES
1072. HIGH TENSILE FASTENERS
1073. HYDROGENATED CASTOR OIL
1074. HYDROGEN GAS PLANT (HYDROGEN & OXYGEN)
1075. HOSIERY MERCERIZING
1076. HOSIERY CLOTH (Cotton) PROCESSING-BLEACHING, DYEING & FINISHING OF CLOTH
1077. HARD GREASE
1078. HAIR DYE IN HAIR OIL FORM
1079. HARD & SOFT FERRITES
1080. HOT MIX PLANT
1081. HDPE PIPE
1082. HARD GELATIN CAPSULES (Empty)
1083. HANK YARN DYEING FOR POWER LOOM
1084. ICE MAKING PLANT
1085. INDIAN PICKLE
1086. INDIAN MADE FOREIGN LIQUOR (IMFL)
1087. IODIZED SALT
1088. IMMERSION HEATER
1089. INDUCTION FURNACE (M.S. INGOTS)
1090. ICE & COLD STORAGE
1091. INJECTION WATER & SALINE
1092. INSULATING VARNISH
1093. INJECTION MOULDED PLASTIC ARTICLES
1094. INDUSTRIAL REFRIGERATION
1095. ICE CREAM STABILIZERS
1096. IRON POWDER FROM MILL SCALE SCRAP ARISING from Iron & Steel Rerolling Mill
1097. INSULATING VARNISH & WIRE ENAMEL
1098. IRON TAWA
1099. INDUSTRIAL KNIFE
1100. I.V. SET
1101. INDIGO BLUE
1102. INVESTMENT CASTINGS
1103. INVESTMENT CAS-TINGS OF BRASS
1104. ICE CREAM
1105. INVERTER
1106. INDUSTRIAL HARD OIL USED IN SOAP MAKING
1107. ICE CREAM CUPS OF PLASTIC
1108. INVERTER & CONVERTER
1109. I.V. CANNULA
1110. INTIMATE SCENT, CHEMICALS ETC. from All Types of Flowers - Cost of Report Rs.2500/-
1111. IRON & STEEL WIRE & NETTING
1112. INSTANT ICE CREAM MIX
1113. ICE CREAM & ICE CANDY
1114. IGNITION CONDENSER
1115. IONES FROM LEMON GRASS OIL
1116. ISO PROPANOL (ISO PROPYL ALCOHOL)
1117. IF/RF COILS
1118. INTEGRATED CIRCUITS
1119. INDUSTRIAL ALCOHOL FROM MOLASSES
1120. ICE CREAM OF DIFFERENT FLAVOURS
1121. INVESTMENT CASTINGS FOR SS & HIGHER ALLOYS - Cost Rs.2500/-
1122. INDUSTRIAL ALCOHOL FROM ETHYLENE
1123. ICE CUBE PLANT
1124. INSTANT TEA & COFFEE
1125. INJECTABLE for Pharmaceuticals
1126. INSTANT SOUP
1127. INSTANT NOODLES
1128. INSULATING LAGGING OF BOILERS & STEAM TUBES
1129. IRON OXIDE PIGMENT
1130. INJECTION & BLOW MOULDED PLASTIC Products
1131. INJECTION MOULDED HOUSE HOLD ITEMS
1132. INSECTICIDES FROM NEEM OIL, LEAVES & NEEM SEEDS
1133. INJECTION MOULDED PLAS-TIC COMPONENTS
1134. IODIZED SALT (MOISTURELESS-FREE FLOWING)
1135. INTERNAL COMBUSTION ENGINE (for Agricu-ltural Equipments)
1136. INTEGRATED COMPLEX OF EASTERS & ALLIED PRODUCTS (DOP, DBP, ETHYL ACET-ATE, BUTYL ACET-ATE, WIRE ENAM-EL, JELLY CABLE COMPOUNDS)
1137. IBUPROFEN
1138. IMITATION JEWELLERY
1139. I.V. PLASTIC BOTTLES
1140. INSTANT FOODS (IDLI MIX, SAMBAR MIX, VADA MIX, GULAB JAMUN, TOMATO SOUP MIX ETC.)

1141. INDUCTION FURNACE BASED C.I. CASTING
1142. INFORMATION MOVING DISPLAY
1143. INJECTION MOULDED PLASTIC COMPONENTS for Electrical/Electronics Indl.
1144. INSULATING VARNISH (Poly Vinyl butyral Based FFC Grade)
1145. IDLER ROLLERS FOR CONVEYERS (PLAIN & RUBBER COVERED)
1146. INDUSTRIAL OXYGEN GAS
1147. ISOPRENE & NEOPRENE BASED RUBBER ADHESIVE
1148. INTRAVENOUS (I.V.) SET
1149. IRON (WROUGHT) & BRASS STAIRCASE, ROD, RAILING, GATE & GRILL
1150. IGNITION CONDENSERS
1151. INDUCTION FURNACE (S.G. Iron Casting)
1152. INSULATING VARNISH (Dry Type)
1153. JUTE TAR FELT
1154. JUTE BAGS
1155. JAM & JELLY
1156. JOB WORK UNIT (FOUNDRY & MACHINING)
1157. JASMINE & LILY FLOWER OIL
1158. JUTE BATCHING OIL
1159. JUTE WASTE PRODUCTS
1160. JAM, CHUTNEY, PICKLE & SQUASHES
1161. J-ACID
1162. JEANS & JACKET (DENIM)
1163. JACQUARD FABRICS
1164. JEAN DYEING & FIXING BY INDIGO BLUE (JIGGER DYE & DIP DYE)
1165. JUTE PROCESSING TWIN & GUNNY BAGS
1166. JUTE TWIN INCLUDING COTTON & COIR
1167. JUTE BAGS FROM RAW JUTE
1168. JELLY FILLED CABLES
1169. JUTE, COIR, GRASS, ROPE SUTLI MAKING
1170. JAUN DEHULLING for Beer Industry
1171. JELLY & JAM
1172. JEWELLERY (Gold)
1173. JUICES (Fruit)
1174. KATECHU (Kattha)
1175. KRAFT PAPER (from Waste Paper)
1176. KRAFT PAPER & MILL BOARD
1177. KRAFT PAPER FROM WASTE CARTON BOXES
1178. KNITTING FABRICS
1179. KALI MEHNDI (HAIR DYE)
1180. KHANDSARI SUGAR
1181. KRAFT PAPER & SPECIAL PAPER
1182. KIMAM MANUFACTURE
1183. KITCHEN SINK (S.S)
1184. KNITTED CLOTH
1185. KATTHA & CUTCH
1186. KATTHA
1187. KERNAL (Cashew nut Kernal Extract)
1188. KANTHAL/NICHRO-ME FURNACE HEATING WIRE
1189. LEMON GRASS OIL BASED IONES
1190. LPG GAS STOVE
1191. LEAD CRYSTAL
1192. LAMINATED OF PAPER WARE (Cards) with Glossy PP (Polyester Film)
1193. LIQUID DETERGENTS (NON IONIC)
1194. LDPE/HDPE FROM ETHYL ALCOHOL
1195. LEATHER GOODS
1196. LUBE OIL & GREASES
1197. LDPE/HDPE MANUFACTURING
1198. LEATHER SHOE (HIGH) & CHAPPALS
1199. LEATHER BINDER (RESIN BASED)
1200. LAUNDRY FOR '5' STAR HOTEL
1201. LEATHER TANNING
1202. LEATHER GOODS (FASHIONABLE)
1203. LATEX RUBBER ADHESIVE
1204. LAUNDRY & WASHING SOAP
1205. LETTER PRESS PRINTING
1206. LIQUID SOAP
1207. LIQUID DETERGENT
1208. LIQUID SHOE POLISH PUFF
1209. LDPE/HDPE PIPES
1210. LEATHER GARMENTS
1211. LITHOPONE
1212. LIQUID GLUCOSE FROM POTATOES
1213. LEASING BUSINESS
1214. LEASING & HIRE PURCHASE
1215. LAUNDRY SOAP
1216. LAMINATED HESSIAN BAG
1217. LAMP CAPS
1218. LIGHT LIQUID PARAFFIN
1219. LAMP FILAMENT
1220. LATEX FOAM (Rubber) Products
1221. LILY FLOWER & JASMINE
1222. LATEX RUBBER CONDOM
1223. LEAD STEARATE
1224. LPG STOVE
1225. LAPTOP COMPUTERS
1226. LEMON GRASS OIL
1227. LEAD REFINING USING LEAD DROSS, LEAD SCRAP, LEAD POWDER AS RAW MATERIAL
1228. LOW PRESSURE CELLULOSE LIQUID
1229. LATHER SHAVING CREAM
1230. LPG CYLINDER TESTING CENTER
1231. LEVELING & DISPERSING AGENT
1232. LEATHER STRAPS for Wrist Watches
1233. LEATHER SHOES
1234. LEATHER BOARD
1235. LATEX FOAM RUBBER (Sponge)
1236. LEATHER TANNING & COLOURING- Cost Rs.2500/-
1237. LOUDSPEAKER
1238. LECITHIN (SOYA BASED)
1239. LIQUID SOAP BY USING PINE OIL
1240. LINK CHAIN
1241. LITMUS PAPER
1242. LEAD SMELTING
1243. LAMINATED JUTE BAGS
1244. LIGHT EMITTING DIODES (LEAD)
1245. LABORATORY CHEMICAL UNIT
1246. LEATHER SUIT-CASES, BRIEF CASES & TRAVELING BAGS
1247. LEAD EXTRACTION from Scrap Battries
1248. LADDU
1249. LPG CYLINDER
1250. LPG GAS REGULATOR
1251. LPG GAS BOTTLING PLANT
1252. LIME STONE, DOLOMITE CHIPS & POWDER
1253. LEAD PENCILS
1254. LUBE OIL from cnsl to Reduce Friction
1255. LOOM OIL
1256. LEATHER AUXILIARIES & CHEMICAL
1257. LEATHER TANNING & LEATHER GARMENTS
1258. LEATHER DYES (NO COSTING)
1259. LUBE OIL RECLAMATION
1260. LAUNDRY & DRY CLEANERS
1261. LACTIC ACID
1262. LINING MATERIAL FOR FLUID FLOWING PIPE (LIQUID PETROLEUM)- Cost of Report Rs.2500/-
1263. LEAD BATTERY PLATES & BATTERY ASSEMBLY
1264. LOW TENSILE TRANS-FORMERS (L.T) upto 400 KVA
1265. LUBE OIL BLENDING
1266. L.T TRANSFOR MER REPAIRING

1267. LIME COLOUR/CEMENT COLOUR/SYNTHETIC RED IRON OXIDE USED FOR FLOORING
1268. LIMIT SWITCHES & METAL PLUG SOCKETS
1269. LEAD NITRATE
1270. LEATHER GARMENTS, SHOES & CHAPPALS
1271. LEATHER WASHERS
1272. LEAD MONOXIDE
1273. LIQUID DETERGENT FOR WOOL
1274. LATEX RUBBER THREAD
1275. LAMINATED SAFETY GLASS
1276. LAMINATED SAFETY & TOUGHENED GLASS
1277. LIPSTICKS
1278. LINSEED OIL
1279. LACTOSE & BYE PRODUCT PROCESSING FROM MILK
1280. LICHEN (JHYAU) (CHARILA)
1281. LIQUID GLUCOSE
1282. LIST OF 100% UNIT
1283. LAMINATION OF CO-EXTRUSION, THREE LAYERS-FILM with Lamination & Printing
1284. LAMINATION OF CO-EXTRUSION MULTI LAYER FILM IN ROLL FORM
1285. LPG GAS PIPE
1286. LUBRICATING OIL & GREASES (Blending of Lubricating Oils) & Manufacturing of Greases
1287. LIQUID BINDI & SINDUR
1288. LIQUID GLUCOSE & ITS BYE PROD-UCTS from Maize
1289. LEAD OXIDE (A) LEAD MONOXIDE (B) REA LEAD (LEAD TETROXIDE) (C) GREY LEAD OXIDE
1290. LEAD EXTRACTION (SECONDARY) FROM SCRAPS (A) BATTERY PLATE (B) PIPES (C) SHEET
1291. METHANE GAS
1292. MILK/DAIRY PRODUCTS
1293. MINI RE-ROLLING MILL
1294. MANUFACTURING OF T-SHIRTS with Knitting Fabrics
1295. MANGO PEEL BASED PECTIN
1296. MASALA/SPICES
1297. MUSTARD OIL (EDIBLE OIL)
1298. MOTEL/SMALL HOTEL
1299. M.S. INGOTS (INDUCTION FURNACE)
1300. METAL CONTAINER
1301. MECHANICAL TOY
1302. MENTHOL CRYSTAL
1303. MARBLE & GRANITE TILES
1304. MINI CEMENT PLANT
1305. MICA PAPER FOR ELECTRICAL INSULATION
1306. MINI SUGAR PLANT
1307. MICRO CRYSTALLINE WAX
1308. MOSQUITO COILS
1309. MINIATURE CIRCUIT BREAKER (MCB)
1310. MELAMINE CROCKERY
1311. METHYL METHA CRYLATE
1312. MINI FLOUR MILL
1313. MANGANESE ORE CONCENTRATION
1314. MINI PAPER PLANT (KRAFT PAPER)
1315. MINI PAPER PLANT (WHITE WRITING & PRINTING)
1316. MAIZE/CORN STARCH
1317. MULTI PURPOSE SPRAY DRIER
1318. MALTED MILK FOOD
1319. M.S. WIRE DRAWING PLANT & ANNEALING
1320. MUSICAL DOOR BELL
1321. MUSHROOM PLANTATION
1322. MUSHROOM CULTIVATION & PROCESSING WITH CANNING
1323. MINERAL WATER IN POUCHES
1324. MINERAL WATER IN POUCHES & PLASTIC BOTTLES
1325. METAL SPECTACLES FRAMES
1326. MIRIT SANJEEVNI SURA
1327. MILD STEEL BOLT
1328. M.S. HINGES
1329. MINI (PERSONAL) COMPUTER
1330. MELAMINE FORMALDEHYDE POWDER
1331. MONOCHROME MONITOR FOR COMPUTER
1332. MOULDED LUG-GAGE (V.I.P. TYPE)
1333. MOULDED LUGGAGE (Cheap Quality)
1334. METAL HARDENING
1335. MOSQUITO REPELLENT MAT
1336. MENTHOL & DEMENTHOLISED OIL
1337. MICRO CELLULAR SHEET FOR SHOE SOLE
1338. MOTHER TINCTURE & BIOCHE-MIC MEDICINES
1339. MATCH BOX MAKING PLANT
1340. MULTI LAYER PRINTED CIRCUIT BOARD (PCB)
1341. MINI PAPER PLANT FORM JUTE STICK & WHEAT HUSK/RICE HUSK
1342. METAL FINISHING
1343. METAL FITTINGS for Leather Goods & Garments
1344. MAGNESIUM CARBONATE MAGNESIUM METAL, CALCIUM CARBONATE FROM DOLOMITE
1345. METAL BONDED DIAMOND IMPREGNATED SEGMENT for Marble Sawing
1346. MILK PRODUCTS
1347. MANGO PULP & MANGO SLICES CANNING
1348. MILK CHOCOLATE
1349. MINI STEEL PLANT BY INDUCTION FURNACE
1350. METALLIC GASKET (SPIRAL WOUND)
1351. METALLIZED POLYPROPYLENE FILM
1352. MODERN RICE MILL
1353. MOSAIC TILES
1354. MALACHITE GREEN
1355. METHYLATED SURGICAL SPIRIT
1356. MANILA ROPES
1357. METAL NAPHTHANATE
1358. MOTOR START ELECTROLYTIC CAPACITORS
1359. METAL PRE TREATMENT CHEMICALS
1360. MINI PAPER PLANT FROM EUCALYPTUS WOOD
1361. MILL & KRAFT PAPER FROM WASTE CARTON BOXES
1362. MOSQUITO MAT RECHARGER
1363. MARINE CONTAINERS
1364. MISHRI PEARL SUGAR CANDY
1365. MONO CHLORO ACETIC ACID
1366. MENTHA OIL
1367. MAIZE STARCH
1368. MINI STEEL PLANT
1369. METALLIC ACID
1370. MAGNESIUM HYDROXIDE POWDER
1371. MAGNESIUM SULPHATE
1372. MERCURIC OXIDE
1374. MALTING PLANT
1375. MILK PRESERVATION & MARKETING (MILK CHILLING PLANT)
1376. METHYL METHA CRYLATE MONOMER & VARIOUS CHEMICAL ADDITIVES FOR PLASTIC BANGLES
1377. METAL POLISH SOAP
1378. MICRO NUTRIENTS MIXTURES
1379. MICRO WAVE TUBES USED IN MICRO WAVE OVEN
1380. MILK POWDER
1381. MULTI PURPOSE COLD STORAGE for Medicines,

Fruits & Vegetables
1382. MILK POWDER & GHEE
1383. MOBILE CATERING VAN
1384. M.S. INGOTS & H.R. STEEL STRUCTURES
1385. MALEIC ANHYDRIDE
1386. MICRO MOTORS
1387. MIXERS/GRINDERS (MIXIE)
1388. MODERN VEHICLE WORKSHOP
1389. MODERN BREAD & BAKERY UNIT
1390. MULTIPLE RELAY FOR LOWVOLTAGE APPLICATION
1391. M.S. WELDING ELECTRODES
1392. MUSHROOM(EOU) CULTIVATION & PROCESSING UNIT (Dehydration & Pickling of Oyster & Paddy Straw Mushroom)
1393. MIRROR (GOLDEN, SILVER & PINK)
1394. MICROVEE & ABSOLUTE FILTER
1395. MEDICAL X-RAY FILM, SLITTING & REPACKING
1396. MAGNESIUM TRI-SILICATE
1397. MICRO PAPER
1398. MUTTON TALLOW for Industrial Use
1399. MILK POWDER, GHEE & SPICES
1400. MINI PAPER PLANT USING BAGASSE
1401. MOSQUITO REPELLENT OIL
1402. METALLIC STEARATES
1403. METHYLINE GLUE
1404. MAIZE/CORN OIL
1405. MOTEL/SMALL HOTEL, BANQUET HALL WITH RESTAURANT
1406. MUFFLERS & SILENCERS FOR TWO WHEELERS
1407. MAINTENANCE FREE RECHARGEABLE BATTERY (Sealed Lead Acid)
1408. METHYL SALICYLATE
1409. MINIATURE TRANSFORMER
1410. MARKING INK FOR FIBER TIP PENS
1411. MONOCHROTOPHOS (Technical)
1412. METTOL FROM HYDROQUINENE & METHYL AMINE
1413. MACHINE SCREWS & SELF TAPPING SCREWS
1414. MUFFLER & SILENCER PIPES for Four Wheelers
1415. MOSQUITO COILS USING EUCALYPTUS LEAVES
1416. MANGO POWDER
1417. MANGO JUICE
1418. MANGO KERNEL POWDER
1419. MUSHROOM & PROCESSED FOOD
1420. MENTHOL CRYSTAL & OTHER CHEMICALS
1421. MAGNET
1422. MODERN ADVERTISING AGENCY WITH DTP & FILM STUDIO
1423. MITHAI/ NAMKEEN
1424. MELAMINE CRYSTALS
1425. MULTI LAYER FILM
1426. MATCH SPLINTERS & INNER BOX MAKING PLANT FROM POPLAR WOOD
1427. METAL CUTTING DIE DESIGN
1428. MICRO CRYSTALLINE WAX FROM SLUDGE of Petro Chemical Reffinery
1429. MANUFACTURING OF PHARMACEUTICALS TABLETS, CAPSULES ETC.
1430. MINIATURE WATCH BATTERY
1431. MICRO NUTRIENT MIXTURE (SOLID)
1432. MULTI STOREY COMMERCIAL COMPLEX ALONGWITH RESIDENTIAL & DELUXE FLATS for Foreign Tourists & Revolving Restaurant
1433. MEASURING TAPES (Steel, Metallic & Plastic)
1434. MUSTARD OIL EXTRACTION & REFINING
1435. MILK TOFFEE
1436. MANGO PROCESSING & CANNING (MANGO PULP)
1437. MANGO PRODUCTS, MANGO JUICE, PICKLES, CHUTNEY ETC.
1438. MOSQUITO COILS & MATS
1439. MILK CHILLING PLANT & PACKING IN POUCHES
1440. MAN POWER EXPORT
1441. METAL POLISHING BAR
1442. MAGNESIUM CARBONATE & BICARBONATE
1443. MURABBA
1444. MOULDED CASE CIRCUIT BREAKER (MCCB)
1445. METHYL ETHYL KETONE
1446. MAGNESIUM INGOTS/ BILLETS CASTINGS
1447. MICRO SCALE STEEL PLANT
1448. MACARONI
1449. MANGALORE TILES & BRICKS
1450. BOTHER BOARD
1451. M.G. KRAFT PAPER FROM WASTE PAPER
1452. MINI CEMENT PLANT (by Rotary Kiln Process-800 TPD)

1453. MULTI LAYER CO EXTRUSION, THREE LAYERS-FILM with Lamination Printing
1454. MICROWAVE OVEN
1455. MEAT PROCESSING (BUFFALO)
1456. MILK PRESERVATION & MARKETING TO WHOLESALERS (In Pouch)
1457. NICOTINIC ACID
1458. NEEM SEEDS INSECTICIDES
1459. NAMKEAN & SWEETS
1460. NON-IONIC LIQUID DETERGENT
1461. NUT, BOLTS, RIVETS/ WASHER
1462. NON-ALCOHOLIC FLAVOURS
1463. NIRMA Type Detergent Powder
1464. NYLON YARN CRIMPING DOUBL-ING, BLEACHING, DYEING ETC.
1465. NON-CARBONATED SOFT DRINK
1466. NURSING HOME
1467. NAPHTHALENE BALLS
1468. NICKEL/CADMIUM BATTERY
1469. NON-FERROUS METAL ALLOY
1470. N.C. SENDING SEALERS
1471. NITRO CELLULOSE
1472. NITRO MUSK
1473. NICKEL PLATING
1474. NYLON POLYESTER & P.P. ROPE MAKING
1475. NON-FERROUS FORGING
1476. NON-EDIBLE & EDIBLE OIL MILL
1477. NICOTINE SULPHATE FROM TOBACCO WASTE
1478. NEON SIGN
1479. NEON BULB
1480. NYLON ZIP FASTENERS
1481. NICKEL PLATING BRIGHTNER
1482. NOTE BOOK, REGISTER & FILES
1483. N.C. PUTTY
1484. NURSERY FARM
1485. NICKEL LINED SCREENS
1486. NEEM OIL FROM SEEDS
1487. NEON LAMP INDICATORS
1488. NAIL ENAMEL (NAIL POLISH)
1489. NEON INDICATOR
1490. NICKEL SULPHATE
1491. NICKEL CATALYST
1492. NAMKEEN INDUSTRY
1493. N.C. THINNER USED IN AUTO PARTS
1494. NON-IONIC SURFACTANTS WETTING AGENTS
1495. NOODLES
1496. NON-BASMATI RICE FROM PADDY
1497. NEWS PRINT PAPER FROM RICE STRAW BAGASSE
1498. NAIL CUTTER WITH FILER & MANICURE
1499. NEOPRENE BASED ADHESIVES
1500. NAPHTHALENE BALLS & POWDER
1501. N-ACETYL, L-TYROSINE
1502. NICHROME WIRE
1503. NON-WOVEN CARPETS (Wadded with Polyester Fiber)
1504. NICHROME/KANTHAL FURNACE HEATING WIRE
1505. NICKEL PLATING BRIGHTNER (Primary or Carrier Brightner & Secondary)
1506. NILGIRI OIL
1507. NEEDLE ROLLERS FOR BEARING
1508. NEROL LAUNDRY SOAP
1509. NURSERY SCHOOL (PRE-NURSERY&NURSERY)
1510. NITRO CELLULOSE (LACQUER)
1511. NON-FERROUS SCRAP MELTING ROD CASTING & WIRE DRAWING
1512. NICKEL SALT
1513. NON-STICK KITCHEN WARES (TEFLON COATED UTENSILS)
1514. NEWS PAPER FOR CHILDREN (DAILY)
1515. NITROGEN & OXYGEN PLANT
1516. NYLON SOCKS
1517. OIL (Cotton Seed)
1518. OIL (Mustard)
1519. OIL (Ground Nut)
1520. OXYGEN GAS
1521. ONE TIME CARBON PAPER
1522. OFFICE PASTE
1523. OIL MILL
1524. ONION POWDER
1525. OIL SEALS
1526. ORTHO BORIC ACID
1527. OXALIC ACID
1528. OFFSET PRINTING PRESS
1529. OFFSET SECURITY PRINTING PRESS
1530. OFFSET COLOUR & TREADLE TYPE PRINTING PRESS (Offset Press)
1531. OLEORESIN OF SPICES
1532. OPTICAL GLASS GRINDING
1533. OCTYL ALCOHOL
1534. OPTICAL WHITENER
1535. OPEN END SPINNING PLANT
1536. OSSEIN FROM ANIMAL BONES
1537. ORGANIC MANURE
1538. OIL BOUND DISTEMPER PAINT
1539. OPTICAL WHITENER & BRIGHT-NER for Plastics
1540. OLEORESIN FROM CHILLY
1541. OSSEIN & GELATIN
1542. ORGANIC SOLVENT PURIFICATION PLANT
1543. ORTHO TOLUENE SOLVENT
1544. OXALIC ACID FROM WASTE VEGETABLES
1545. OXYGEN & NITROGEN PLANT
1546. OYSTER MUSHROOMS (CULTIVATION & PROCESSING UNIT)
1547. OXALIC ACID FROM SAW DUST
1548. OXIDISED WAX
1549. OPTICAL FIBER CABLE
1550. OFFSET PRINTING INK
1551. ONION & POTATO POWDER
1552. OIL (Castor)
1553. OIL (Rice Bran)
1554. OIL (Essential)
1555. PVC FABRIC YARN ON POWER LOOM (TERRYCOT)
1556. POWER LOOM
1557. PETROMAX CONTAINER
1558. PUBLISHING & PRINTING UNIT
1559. POTATO STARCH
1560. POLYTHENE BAGS & AUTOMATIC PRINTING
1561. PAINT INDUSTRY
1562. PHARMACEUTICAL ALCOHOL FROM NON-MOLASSES BASED
1563. PVC CONDUIT PIPE
1564. PVC PIPE & FITTINGS
1565. PHARMACEUTICAL UNITS (TABLETS, CAPSULES, SYRUPS, LOTION & OINTMENT)
1566. PRINTED TIN CONTAINERS
1567. PIGGERY FARM
1568. PAPER FROM WASTE PAPER (KRAFT PAPER)
1569. PAPER FROM WASTE PAPER (WRITING & PRINTING PAPER)
1570. PAPER FROM BAGASSE
1571. PAPER FROM RICE STRAW
1572. PAPER CONES & TUBES
1573. PAPER & PULP
1574. PAPER FROM EUCALYPTUS
1575. PAPER ENVELOPS
1576. PAPER FROM RICE HUSK & WHEAT HUSK
1577. PAPER FROM PAPYRUS GRASS
1578. PAPER (HAND MADE PAPER)
1579. PAPER CUPS
1580. PAPER PLANT from Tree Bark & Eucalyptus Wood
1581. PAPER BASED PHENOLIC SHEET (FOR ELECTRICAL APPLIANCES)
1582. PAPER WASTE RECYCLING PLANT
1583. PVC INSULATION TAPES

1584. POTATO CHIPS/WAFERS
1585. PESTICIDES FORMULATIONS
1586. PVC WIRES & CABLES
1587. PVC WIRES/TWIN FLAT CABLE
1588. PET BOTTLE/CONTAINERS
1589. POWER SUPPLY (SWITCH MODE)
1590. PHOTO COLOUR LAB (QSS)
1591. POTATO GRANULE
1592. PRINTING INKS
1593. PLASTIC MOULDED ARTICLES
1594. PARAFFIN WAX FROM SLACK WAX
1595. PLYWOOD & PLY BOARD
1596. PLYWOOD
1597. PRINTED CIRCUIT BOARD (PCB)
1598. PROCESSING OF FRUIT & VEGETABLES
1599. PLASTIC WARES
1600. PLASTIC SPRAY LAMINATED ARTICLES
1601. PRUSSIAN BLUE
1602. POTATO POWDER
1603. PVC PIPES & FITTINGS
1604. PILFER PROOF CAPS & CROWN CAPS
1605. PILFER PROOF CAPS (P.P. CAPS)
1606. PVC GRANULES/ COMPOUNDS BY CHEMICAL PROCESS
1607. PVC GRANULES/ COMPOUNDS BY PLASTIC WASTE
1608. PHOSPHORIC ACID FROM ROCK PHOSPHATE
1609. PVC RIGID PIPE
1610. POLYESTER RESIN
1611. PERFUMERY COMPOUND
1612. PERFUMERY COM-POUND, COSMETICS ETC.
1613. PICKLES
1614. PLASTIC SYRINGES (Disposable)
1615. PROCESSED FRUITS
1616. POULTRY & CATTLE FEED
1617. POULTRY FEED
1618. PHENYL (BLACK) IN LIQUID FORM
1619. PRINTING PLATE for Offset Printing Machine
1620. PROCESSED FOOD (Readymade)
1621. PRECIPITATED CALCIUM CARBONATE
1622. PLASTER OF PARIS BANDAGE (POP BANDAG)
1623. PLASTER OF PARIS
1624. PLASTER OF PARIS BANDAGES & COTTON ADHESIVE TAPE
1625. POLYESTER YARN (TEXTURIZED)
1626. PULSE MILL (DAL MILL)
1627. PVC INSULATED CABLES
1628. PHENYL (BROWN & WHITE)
1629. PROCESSED CHEESE
1630. PAINT BRUSHES
1631. PAPER BAGS
1632. PVC PROFILES (DOOR & WINDOW)
1633. PLASTIC BUTTONS
1634. PAPPAD PLANT
1635. PRE STRESSED CONCRETE RAILWAY SLEEPER
1636. PLASTIC CONFERENCE BAGS, FOLDERS ETC.
1637. PHOTO TYPE SETTING
1638. PLASTIC MOULDED FURNITURE
1639. PVC FOOTWEAR
1640. POUCHES for Oil & Ghee Packing
1641. PAN MASALA IN POUCHES & TIN PACKS
1642. PLANT PROTECTION EQUIPMENTS
1643. PARACETAMOL
1644. PRINTING PRESS (LETTER PRESS)
1645. PRINTING PRESS (OFFSET)
1646. POLYSTYRENE MOULDING (EXPANDED)
1647. PULVERIZED FLOUR MILL
1648. PLASTIC WASTE REPROCESSING
1649. POLY PROPYLENE BOX STRAPPING
1650. PLASTIC SUTLI
1651. POWER SUPPLY (Liner & Switch Mode)
1652. PVC SOLES FOR LEATHER SHOE UPPERS
1653. POLYURETHANE FOAM FLEXIBLE & RIGID
1654. PRESSURE DIE CASTING ALUMINIUM
1655. PROTEIN & PROTEIN BASED PRODUCTS
1656. POLYPROPYLENE/HDPE BOX STRAPPING
1657. POULTRY & BROILER FARMING
1658. POULTRY & HATCHERY FARMING
1659. POULTRY FARM
1660. POTABLE ALCOHOL from Grains & Rotten Fruits
1661. PUMIC WHITE ABRASIVE CAKE/STICK
1662. PEPSI COLA IN POLY TUBES
1663. PCC ELECTRIC POLES
1664. PHTHALOCYNINE BLUE & GREEN
1665. PVC/XLPE (Armoured) CABLES
1666. PCB SHEETS
1667. PALM OIL
1668. POWER TRANSFORMERS UPTO 600 KVA
1669. PVC WIRE & CABLES/PIPES & FITTINGS
1670. PAPER & PAPER BOARD
1671. POUCH FILLING for SAUNF, SUPARI & ELAICHI ETC.
1672. P.I.D. CONTROLLER
1673. PVC CASING CAPING MATERIAL FOR ELECTRICAL FITTING
1674. POLYTHENE BAGS & TUBES
1675. PIGMENT BINDER FOR TEXTILE PRINTING
1676. POLYESTER RESIN for WIRE ENAMEL
1677. PRECIOUS METAL PLATING & MANUFACTURE OF THEIR SALTS
1678. PLASTIC CONTAINER (BLOW MOULDED)
1679. PICKLE & SAUCES
1680. PAPAIN FROM PAPAYA (Papaya Latex)
1681. POLYPROPYLENE SPINNING FILAMENT YARN
1682. PRESSURE COOKER & ALUMINIUM UTENSILS
1683. PERSONAL COMPUTER
1684. PORTABLE TELEVISION
1685. PECTIN FROM RAW PAPAYA
1686. PECTIN FROM APPLE POMACE
1687. PECTIN FROM CITRUS, LEMON & ORANGES
1688. PECTIN FROM MANGO PEELS
1689. PECTIN FROM ORANGE/ LIME PEELS
1690. PAPAIN
1691. PAPAIN FROM PAPAYA
1692. PAPAYA CULTIVATION
1693. PAPAYA & TOMATO CULTIVATION
1694. PAPAYA CULTIVATION & PAPAIN MANUFACTURE
1695. PARTICLE BOARD
1696. PHOSPHORIC ACID FOR POLLUTION CONTROL
1697. PERFUME FOR SOAP, DETERGENT & AGARBATTI (YARA YARA)
1698. PIGMENTS (DYE PIGMENTS)
1699. PISTON ASSEMBLY (Aluminium Alloy)
1700. PVC/PLASTIC/SOFT/RIGID/ FILM SHEETS
1701. PLASTIC INJECTION MOULDING PROJECTS
1702. POLYSTER YARN FROM WASTE
1703. PHOTO POLYMER COATING for Plate & Block Making
1704. POUCH MAKING & GRAVURE PRINTING

1772. PROCESSED CONTROL TIMER (Electronic Timer)
1773. PLYWOOD BOARD
1774. PLYWOOD & PLY BOARD (PHENOL BONDED, BOILING WATER PROOF, TERMITE, RESISTANCE, LAMINATED & COMMERCIAL PLYWOOD & PLY BOARD)
1775. POLYURETHANE FOAM & ITS PRODUCTS
1776. PEPPERMINT OIL
1777. PRAWN FISH FARMING
1778. PAN MASALA & POUCH MAKING PLANT
1779. PLASTIC SHEET from Plastic Scraps
1780. PICKLES, MURABBAS, SAUCES ETC. (VEGETARIAN & NONVEG. PICKLES)
1781. POUCH PACKING FOR MILK
1782. POWER PLANT
1783. PARTICLE BOARD FROM RICE HUSK
1784. PAN MASALA, TOBACCO, ZARDA & KIMAM
1785. PAINT-BITUMINOUS BASED CORROSION RESISTANT
1786. PLASTIC STRIPPABLE COATING MATERIAL
1787. PLASTER OF PARIS (CALCIUM SULPHATE)
1788. PORK PROCESSING & FARMING
1789. PVC FLEXIBLE PIPES
1790. PHOTO ETCHING OF STAINLESS STEEL PLATES
1791. POLYETHENE POUCHES FOR GHEE, BUTTER, OIL, MILK ETC.
1792. PVA BASED ADHESIVES
1793. PURIFICATION OF CASEIN
1794. PAINT REMOVERS
1795. PLASTIC DRINKING STRAW
1796. PRESSURE COOKER
1797. PVC ON G.I. WIRE
1798. PICTURE VARNISH
1799. PAPER VARNISH
1800. PLASTIC FILM CAPACITOR-COST OF
1801. PAPER FROM AKRA
1802. PERFUMED PHENYL (PINE OIL DISINFECTANT)
1803. PHENOLIC RESIN
1804. PLAIN PAPER COPIER
1805. PHENOLIC FORMALDEHYDE RESIN (PF RESIN)
1806. PHOTO GRAPHIC DEVELOPERS & FIXERS
1807. PARTICLE BOARD WOOD CHIPS
1808. PHENYL ACETIC ACID
1809. PLASTIC GRANULES (HDPE, LDPE, PP) FROM PLASTIC SCRAPS/WASTE
1810. PETHA PACKAGING
1811. POLYPROPYLENE & MULTIFILAMENT SPINNING YARN
1812. POLYESTER MICRO FIBER
1813. PARTICLE BOARD & BLOCK BOARD WITH SENDING & LAMINATION OF PARTICLE BOARD
1814. PARA CHLORO NITRO BENZENE
1815. POWER PLANT (HYDRO BASED)
1816. PHENOL
1817. PASTEURIZATION OF MILK (FLAVOURED MILK)
1818. PLATINUM LABORATORY APPARATUS
1819. PVC ROOFING SHEET
1820. PEANUT COATING (SPICES, HONEY, CHEESE, CHOCOLATE, SALT) (WITHOUT COST ESTIMATION)
1821. PAPER CONES FOR LOUDSPEAKER
1822. POPLAR PLANTATION
1823. PLASTIC TOOTH PICK
1824. PCC/RCC PIPES
1825. PLASTIC I.V. BOTTLES
1826. PHOSPHORIC ACID (Purification) FROM CRUDE
1827. POLISH (WAX)
1828. POLISH (CAR)
1829. POTASSIUM DI-CHROMATE/BI-CHROMATE
1830. PLASTIC FILM & SHEETS WITH PRINTING (FLEXO & ROTO) LDPE/HDPE/PP/HM/PVC
1831. POWER CAPACITOR

1832. PISTON ASSEMBLY (Aluminium Alloy)
1833. POLYESTER STAPLE FIBER FROM POLYESTER FIBRE WASTE
1834. POLY VINYL ACET. EMULSION for Textile Process (Dyeing & Printing)
1835. PVC FILM
1836. PLASTIC CORRUGATED SHEET & BOXES
1837. PLASTIC BUTTONS FROM POLYESTER SHEET & RODS
1838. POWER INVERTER
1839. PLASTIC ADVERTISEMENT BALLOONS
1840. PELLETIZER Plant (for Cattle Feed, Poultry Feed, Sheep Feed, Pig & Other Feed)
1841. POTASSIUM IODIDE
1842. POTATO POWDER AUTOMATIC IMPORTED PLANT
1843. PAINT INDUSTRY (PRIMER)
1844. POTABLE LIQUOR
1845. PHOTO DEVELOPER & FIXER
1846. PAPER PLANT (Kraft & White Writing & Printing Paper)
1847. POLYESTER YARN
1848. PENCIL (LEAD)
1849. QSS COLOUR PHOTO LAB
1850. QUICK LIME
1851. REFINED SUNFLOWER SEED OIL
1852. RESIDENTIAL APARTMENTS
1853. RECLAMATION OF USED ENGINE OIL
1854. READY MADE GARMENTS
1855. READY MADE GARMENTS & HOSIERY
1856. RICE MILL
1857. RICE TRADING (BASMATI RICE)
1858. RECONDITIONING OF EMPTY CEMENT JUTE BAG
1859. RED OXIDE Primer
1860. ROLLER FLOUR MILL
1861. RUBBER ROLLERS
1862. RUBBER ROLLER for Printing Machine
1863. RUBBER ROLLER FOR RICE MILL
1864. RUBBER CONVEYER BELT
1865. REFINING OF GROUNDNUT OIL
1866. REACTIVE DYES
1867. READY MADE PROCESSED FOOD
1868. RCC SPUN PIPES
1869. RECTIFIED SPIRIT FROM MOLASSES & MAHUA FLOWER
1870. REROLLING OF SARIYA (TOR)
1871. RESTAURANT
1872. RUBBER HOSE PIPE
1873. REFINED OILS (COTTON SEEDS, GROUNDNUT, SUNFLOWER etc.)

Price Rs.3000/- for each "Detailed Project Report" Payable in advance through Draft/Cash/M.O. in favour of "ENGINEERS INDIA RESEARCH INSTITUTE". Immediate Delivery or Ask by V.P.P. PH.: 2918117/ 2916431 Fax : 291 6431

1945. RED OXIDE PIGMENTS
1946. ROTO GRAVURE PRINTING (for Flexible Packaging)
1947. RUBBER BUSHING
1948. RUBBER HOSE PIPES & RUBBER GLAZING
1949. RAINBOWCOLOUR ON METALS
1950. RUBBER PLANTATION
1951. RECTIFIED SPIRIT FOR POTABLE ALCOHOL, INDUSTRIAL ALCOHOL & MEDICAL ALCOHOL
1952. RECTIFIED SPIRIT FROM RICEPADDY STRAW
1953. RED OXIDE PRIMER (ANTI CORROSIVE)
1954. RUBBER MOULDING & LINING OF RUBBER SHEETING
1955. RE-REFINING OF USED LUBRICANT
1956. RHODIUM PLATING ON SILVER & GOLD JEWELLERY
1957. RED PHOSPHORUS
1958. RUBBER ADHESIVE (All Purpose)-NEOPRENE & AISOPRENEBASED
1959. RUBBER ADHESIVE for Plywood
1960. ROASTED/SALTED/ MASALA CASHEWNUTS, ALMONDS & PEANUTS
1961. RUBBER ROLLERS FOR TEXTILE MILLS & PAPER INDUSTRIES
1962. RUBBER ROLLER & EBONITE ROLLER
1963. ROTARY PRINTING & DYEING ON COTTON/ SYNTHETIC TEXTILE
1964. RAZOR BLADE
1965. RECONDITIONING OF T.V PICTURE TUBE
1966. ROASTED & FRIED DRY FRUITS, GROUNDNUTS/ PEANUTS WITH PACKAGING UNIT
1967. RUBBER (LATEX) LINED JUTE MATS
1968. RUBBER PROCESS OIL
1969. RECLAMATION OF HYDRAULIC OIL
1970. RIGID PVC PIPES & FITTINGS (RIGID PIPES PIPE FITTINGS LIKE ELBOWFITTINGS, T-JOINTS ETC.)
1971. RAINBOW COLOUR ON PVC FILM & SHEET
1972. REACTIVE DYE M5B DYE
1973. RUBBER BELTING (FAN/V BELT)
1974. RED MIRROR BY ELECTROLESS DIPPING

METHOD
1975. ROASTED/SALTED/ COATED CASHEWNUT, PEANUT, ALMOND (ImportedAutomatic)
1976. RE-WINDING OF BURNT ELECTRIC MOTOR
1977. RECLAMATION OF NICKEL from Spent Catalyst of Vanaspati Industry
1978. REFRIGERANT ALFA-R134
1979. RICE & CORNFLAKE
1980. READY MADE GARMENTS (100% EOU)-STITCHING, WASHING, DYEING, PRINTING & FINISHING)
1981. RUBBERIZED CLOTH
1982. RIGID & ELASTIC TAPES
1983. RUBBER (FIELD) CONVERTED TO THE 60% LATEX RUBBER
1984. RUBBER ERASERS (School Rubber)
1985. RUBBER AUTO GASKET
1986. RUBBERISED CANVAS SHOES
1987. RUBBER(Synthetic)
1988. RUBBER HOSES FOR AUTOMOBILE
1989. REROLLING OF STEEL CUTTING
1990. SOLVENT EXTRACTION PLANT FROM COCONUT CAKE
1991. STEEL TUBE/PIPE
1992. SILICON RUBBER NIPPLE/ TEAT
1993. SULPHUR CRYSTAL (100% PURE)
1994. STARCH, DEXTROSE, SORBITOL, VITAMIN - C, etc. from Maize
1995. SILICONEMULSION
1996. SOFT DRINKS (Non Carbonated)
1997. SURGICAL EXAMINATION GLOVES(Disposable)
1998. STRAWBOARD
1999. SAFETY GLASS
2000. SODIUM DICHROMATE & SODIUM SULPHATE
2001. SILVER EXTRACTION from Waste HypoSolution, X-Ray Film & Cimema Film
2002. SCREEN PRINTING ON TEXTILES
2003. STEARIC ACID
2004. SODIUM SILICATE form Silica Sand
2005. SODIUM SILICATE FROM RICE HUSK/PADDY HUSK
2006. STAINLESS STEEL PATTA
2007. STEARATES MANUFACTURE
2008. SOLVENT EXTRACTION & REFINING OF SOYA BEAN
2009. SOLVENT EXTRACTION PLANT
2010. SOCKS KNITTINGS
2011. SODA ASH

2096. SCENTS/PERFUME
2097. SODIUM SULPHIDE by Barium Sulphate Process
2098. SODIUM HYDRO CHLORITE (Bleach Liquor)
2099. SHIP CONTAINERS
2100. STEEL PLANT (EAF-BASED)
2101. STANNOUS CHLORIDE
2102. STEEL ROLLING MILL
2103. SINGLE SUPER PHOSPHATE (s.s.p) & SULPHURIC ACID
2104. SILVER & GOLD PLATING ON PVC & NYLON-6
2105. SKIMMED MILK POWDER
2106. SILICON
2107. STAINLESS STEEL UTENSILS (Copper Electroplated)
2108. SAGOL
2109. SCENT & Perfume for Agarbati
2110. STEEL FORGING (Automobile Parts)
2111. SODIUM HYDRO SULPHITE (ZINC REDUCTION PROCESS)
2112. SMOKE LESS COAL
2113. SILVER EXTRACTION FROM WASTE HYPO SOLUTION, X-RAY FILM & CINEMA FILM (ELECTROLYSIS PROCESS)
2114. SHEET METAL PRODUCTS (FERROUS/NON-FERROUS)
2115. SPRAY DRIER
2116. S.G. IRON & MALLEABLE IRON CASTING
2117. SINDHUR
2118. SAFETY PINS
2119. SINTERED BEARINGS
2120. SODIUM BI-SULPHITE
2121. SESAME OIL FROM SESAME SEEDS
2122. S.G. IRON & ALLOY STEEL CASTINGS
2123. STARCH & DEXTRIN BASED ADHESIVES
2124. SODIUM SULPHIDE FROM SALT CAKE
2125. STEEL WOOL
2126. SODIUM NAPHTHOANATE
2127. SOLVENT & THINNERS
2128. STUFFING JOINT BOX OF PLASTIC
2129. STARCH & ALLIED PRODUCT FROM MAIZE
2130. SURGICAL/ABSORBENT COTTON
2131. SCIENTIFIC INSTRU-MENTS
2132. SPONGE RUBBER (LatexFoamRubber)
2133. SCREEN PRINTING ON COTTON, POLYESTER & ACRYLIC
2134. SORBITOL
2135. SPECIAL STEEL (HIGH ALLOY)
2136. SEWING THREADS, REELS, BALLS
2137. SALSEED FAT
2138. SODIUM TRI-POLY PHOSPHATE
2139. SHUTTLE COCKS FOR BADMINTON
2140. SEMI CONDUCTORS FOR TRANSISTORS & DIODE
2141. SEMI CONDUCTOR DEVICES
2142. STONE CRUSHER
2143. SODIUM THIO-SULPHATE FROM SODIUM SULPHATE
2144. SURFACE FLOOR & CAR POLISHES
2145. SODIUM SULPHATE
2146. STRAW BOARD & GREY BOARD
2147. SERVO CONTROLLED STABILIZER (1 KVA - 100 KVA)
2148. SHOTS & GRITS OF HIGH CARBON STEELS
2149. STEEL CASTING FOR RAILWAYS
2150. SALTED GROUNDNUT
2151. SAGO SEED FROM POTATO & SWEET POTATO (SABOO DANA)
2152. SHOE LACES
2153. SOLID FUEL CAKE
2154. SILVER NITRATE
2155. SUPER ENAMELED COPPER WIRE (COPPER SCRAPS)
2156. SUGAR MANUFACTURING PLANT BY CARBONATION PROCESS
2157. SEWING MACHINE (PARTS MACHINING & ASSEMBLY)
2158. SILICA SAND
2159. SWEATER, MUFF-LER & KNITTING INDUSTRY
2160. SALINE & INJECTION WATER
2162. SPEAKER PARRY RING (FORMULAE)
2163. SILICON RELEASE PAPER
2164. STICKER MAKING-AUTOMATIC Plant
2165. STICKER & LABELING PLANT
2166. STAIN REMOVERS
2167. SEMI AUTOMATIC BRICKS PLANT
2168. SEMI AUTOMATIC CONFECTIONERY PLANT
2169. SILVER JEWELLERY
2170. SEAMLESS M.S. TUBES & PIPES
2171. SHERBAT
2172. STEEL WIRE DRAWING & GALVANIZING
2173. STORAGE BATTERY
2174. SOFT DRINK CONCENTRATE (Saccharine Based)
2175. SILICON COMPOUND
2176. SOAP COATED PAPER
2177. STARCH FROM WHEAT FLOUR
2178. SHOES, CANVAS AS WELL AS BOOT, RUBBER KNEES, JUNGLE BOOT COMBAT, RUBBER LINED
2179. STEEL PIPES
2180. SUBMERGED ARC WELDED PIPES (SAW PIPE)
2181. STAINLESS STEEL CUTLERY
2182. STEEL INGOTS (Gas Fire Furnace)
2183. SODIUM SULPHIDE FROM AMMONIUM SULPHITE & SODIUM CHLORIDE
2184. STARCH & ALLIED PRODUCTS FROM BROKEN RICE, LIQUID GLUCOSE, DEXTROSE ANHYDROUS
2185. SUNFLOWER OIL
2186. SUBMERSIBLE PUMP
2187. SODIUM BENZOATE
2188. SPONGE IRON
2189. STEEL WIRE HEALDS
2190. STARCH FROM TAPIOCA
2191. STREET LIGHT FITTING
2192. SKYLATED PHENOL
2193. SKY BAGS
2194. STAMPING HOT FOILS
2195. STEEL REROLLING MILL (STEEL RODS & COILS FROM SCRAPS)
2196. SULPHUR POWDER FROM SULPHUR CRYSTALS/ LUMP
2197. SPORT SHOES
2198. SPORT SHOES (Imported) AUTOMATIC PLANT-ACTION, LIBERTY ETC. TYPE
2199. SODIUM HEXA META PHOSPHATE
2200. SUGAR CANE WAX FROM PRESS MUD
2201. SIZING OF YARN
2202. SHAVING CREAM (LATHER)
2203. SCREEN PRINTING INKS
2204. SILK MANUFACTURES
2205. SCREEN PRINTING
2206. STEEL DRUM & BARRELS
2207. SILK WASTE PROCESSING & SPINNING
2208. SPRAY DRIED DETER-GENT POWDER
2209. SOLAR ENERGY WATER HEATER (GEYSER)
2210. SCREEN PRINTING ON PAPER/CARDS
2211. S.S. HINGES
2212. SOFT DRINK ESSENCES
2213. SPARK PLUGS
2214. SOLAR POWER EQUIPMENTS
2215. SURGE SUPPRESSER
2216. SINTERED BUSHES
2217. SINTERED BUSHES (SELF LUBRICATED)

2218. SHISHAM PLANTATION
2219. STENCIL COATING SOLUTION
2220. SURGICAL COTTON & SURGICAL ADHESIVE TAPES
2221. SODIUM PERBORATE (TETRA HYDRATE)
2222. SULPHUR BLACK DYES
2223. SILICON FROM RICE HUSK
2224. SOFT & HARD FERRITES
2225. STEP DOWN TRANSFORMER
2226. SOAP SHOP
2227. SHAVING CREAM & SHAVING SOAP
2228. SHOE TACKS
2229. SILICA GEL
2230. SURGICAL GLOVES from Latex
2231. SANITARY NAPKINS (Tab Ended-Tube Filled)
2232. SODIUM SULPHATE (ANHYDROUS)
2233. SALT LICKS FOR CATTLES
2234. SURGICAL BANDA-GE, SANITARY NAPKINS & ALLIED PRODUCTS
2235. SODIUM ALGINATE
2236. SOLVENT EXTRACTION & REFINING PLANT (COTTON SEED OIL)
2237. SHOVELS
2238. SODIUM CYCLAMATE
2239. SPINNING OF VISCOSE STAPLE FIBER INTO YARN
2240. SULPHUR RECOVERY FROM SLUDGE
2241. SUNFLOWER SEED OIL EXTRACTION
2242. STAINLESS STEEL TIFFIN BOX (LUNCH BOX)
2243. SOLAR ELECTRICAL CELLS & PANELS
2244. SOLAR PUMP
2245. SELF TAPPING STEEL SCREWS
2246. STEEL TAPES FOR CABLE ARMOURING
2247. SNACK FOOD (CRAX TYPE-ROLL & BALL TYPE)
2248. SYNTHETIC ASAFOETIDA(Hing)
2249. SAFFTY MATCHES & FIBER BOX
2250. SCREEN EMULSION
2251. SODA LIME
2252. SNUFF FACTORY
2253. SWEET AROMA OF BETAL NUT
2254. 2-4-D SODIUM SALT
2255. SOYA MILK & PANEER
2256. SILVER BRAZING FOIL
2257. SUGAR COATED CASHEWNUT, ALM-ONDS & PEANUTS
2258. STUFF TOYS
2259. SILK FABRICS (POWER LOOM)
2260. STAINLESS STEEL KNIFE (Table Knife)
2261. SEALING MATERIAL COMPATIBLE TO CERAMIC & NICHROME WIRE
2262. SOAP RIVETS (HOLLOW TYPE)
2263. STAINLESS STEEL VACUUM FLASK (UNBREAKABLE)
2264. SOYABEAN BARIYAN
2265. STEEL BALLS
2266. SOAP FROM SOAP STOCK (SOAP INDUSTRY)
2267. SURAT JARI
2268. SAFETY BELT
2269. STARCH BOOK BINDING CLOTH
2270. STEEL STRIPS (COLD ROLLED) ELECTRICAL SILI-CON WITH ORIENTED GRAINS FOR ELECTRICAL MACHINES & TRANSFORMERS
2271. SILVER DIP (Cleaning Solution)
2272. SHEHNAZ HUSSAIN'S INSTITUTE FOR SKIN, HEALTH & HAIR CARE (HEALTH CLUB CUM BEAUTY PARLOUR TRAINING INSTITUTE)
2273. SYNTHETIC ALMOND OIL
2274. SYNTHETIC TALLOW
2275. SPINDLE OIL
2276. SODIUM SULPHITE FROM SODIUM DIOXIDE
2277. SYNTHETIC DETERGENT (BLUE POWDER)
2278. STEEL TANKS FOR DRINKING WATER (WATER STORAGE TANKS OF M.S)
2279. SPIKENARD (JATAMANSI)
2280. SOAP JELLY
2281. SKIMMED MILK POWDER & GHEE
2282. SODIUM ACETATE
2283. SPRAY PERFUME
2284. STEEL PLANT (25-T UHF ELECTRIC ARC FURNACE & HOT ROLLING)
2285. SPICE OILS OR OLEORESINS (EXTRACTION OF ESSENTIAL OILS CARDAMOM, JEERA, AJWAIN, GINGER OIL & OTHER SPICES)
2286. SYNTHETIC ADHE-SIVE FOR DECORATIVE LAMINATE BONDING
2287. STEEL WIRE/ROD (CONTINUOUSLY CAST)
2288. SODIUM PETROLEUM SULPHONATE (EMULSIFIER)
2289. SECURITY SYSTEM
2290. S.W. PIPES
2291. SECONDARY LEAD

EXTRACTION FROM SCRAPS (A) BATTERY PLATE (B) PIPES (C) SHEETS
2292. SEWING NEEDLES (FOR USED WITH DOMESTIC/ INDUSTRIAL SEWING MACHINE)
2293. SODIUM META SILICATE
2294. SODIUM CHROMATE
2295. SOLAR PHOTO VOLTAGE MODULES (SOLAR ELECTRICAL CELLS & PANEL)
2296. SUNFLOWER PLANTATION
2297. SHEEP AND GOAT FARMING
2298. SABOO DANA
2299. SOFTWARE (COMPUTER)
2300. SOYABEAN OIL
2301. TIN PRINTING & ANODIZING ON ALUMINIUM
2302. TYRE RETREADING BY COLD PROCESS
2303. THREE STAR HOTEL
2304. TOMATO CONCENTRATE
2305. TAMARIND JUICE CONCENTRATE
2306. TOYS (PLASTIC)
2307. TOYS (Electronics)
2308. TOYS (STUFF)
2309. TIN CONTAINER
2310. TEFLON TAPES
2311. TEA PACKAGING
2312. TELEPHONE AMPLIFIER
2313. TEXTURISED POLYESTER YARN
2314. THINNERS
2315. THERMOCOLE PACKAGING
2316. TYRE RETREADING (Hot Process)
2317. TAB ENDED PULP FILLED NAPKINS (Sanitary Napkin)
2318. TABLET&CAPSULE
2319. TABLET, CAPSULE, SYRUPS, LOTION & OINTMENT
2320. TELEVISION ARIELS (ANTENNA)
2321. TOILET SOAPS
2322. TOMATO PRODUCT IN POUCHES
2323. TELEVISION (COLOUR & B W)
2324. TELEVISION (PORTABLE)
2325. TILES (MOSAIC)
2326. TILES (GLAZED CERAMIC)
2327. TRANSFORMER
2328. TRANSFORMER (DISTRIBUTION)
2329. TENT & TARPAULINE
2330. TIE ROD ENDS
2331. T.V CUM VIDEO GAMES
2332. TOOTH BRUSH
2333. TOOTH BRUSH, TOOTH PASTE & POWDER
2334. TURKEY RED OIL
2335. TOOTH PASTE (GEL-COLGATE, CLOSE-UP TYPE)
2336. TOOTH PASTE & POWDER
2337. TOOTH PASTE
2338. THERMOCOLE MOULDING
2339. TEXTILE DYEING BLEACHING FINIS-HING & PRINTING
2340. TAPE DECK MECHANISM
2341. TITANIUM OXIDE
2342. TRANSFORMER OIL
2343. TELEPHONE CABLES/CORD
2344. TITANIUM NITRIDING
2345. TERELENE PRODUCTS
2346. TARTARIC ACID
2347. THREAD, CUSHION COMPOUND & VOLCANIZING SOLUTION FORMULATION & MANUFACTURE
2348. TUBULAR POLES, TRANSMISSION LINE, HARDWARE & MAIN SWITCHES FOR ELECTRICAL TRANSMISSION
2349. TUBULAR POLES FOR ELECTRICAL TRANSMISSION
2350. TUNGSTEN FILAMENT
2351. TITANIUM DIOXIDE BY CHLORINE
2352. TEFLON COATED ELECTRIC CABLES
2353. TRANSFORMER OIL RECLAMATION
2354. THERMOMETER (CLINICAL)
2355. TURPENTINE & ROSIN DISTILLATION
2356. TEXTILE PRINTING PIGMENT BINDERS
2357. TWO WHEELERS REPAIR & SERVICE WORKSHOP
2358. TOBACCO TOOTH PASTE FROM TOBACCO DUST
2359. TOBACCO TOOTH PASTE FROM TOBACCO
2360. TAR FROM PINE WOOD
2361. TRAVELLING AGENCY
2362. TEFLON COATED UTENSILS (NON-STICKS)
2363. THERMO PLASTIC ELECTRICAL SWITCHES & FITTINGS
2364. TRACING PAPER
2365. TENNIS BALL
2366. TISSUE & AIR MAIL PAPER
2367. TYRE RETREADING
2368. TEXTILE GOLD STAMPING PASTE
2369. THERMOSTATE FOR REFRIGERATOR
2370. TABLE FAN
2371. TOMATO POWDER
2372. TURPENTINE OIL FROM EXTRACTIONS OF DIPETR-OCORPUS TREE
2373. TISSUE & TOILET PAPER ROLL & AIR MAIL PAPER
2374. TUTI FRUITY FROM PAPAYA FRUITY
2375. TARTARIC ACID FROM MALEIC-ANHYDRIDE
2376. TETRA PACK FOR MILK PACKAGING & OTHER LIQUIDS
2377. TURMERIC POWDER (EDIBLE GRADE)
2378. TENNIS BALL & CRICKET BALL
2379. TIN PRINTING
2380. TYRE & TUBES FOR SCOOTER, MOTOR CYCLE, RIKSHAW, 2/3 WHEELERS
2381. THREE WHEELER ASSEMBLY
2382. TREAD RUBBER (CAMEL BLACK)
2383. TRI SODIUM PHOSPHATE
2384. TALLOW PROCESSING for Soap Manufacturing
2385. TEA PLANTATION
2386. TEA INDUSTRY
2387. TOMATO PASTE
2388. TOMATO KETCHUP, JAMS, JELLY ETC.
2389. THINNER/SOLVENTS & ITS ALLIED PRODUCT
2390. TEAK & MUSHROOM PLANTATION
2391. TEAK PLANTATION
2392. TANNIC ACID
2393. TABLE TENNIS BALL
2394. TOGGLE SWITCHES
2395. T.V. PICTURE TUBE (B/W) & COMPUTER MONITOR TUBE
2396. TONER INK
2397. TAILORS CHOKES
2398. TEFLON MANUFACTURING
2399. TANTALUM CAPACITOR
2400. TOILET SEATS & COVERS
2401. TOUGHENED GLASS & SILVER MIRROR GLASS
2402. TORCH & TRI LIGHT UNITS INTEGRATED PLANT INCLUDING MINIATURE BULB & TUBES, ENGINEERING PLASTIC MOULD/DIES MANUFACTURE
2403. TEA PACKAGING & DISTRIBUTION JOB WORK
2404. TUBE VALVES
2405. T.V. SIGNAL BOOSTERS
2406. THERMO COUPLE TIPS
2407. TWISTED YARN (NYLON)
2408. TERRY TOWEL
2409. TEXTILE AUXILLIARIES & CHEMICALS
2410. TEFLON TAPES & CAABLE
2411. TABLE WARE & CERAMIC TILES
2412. TOMATO PULP
2413. THERMOCOUPLES
2414. TEXTILE PRINTING PASTE (GUM)
2415. TALCUM POWDER (FACE & TOILET)
2416. TAPER ROLLER BEARINGS
2417. TOMATO WAFFERS
2418. TOBACCO & ITS PRODUCTS
2419. TOILET PAPER

2420. TELEVISION
2421. TOXIC COMPOUNDS EFFECTS ON HUMAN BODY
2421. TEA PACKAGING & DISTRIBUTION
2422. TERRY TOWELS/TERRY FABRICS WEAVING UNIT
2423. TRICYCLE RIKS-HAW ASSEMBLY
2424. TABLET, CAPSULE, SYRUP & LOTION
2425. TISSUE CULTURE (100% EOU)
2426. TELEVISION (B/W)
2427. TRI-METHOPRIME
2428. TELEPHONE CABLE (Jelly Filled)
2429. TRI BASIC LEAD SULPHATE
2430. TOILET & HERBAL SOAP
2431. THERMOCOLE SHEET & MOULDED PRODUCTS
2432. TEXTILE DYEING
2433. TEXTILE MINI SIZING PLANT
2434. TELEPHONE (Push Button Type)
2435. 2-4-D SODIUM SALT
2436. THERMOCOLE
2437. THERMOFORMED PACKAGING (Blister & Pouch Packing)
2438. TOUGHNED GLASS for Wrist Watch
2439. THERMO PLASTIC POLYURETHANE
2440. TABLE OFFSET & D.T.P
2441. TWO-T 2-STROKE OIL
2442. TOMATO & PAP-AYA CULTIVATION
2443. T-SHIRTS
2444. TOILET PAPER & NAPKIN
2445. TEA BAGS
2446. TEA (INSTANT)
2447. TOY BALLOONS, DECORATIVE BALLOONS
2448. TURPENTINE OIL
2449. TIMBER/WOOD SEASONING
2450. TRANSPARENT LACQUER (CLEAR) for Coating on Brass Bangles to Make it Weather Resistant
2451. TOFFEE (MILK)
2452. TOWEL, SOCKS & HOSIERY
2453. ULTRAMARINE BLUE
2454. UNINTERRUPTED POWER SUPPLY (UPS)
2455. UN ARMOURED, PVC INSULATED CABLES
2456. UTENSILS (SILVER PLATED)
2457. UTENSILS (ALUMINIUM)
2458. UTENSILS (BRASS)
2459. UREA FORMALDEHYDE POWDER
2460. UREA FORMALDEHYDE RESIN
2461. UREA
2462. U.J. CROSS & KING PIN
2463. UREA FERTILIZER PLANT
2464. UMBRELLA
2465. UNDECYLENIL ACID
2466. UREA FORMALDEHYDE & MELAMINE FORMALDE-HYDE MOULDING POWDER
2467. UNSATURATED POLYSTER RESINS
2468. U-CLAMPS, U-BOLTS & NUTS
2469. U-BOLTS & CENTRE BOLSTS FOR AUTO LEAF SPRING
2470. UTENSILS (STAINLESS STEEL)
2471. UTENSILS (TEFLON COATED)
2472. U.V. PAINT
2473. VACUUM METALIZING
2474. VANASPATI GHEE
2475. VAT DYES
2476. VIDEO & T.V. GAMES
2477. VIDEO & AUDIO CASSETES
2478. VIDEO CASSETES
2479. VIDEO STUDIO
2480. V-BELTS
2481. VIDEO & AUDIO MAGNETIC TAPES
2482. VIDEO CASSETE ASSEMBLING & RECORDING
2483. VITAMIN-C FROM POTATO EXTRACT
2484. VALVE GUIDES
2485. VISCOSE RAYON YARN FROM COTTON LINIERS
2486. VARNISH & PAINT INDUSTRY
2487. VOLTAGE REGULATOR (FOR AUTOMOBILES)
2488. VIDEO CAMERA
2489. VIDEO FILM STUDIO
2490. VOLTAGE STABILIZER using IC Timer
2491. VCP & VCR
2492. VINEGAR & MALT VINEGAR FOR INDUSTRIAL & DOMESTIC USE
2493. VENETIAN BLIND
2494. VIDEO CASSETTES (COMPLETE MANUFACTURING & ASSEMBLING UNIT)
2495. VIDEO TAPE
2496. VOLTAGE STABLIZER
2497. VACUUM CLEANER
2498. VIDEO FILM STUDIO TO MAKE FILMS ETC. IN VIDEO CASSETTES & FILM ROLLS
2499. VIDEO CASSETTES LIBRARY
2500. VARNISH THINNER (SOLVENT)
2501. VACUUM-METALLISING

LACQUER
2502. VISCOSE STAPLE FIBRE (RAYON STAPLE FIBER)
2503. VELVET CLOTH BY FLOCKING PROCESS
2504. VEGETABLE OIL REFINING (by Physical Process)
2505. VASELINE
2506. VELCROW FASTENING TAPE (Fastner Hoop Loop Tape & Synthetic)
2507. VODKA FROM WASTE GRAIN
2508. VETENERY MEDICINES (ONLY FORMULAE)
2509. VERMICELLI
2510. WIRE (Mild Steel)
2511. WIRE/CABLE (PVC)
2512. WIRE (COPPER)
2513. WAX CRAYON
2514. WAX FLOOR POLISH
2515. WRITING & PRINTING PAPER
2516. WOODEN BOXES
2517. WASHING & LAUNDRY SOAP
2518. WIRE MESH
2519. WELDING ELECTRODES
2520. WOOD CHARCOAL & BYE PRODUCTS
2521. WIRE DRAWING & ENAMEL
2522. WALL TILES/FLOOR TILES/ SANITARY TILES
2523. WASHING MACHINE (AUTOMATIC ELECTRO COMPUTERISED)
2524. WAX (PARAFFIN)
2525. WAX (MICRO CRYSTAL-LINE)
2526. WIRE RODS (ALUMINIUM)
2527. WINE & BEER
2528. WOOLLEN KNITWEAR
2529. WASHING MACHINE & GEYSER
2530. WIRE DRAWING (ALUMINIUM)
2531. WIRE DRAWING (COPPER)
2532. WIRE DRAWING (MILD STEEL)
2533. WIRE WOUND RESISTORS
2534. WORSTED WOOLLEN YARN
2535. WIRE DRAWING & ANNEALING
2536. WATER PROOFING BITUMINISED COMPOUND
2537. WIRE NAIL
2538. WAX FOR PAPER INDUSTRY
2539. WATCH CASE BUFFING
2540. WINDING WIRES, PVC INSULATED SUBMERSIBLE MOTOR
2541. WICK STOVE
2542. WAX EMULSION
2543. WOODEN ACCESSORIES FOR SEWING M/C
2544. WAX FOR PAPER
2545. WOOLLEN YARN
2546. WATER PROOF CEMENT COMPOUND
2547. WIRE ROPE (STEEL)
2548. WOOL YARN SPINNING
2549. WHITE CEMENT
2550. WRIST WATCH-DIAL
2551. WIRE PRODUCTS
2552. WAX EMULSION
2553. WIRE ROPE SLING
2554. WATER FILTER CANDLES
2555. WATER FILTER & PRESSURE COOKER
2556. WOOLLEN YARN CARPET DYEING
2557. WATCH LEATHER STRAP
2558. WALL PAPER PRINTING
2559. WELDING FLUXES
2560. WOODEN DOORS, & WINDOWS
2561. WELDING RODS (SPECIAL) & M.S. WELDING ELECTRODES
2562. WELDING BRASS ROD
2563. WASHING POWDER & WASHING SOAP
2564. WIRE MESH & GAUGE
2565. WETTING OIL
2566. WELDED WIRE MESH
2567. WASHING CUM DRYING MACHINE (FULLY AUTOMATIC, PROGRAMME CONTROLLED)
2568. WATCH GLASS
2569. WHEEL RIMS
2570. WOOD WOOL INDUSTRY
2571. WATER PROOF MARKING INK
2572. WATER FOR INJECTION AMPOULES PLANT
2573. WIRE NAILS & WIRE DRAWING
2574. WHITE PHENYL
2575. WHITE OIL
2576. WOOD POLISH
2577. WOODEN DRUM FOR AA/ ACSR CONDUCTOR STORAGE
2578. WATTLE EXTRACT (TANNIN POWDER)
2579. WAX PAPERED MATHC STICK
2580. WOOL BATCHING OIL
2581. WHISKY FROM COMMERCIAL ALCOHOL
2582. WELDING CABLE
2583. WIND MILL
2584. WOOLLEN FELT
2585. WOOD SEASONING
2586. WAX & CHEMICAL COATED BRAIDED TINSEL WIRE
2587. WINE, BRANDY, WHISKY & CHAMPAGNE
2588. WOODEN FURNITURE
2589. WALL PAPER
2590. WOOLLEN YARN SPINNING PLANT
2591. WEET AROMA OF BETAL NUT
2592. WHTIE OIL FROM KEROSENE OIL
2593. WOOLLEN SWEATERS
2594. WOVEN HOSIERY LABELS
2595. WASHING CAKE, DETERGENT CAKE & POWDER
2596. WATER PROOFING FORMULATIONS FOR PAPER CONES USED FOR SPEAKERS
2597. WOOLLEN CARPET
2598. WATER PROOFING FOR COTTON CLOTH
2599. WOODEN CANE FURNITURE
2600. WRIST WATCHES
2601. WROUGHT IRON & BRASS STAIRCASE ROD
2602. WHEAT PUFF
2603. WINE (I.M.F.L)
2604. WHEAT PORRIDGE
2605. WOOD GASIFIER
2606. WHEAT FLOUR MILL
2607. WATER METER
2608. WATER STORAGE TANK
2609. WATER PROOFING PAINT
2610. WATER (MINERAL)
2611. WIND ENERGY POWER
2612. X-RAY MACHINE
2613. XLPE CABLES
2614. X-RAY DEVELOPERS
2615. X-RAY FILM SLITTING & REPACKING (MEDICAL)
2616. XEROX PAPER
2617. XANTHATES
2618. X-RAY TUBES
2619. X-RAY FILMS
2620. YARN INDUSTRY
2621. YEAST INDUSTRY
2622. YARN - COTTON
2623. YARN - WOOLLEN
2624. YARN DYEING (Cotton)
2625. YARA YARA
2626. YARN DYEING & TEXTURISING
2627. YARN DYEING (COTTON)
2628. YARN (PVC Fabric)
2629. YARN (Viscose Rayon)
2630. YARN (POLYESTER YARN FROM WASTE)
2631. YARN DYEING (Carpet Woollen)
2632. YARN (NYLON)
2633. YARN (TWISTED)
2634. YARN SPINDLES
2635. YARN - Sizing
2636. YARN - HANK
2637. ZINC OXIDE
2638. ZINC SULPHATE
2639. ZARDA & KIMAM
2640. ZINC CHLORIDE
2641. ZINC METAL
2642. ZARDA-BABA CHHAP
2643. ZARDA & PAN MASALA
2644. ZINC BRIGHTNER
2645. ZINC COATING ON WIRE
2646. ZINC STEARATE